BRITISH
TRAITORS

Pocket Essentials by Gordon Kerr

BRITISH TRAITORS

Betrayal and Treachery in the Twentieth Century

GORDON KERR

Oldcastle Books

First published in 2022 by
Oldcastle Books,
Harpenden, UK
www.oldcastlebooks.com
@oldcastlebooks

Editor: Nick Rennison

A CIP catalogue record for this book is available from the British Library.

ISBN
978-0-85730-479-7 (print)
978-0-85730-480-3 (ebook)

2 4 6 8 10 9 7 5 3 1

Typeset in 11.5 on 13.5pt Adobe Garamond Pro
by Avocet Typeset, Bideford, Devon, EX39 2BP
Printed and bound in Great Britain by CPI Group (UK) Ltd,
Croydon, CR0 4YY

For Jack Boulter, whose idea it was

Contents

'A nation can survive its fools, and even the ambitious. But it cannot survive treason from within. An enemy at the gates is less formidable, for he is known and he carries his banners openly against the city. But the traitor moves among those within the gates freely, his sly whispers rustling through all the alleys, heard in the very halls of government itself. For the traitor appears no traitor; he speaks in the accents familiar to his victims, and he wears their face and their garments, and he appeals to the baseness that lies deep in the hearts of all men. He rots the soul of a nation; he works secretly and unknown in the night to undermine the pillars of a city; he infects the body politic so that it can no longer resist. A murderer is less to be feared.'

Cicero

Glossary & Abbreviations

ARCOS	All-Russian Cooperative Society
BBC	British Broadcasting Corporation
BUF	British Union of Fascists
'C'	Chief of Secret Intelligence Service
CIA	United States Central Intelligence Agency
Comintern	Third Communist International (Soviet Union 1919-43), organisation advocating world communism
CPC	Combined Policy Committee
CPGB	Communist Party of Great Britain
FBI	US Federal Bureau of Investigation
GC&CS	British Government Code and Cypher School
GCHQ	British Government Communications Headquarters (1946 to present day)
GRU	Soviet Main Intelligence Directorate, Army General Staff (*Glavnoye Razvedyvatel'noye Upravleniye*) (1942, 1945-46, 1953 to present day)
HMS	Her/His Majesty's Ship
Illegal	A Soviet agent operating without diplomatic status or protection
JBC	Joint Broadcasting Committee
KGB	Committee for State Security (*Komitet Gosudarstvennoy Bezopasnosti*) (USSR: 1954-91)
KPD	Communist Party of Germany (*Kommunistische Partei Deutschlands*)
MI1	Secret Intelligence Service (1916-21)
MI5	Security Service
MI6	See SIS

MI9	Intelligence agency specialising in POW escapes
MI14	Intelligence agency specialising in intelligence about Germany
NKGB	People's Commissariat for State Security *Naródnyï Komissariát Gosudárstvennoï Bezopásnosti*
NKVD	People's Commissariat for Internal Affairs (*Naródnyy Komissariát Vnútrennikh Dyel*) (1934-46)
OTP	One-time cipher pad
POW	Prisoner of war
RAF	Royal Air Force
Rezident	Head of Soviet intelligence station
Rezidentura	Soviet intelligence station
SIGINT	Signals intelligence
SIS	Secret Intelligence Service (1921 to present)
UB	Polish Secret Police (*Urząd Bezpieczeństwa*)
UDE	Underwater Detection Establishment at Portland
YCL	Young Communist League

Introduction

The dictionary definition for the complex little 7-letter word 'traitor' is, to say the least, succinct:

> **traitor** a person who commits treason
> *Chambers Dictionary, 10th Edition*

The operative word is, of course, 'treason' which the same tome defines as 'betraying or attempting to overthrow one's government, country or sovereign; treachery; disloyalty'. In terms of human behaviour, it really does not get much worse. Murder, certainly, is about as low as a human being can stoop, but treachery, being a traitor, perhaps runs it a close second. Some might even say it is a more heinous crime. Of course, there are degrees of treachery and these have historically brought different levels of punishment. Treachery in time of war, for instance, was once not at all the same as treachery in time of peace. The punishment during war throughout much of the twentieth century until the Crime and Disorder Act 1998 abolished it, was death. This, even though capital punishment had ceased to be the punishment for murder as far back as 1965. Being a traitor is, without doubt, a serious matter.

With such a momentous penalty, what motivates a person to become a traitor? As this book demonstrates, there are a number of reasons why an individual would make the decision to betray his or her country. Ideology for one. Many of the major conflicts and confrontations that blighted the last century were, of course, driven by differing ideologies. The Second World War, for instance, produced traitors who fell for the fascist rhetoric of men such as Adolf Hitler, Benito Mussolini and, in Britain, Sir

11

Oswald Mosley. The hatred of people like William Joyce – the infamous 'Lord Haw-Haw' – and John Amery, was fuelled by the anti-Semitic policies of the Nazis and, to some extent, by the posturing of Mosley and his British Union of Fascists. They broadcast to Britain from Germany, undermining the war effort and promulgating fake news.

The Cambridge spies and others, such as Douglas 'Dave' Springhall and Wilfred Macartney, were driven by their unwavering commitment to communism, their belief in the myth of the Soviet worker-peasant state. And, certainly, in the case of the Cambridge group, there was a belief that the Soviet Union was the only country that would stand up to the spread of Nazism and authoritarianism.

Then there was George Blake, converted to communism during captivity in the Korean War, who famously said: 'To betray, you must first belong', pointing out that he was an outsider, a man who failed to fit into British society and its class system. The fact that he was a fervent communist made betrayal relatively easy for him.

The development of the atom bomb during the Second World War in the British-Canadian 'Tube Alloys' project and the American Manhattan Project turned several communist British scientists into traitors, men such as Alan Nunn May and Klaus Fuchs, who believed they were levelling the playing field and enabling world peace by passing atomic secrets to the Soviet Union.

Of course, there were others who betrayed their country for more mundane reasons. John Herbert King, who worked in the Foreign Office cipher department in the 1930s, sold secrets to the Russians in order to maintain an expensive mistress and finance his lifestyle. Unknown to him, however, some of the secrets he sold made their way to the Germans and the Italians against whom Britain was fighting. Harry Houghton displayed his desire for cash while working at the British Embassy in

Warsaw when he imported goods for sale on the black market. He still had that hankering when he and his mistress, Ethel Gee, began to smuggle top-secret documents out of the Underwater Detection Establishment on Portland in the mid-1950s.

In various differing ways, the thread of sex runs through espionage activities in the twentieth century. The Cambridge spies contained a couple of gay men in Anthony Blunt and the outrageous Guy Burgess, and one bisexual man, Donald Maclean. These men were already in danger of exposure and imprisonment for their lifestyles and so, as people who were adept at living a double life and operating in the shadows, they were probably ideally suited to the double life of the spy. Sex also rears its head in the case of John Vassall, who was caught in a classic homosexual honey-trap which led to him spying for the Soviet Union from 1954 to 1962. Geoffrey Prime, a traitor during the 1960s and 1970s, was only caught because of his arrest for a series of vile sex offences he committed.

Of course, stupidity and arrogance sometimes create traitors. Michael Bettaney was an attention-seeker, but his pleas to spy for the Soviets fell on deaf ears, no matter what material he tempted them with. The Second World War traitors, Theodore Schurch, George Armstrong and Duncan Scott-Ford, were foolish young men who made naïve errors and paid for them with their lives.

All these men were brought to justice under the Official Secrets Acts. The first such act was passed in 1889, creating offences for disclosure of information by officials and for breach of official trust. This was bolstered in 1911 by the Official Secrets Act 1911, introduced in response to public alarm at the threat posed by Germany at the time. This alarm arose from popular novels and plays that dramatised the threat and exaggerated it. Books such as William Le Queux's 1909 novel, *Spies of the Kaiser: Plotting the Downfall of England* and reports such as one in the *Morning Post* in 1907, claiming that there were 90,000

German reservists and spies in Britain, helped to create a febrile atmosphere. Invasion fiction had become popular, represented by books such as Erskine Childers' *The Riddle of the Sands* from 1903 and Le Queux's *The Invasion of 1910*, published in 1906. The Agadir Crisis, in which Germany dispatched a gunboat to the Moroccan port in response to the deployment of a force of French troops in Morocco, tested Britain's alliance with France, created near-hysteria and led not only to the passing of the Official Secrets Act 1911 but also to the creation of the British Secret Service. There were heavy penalties for the breach of the Act by reporting on or making sketches of military or naval installations or even giving protection to people who had been engaged in such activities. It was amended in 1989, but the individuals in this book were brought to book by the 1911 Act.

The *sturm und drang* of the twentieth century produced a seemingly endless supply of traitors. Harold Macmillan's government of the late 1950s and early 1960s teetered on the brink of collapse as the Kim Philby scandal played out. It was then rocked by the exposure of the Portland spy ring, closely followed by the arrest and conviction of John Vassall. '… … you just can't shoot a spy as you did in the war,' Macmillan is reported to have said to the head of the Security Service, 'There will be a great public trial. Then the security services will not be praised for how efficient they are, but blamed for how hopeless they are. Then there will be an enquiry. There will be a terrible row in the press. There will then be a debate in the House of Commons, and the government will probably fall. Why the devil did you catch him?' Eventually, of course, it was the Profumo scandal that brought his government down, but the relentless sequence of spy scandals irreparably damaged the public's perception of its government.

Treachery is a momentous act that impacts upon the fate of nations and the lives of everyone. The men whose stories are told in this book were responsible for countless deaths, for swings in history and for the devastation of their own lives and families. But their stories are extraordinary, and they could even be called courageous, risking all as they did, very often for what they deeply believed in. I hope this book demonstrates that as well as the evil for which they were often responsible.

Communist Spies of the 1920s and 1930s

The Secret Service Bureau

The United Kingdom's Secret Service emerged in 1909 from the government's nervousness in the early 1900s about the threat posed to the British Empire by Germany's imperial ambitions. Germany had adopted an imperialist policy – known as *Weltpolitik* – with the ultimate aim of making the country – recently unified under Kaiser Wilhelm I – a global power. In a debate in the Reichstag on 6 December 1897, German Foreign Secretary Bernhard von Bülow famously said: 'We wish to throw no one into the shade, but we also demand our own place in the sun.' The British Empire was the obvious rival to German ambitions and scare stories began to spread that German spies were operating in Britain, undermining the country's defences and its maintenance of imperial control. As it transpired, these suspicions proved largely unfounded, but there was considerable public concern. In response, the Prime Minister of the day, Herbert Asquith, ordered the Committee of Imperial Defence to look at ways to counter German espionage. Their recommendation in 1909 was the establishment of a Secret Service Bureau.

With its focus on Germany, the Bureau was shared between the Admiralty and the War Office, its brief to control secret intelligence operations in the United Kingdom. It was split into two sections – naval and military. Initially, the naval section was principally engaged in scrutinising the strength of the Imperial German Navy, but over time it began to specialise in foreign espionage. The military section, meanwhile, focused on internal counter-espionage operations. During the First World War, the separation of the two sections was made official and in 1916, the foreign section was renamed MI1(c) of the Directorate of Military Intelligence. A 50-year-old Royal Navy officer, Captain Mansfield Smith-Cumming, was selected to lead it. He was in the habit of signing communications with the letter 'C' written in green ink and this codename has famously been used by every director of the service since then.

The home section, meanwhile, became Section 5 (MI5) and was headed by Vernon Kell, an officer in the South Staffordshire Regiment who would remain in the role until 1940. Its initial brief was limited – protecting national security through the use of counter-espionage. Working closely with the Special Branch, a unit of the London Metropolitan Police that had been established in 1883 as a counter-terrorism unit, it identified foreign agents while Special Branch took on the work of investigation, arrest and interrogation.

During the First World War, MI5 enjoyed a great deal of success in identifying German agents who had managed to embed themselves in Great Britain. This was achieved mostly by inspection of mail and strict border controls. Once Germany had been defeated, however, attention very quickly turned to the Soviet Union whose international organisation, the Comintern, advocated world communism. The Comintern sponsored Soviet spies working in Britain, but their operatives were inexperienced and fairly incompetent as evidenced by the fact that MI5 caught most of them. Meanwhile, the service's responsibilities grew. It began to scrutinise not only foreign agents, but also trade unions, pacifist and anti-conscription organisations, amongst others. They justified such activities by insisting that foreign money was, more often than not, involved in their activities. It still had no powers of arrest, and continued to be reliant on Special Branch for that, but it was now a powerful investigative Force.

Immediately after the war, MI5 had its budget slashed from

£100,000 to a mere £35,000 which meant its complement was cut from 800 officers to just a dozen. The result was that it played no significant part in the Irish War of Independence but Kell soon began the process of re-establishing MI5 as Britain's most important domestic spy agency. In the 1920s, however, it was mainly concerned with security issues involving the armed forces. Only in 1931 did it assume responsibility for all counter-intelligence in Britain.

In the world of spying, much changed in the 1930s and MI5 lagged behind. An inherently conservative organisation, it had changed little in its approach to counter-intelligence for many years. It still imagined that Soviet Intelligence, in the form of the NKVD (People's Commissariat for Internal Affairs), obtained information by bribing officials, or from observation. Or perhaps agents would infiltrate trade unions or the military, gathering intelligence that way. Things had moved on, however, and, as we shall see later in this book, Soviet methods had become much more long-term in strategy. The aim was to recruit from the elite and wait patiently until their recruits had gained positions of influence.

Following the end of the First World War, Britain, formerly the most powerful nation on earth, was drained of energy and burdened with huge debt. In the east, the Russian Revolution provided a huge threat to the status quo, with its stated aim of destroying capitalism and imperialism, thereby irrevocably changing society and the world economy. Britain's position as the dominant power was in danger. She faced an ideologically driven enemy that operated not in the conventional way to remove opposition, but, rather, worked subversively, in cells, its operatives infiltrating the local population and blending in with it. An almost mythical image of the Soviet Union as a kind of Utopia was promulgated at the same time, an image of the country that was increasingly removed from the reality, but which was enthusiastically embraced by many.

The biggest opportunity for the change sought by the Comintern came with the General Strike of 1926, an event that Prime Minister Stanley Baldwin worried had brought the country 'nearer to proclaiming civil war than we had been for centuries past'. It was certainly a remarkable moment in British history; more working days were lost in that one year than in 1912, 1921 and 1979 – years of large-scale strikes – put together. The nine-day strike, however, achieved little and proved a huge disappointment to the Communist Party of Great Britain (CPGB) and the Comintern. They had hoped for revolution and were now faced by militant trade unionists who had been encouraged to withhold their labour by communist propaganda but had achieved very little as a result. Revolution did not seem to be something the British were that partial to.

Two of the three traitors in the following chapter – Wilfred Macartney and 'Dave' Springhall – were ideologically driven towards espionage, although the remarkable Macartney was a born seeker of adventure and this may also have been a large part of his motivation. Springhall was the real thing – a dyed-in-the-wool communist. The third, John Herbert King, was a weak and foolish man whose motivation was purely financial, betraying his country simply in order to support a mistress. They all did irreparable damage to the interests of Great Britain at a perilous time in world history, when forces were positioning themselves for the war that would inevitably erupt at the end of the 1930s.

Wilfred Macartney:
The Man Who Never Told the Truth

A Stout, Short-sighted Scotsman

An acquaintance described him as 'a rosy-faced, innocent-looking little man who wore bottle-top glasses... a stout, short-sighted Scotsman'; not the idealised image of a spy of the dashing James Bond type, but a seemingly ordinary little man whose 70 years on this planet were, nonetheless, filled with excitement and derring-do of a rather old-fashioned kind.

Wilfred Francis Remington Macartney, AKA the 'Monocle Man', was an enigma, a Zelig-like character who seems to have lived a dozen lives and, if what he lived was insufficiently adventurous, perhaps he was happy to embellish it a little. He claimed to have received war decorations from both Serbia and Greece and had friends in high places... and most certainly in low ones, too. One thing is for certain, however, he passed secrets to the Russians and was sentenced to ten years in prison for it.

But, who exactly was Wilfred Macartney? He came into the world in Cupar in Scotland in 1899... or, perhaps, he was born in Malta. As with many things about Macartney, the facts are unclear. His mother was American and his father a mélange of Irish, Scottish and American, the family wealth resulting from the success of his father's business, the Malta-based engineering company, Macartney & McElroy, specialists in the construction of electric tramway systems around the world. His father was able to provide young Wilfred and his brother with expensive educations and in pursuit of his father's business interests, the family travelled the world. As a boy, Macartney visited Jamaica, the United States, Malta and many other places. In Ukraine when he was aged six, he saw his mother arrested and accused of espionage by the Tsar's police. Fortunately, the authorities quickly realised that it was a case of mistaken identity and she was released.

Unusually, his father made Wilfred and his brother directors of his company when Wilfred was just 13 and his brother 18 and, when he died, the boys inherited his substantial fortune. Wilfred received £67,000, equivalent to around £5 million in 2021, but, characteristically, he would later gamble away his inheritance.

In early 1914, he travelled across the Atlantic to Pittsburgh to attend university, leaving his brother to attend to the business and deal with litigation over their father's will. His trip coincided, however, with a tense period in European politics and, when war eventually broke out in July of that year, Macartney, ever the romantic in search of adventure, hurried home to join the flood of young British men rushing to enlist. The problem was, of course, that at 15 he was too young. After trying to get into uniform by lying about his age he was devastated to be rejected on account of his poor eyesight. The following year, with the war escalating, he tried again and this time his application was successful. Due to the weakness in his eyes, however, he was sent to the Western Front as a driver for the Third London Ambulance Corps. After a time, he secured a commission in the Royal Scots and was sent to the Eastern Mediterranean where his commanding officer was the Scottish writer, Compton Mackenzie, a captain in command of British intelligence operations there. Macartney later wrote: 'Ciphers, agents' reports, inter-departmental jealousies, international intrigues added to my not inconsiderable experience, making me regard life and the war less credulously than was usual among boys of my age.'

In 1917, Macartney was reassigned to France, where, fighting in the battle of Cambrai, he was wounded and taken prisoner. He almost lost an eye which was saved by his captors and shrapnel in his shoulder was only removed ten years later. Characteristically, on 17 October 1918, he escaped captivity by jumping from a moving train at Aachen that was taking him from Parchim in Germany to Aix-la-Chapelle. Instead of making his way to Holland and safety, he found himself in the Belgian town of Bilzen where he knocked on the door of a large house. Luckily for him, the owner was sympathetic and gave him shelter. Some weeks later, Macartney finally made his way back to London where he was in danger of being court-martialled for desertion. Once his story became known, however, he instead received a commendation.

After the War

Macartney was next attached to the Berlin-Baghdad Railway Mission in Constantinople, working in the role of Railway Transport Officer in the course of which he became friendly with Kemal Atatürk, the founding father of the Turkish Republic and its first president. He left the army eventually in 1919, by which time he had risen to the rank of lieutenant but had also developed a serious drinking habit that led to him associating with some unsavoury characters.

Astonishingly, despite his experiences and adventures, when Macartney was demobbed he was still a minor and unable to access his share of his father's estate. Living above his means, he became very bitter about what he saw as a grave injustice. He was also bitter about what he saw around him, and felt, like many of his generation, that he had been let down by the government and the society for which he had risked his life in the war. This led to an interest in communism. 'The only chance for the huge majority of mankind,' he wrote, '… is a communistic revolution leading to the replacement of a system of universal exploitation, degradation and horror by a communistic economy in which human beings shall enjoy the full fruits of an [sic] universal abundance'.

In 1920, he joined the Spanish Foreign Legion, but returned from Morocco just over a year later, telling *The Times* of the privation and suffering endured by him and the 53 other British legionnaires who returned.

In 1923, he married Martha J Warden, daughter of an actor, but he was still always broke. Some sources suggest that he next enrolled, like many ex-soldiers, for British intelligence with the Black and Tans. These were constables forming a paramilitary unit recruited during the Irish War of Independence to support the Royal Irish Constabulary against the Irish Republican Army. He is said to have worked alongside George Nathan, another English recruit to the Black and Tans who has been associated with the so-called Curfew Murders in Limerick, three killings perpetrated on 7 March 1921. The Sinn Féin mayor of Limerick, George Clancy, and councillor and former mayor, Michael O'Callaghan and a town hall clerk, Joseph O'Donahue, were each shot to death at home. The wife of one of the dead men identified George Nathan as being amongst her husband's murderers but he was never charged.

Back in London, in February 1926, Macartney was penniless and on the wrong end of a nine-month sentence for smashing the window of a jeweller's shop in Albemarle Street in Mayfair. When he left prison, he did the rounds in Fleet Street, offering them the inside story of his activities as an agent of the Secret Service which came to the attention of MI5 who decided to keep an eye on him. He joined the Communist Party of Great Britain around this time, and two articles written by him appeared in the communist newspaper, the *Sunday Daily Worker*, which drew further interest from MI5. He was, as ever, quite a dapper chap, an MI5 report describing him at the age of 28 as 'very neatly dressed, usually wears an eyeglass, and of excellent address and good education; small to medium height, clean shaven, dark hair usually worn brushed right back from his forehead…' This report went on to say that 'Macartney is completely unscrupulous, can never tell the truth about any matter, is very clever but not quite so clever as he thinks.' MI5 decided around this time not to proceed with their enquiries into his activities.

Things started to go seriously wrong for Wilfred Macartney in 1927. He had already been recruited, the circumstances are unknown, by the Soviets and was given a handler named Georg Hansen who went by the codename 'Johnson'. In March of that year, he asked a Lloyds underwriter, George Monckland, one of his gambling partners, to give him information on arms shipments to the Baltic States. Monckland, uncharitably described in MI5 files as 'an undesirable man about town', could access this information through the cargo documents that were lodged with insurance companies. He was at first unaware of exactly what Macartney was up to, but when he was given a detailed questionnaire on military matters to complete, Monckland became suspicious and contacted Admiral Sir Reginald 'Blinker' Hall, Director of Naval Intelligence during the First World War who took the matter to Freddie Browning, former head of SIS. The case was then passed to Desmond Morton who worked at the War Office rather than to MI5. He took charge of Monckland, using him as a double agent against Macartney. On 2 May 1927, Morton sent a message to MI5:

'We have received a report originating from the G.P.U. [Soviet foreign intelligence] in Paris as follows: 'W. F. R. Macartney… is now acting as an agent for the Soviet Union in connection with British Aircraft matters and the British Air Force. He arrived in Paris on the morning of April 29th, having crossed from England by the previous night's boat.

Here he is going under the name W. F. Hudson... He is in touch with a certain George Monckland... expects to receive reports on British Air Force matters from England... He intends to post these reports when received back to England to George Monkland, who has been instructed to pass them on to the head of the USSR espionage.'

The case became a joint effort between MI5 and SIS with Morton and Jasper Harker of MI5 managing it. While evidence was being collected to build a case against Macartney, it was decided to do no more than observe. Meanwhile checks were made into Monckland's background and a tap was put on his phone. It was learned that he slept late and did not seem to work much and as a result of that, plus his gambling losses, his finances were in a bad state, which could give someone leverage over him.

One day, a call came in to Monckland's phone from a man named 'McCarthy' – undoubtedly Macartney. He warned Monckland to hide 'those papers' as the Soviet espionage headquarters in London had been raided that day. A few days previously a trap had been set. Monckland had been given a Signals Training pamphlet that was about to be replaced with a new version and was told to give this to Macartney who would be kept under close observation by Special Branch operatives. He was seen passing the manual to Soviet officials who worked at the All Russian Cooperative Society (ARCOS), a Soviet body responsible for developing Soviet-British trade in the early years of the Soviet Union. The organisation had been suspected of being a cover for espionage operations ever since 1925 when an MI5 operative, John Ottaway, had followed a suspected Russian spy back to its Moorgate offices. It was also believed that in the basement of the offices, the Soviets had a Photostat machine that was used specifically to copy secret documents.

Late in the afternoon of 12 May, around 100 uniformed policemen, 50 Special Branch officers and a number of Foreign Office interpreters entered the offices of ARCOS where they seized control of the telephone system and started sifting through documents. Drilling equipment was used to open safes and strongboxes. In the basement a secret cipher room was discovered inside which officials were hastily burning documents. The Signals Training pamphlet was never recovered.

Arrest and Trial

This incident had a dramatic consequence. Britain severed diplomatic and economic ties with the Soviet Union and the British government accused the Soviets of engaging in subversive activities 'in abuse of diplomatic privilege'. The Soviets were horrified and, paranoid as ever, became convinced that this must be the prelude to war, to a British invasion of the USSR. Wilfred Macartney now took on greater importance in the eyes of the authorities. At the time, as he moved back and forward between Paris, London and Berlin, he was writing letters to Monckland, all of which were intercepted by British intelligence. Monckland informed Morton that, using a false passport, Macartney was heading for a meeting in Paris with agents who were going to be running Soviet operations in Britain. This was important information as, without knowledge of Macartney's fake passport, the security services would never have been able to trace his movements. He was in Paris by the middle of July and Morton was receiving reports via Monckland. In one intercepted letter, Macartney boasted that he was travelling to Berlin, at the time a hotbed of European espionage, to meet 'somebody of great importance'. On another occasion, Macartney spoke of unsuccessfully offering his services to Prince Carol of Romania.

On 17 November, he and Johnson/Hansen were arrested and

charged with offences under the Official Secrets Act, following which they were held on remand at Brixton Prison until their trial which started at the Old Bailey in January 1928. Macartney's defence counsel attempted to destroy George Monckland's character, by claiming that he associated with 'mainly criminal types' while also maintaining that Macartney had merely been working as a journalist, trying to find evidence to prove that the infamous Zinoviev letter had actually been forged by MI5. The Zinoviev letter had been published and sensationalised by the *Daily Mail* just before the October 1924 general election. Purportedly written to the Communist Party of Great Britain by Grigory Zinoviev, head of the Comintern, it ordered the party to engage in seditious activities. The letter's objective was to turn voters against the Labour Party and, although generally accepted now to have been a forgery, it did huge damage to Labour's election prospects, helping the Conservatives to a landslide victory.

Macartney was put on trial alongside his Soviet handler, Johnson/Hansen, and was found guilty of several charges, including 'attempting to obtain information on the RAF' and 'collecting information relating to the mechanised force of His Majesty's Army'. He was sentenced to ten years' hard labour with a further two years, to be served concurrently. Unrepentant and indignant, he later said of his offence, speaking of himself in the third person:

'It cannot be denied that for money Macartney took on the job of obtaining information for a foreign power. The power was the Soviet Union and Macartney believed in communism. The first task Macartney's employers set him was to ascertain the amount and quality of war material shipped from Great Britain to the Baltic States, Poland, Latvia etc. Now to obtain and pass on this information is not a criminal offence and therefore it would be interesting to know at just what points Macartney's activities actually became criminal.'

He served his sentence at Parkhurst prison on the Isle of Wight, and was released after eight years. But his life after prison was hardly any less exciting than before. In 1936, he published a book about his experiences in Parkhurst. In *Walls Have Mouths* he was scathing about the conditions in which prisoners were kept. 'The food I received in German prison camps was,' he wrote, 'with the exception of the bread, cleaner and more nutritious and more palatable than what was grudgingly given me at Parkhurst. The food on certain days was uneatable even to a hungry man.' When he had complained in prison, he had been told his conditions would be improved if he would inform on other prisoners. He refused.

In December 1936, Wilfred Macartney travelled to Spain, like many other young, left-leaning men, to fight for the Republican cause in the Spanish Civil War. Of course, his previous military experience was of great value and in December of that year he was appointed the first commander of the British Battalion. His colleagues were not entirely impressed, however, by his military credentials. As one said: 'it soon became evident that [Macartney] had very little idea of the duties of a Battalion Commander.' Another said: 'He was not terribly popular in the battalion but I think he was respected for his ability. He was a capable military officer. He had a rather arrogant style.'

During the Second World War, Macartney is said to have carried out an undercover operation alongside Eddie Chapman – also known as Agent Zigzag – that involved them in sending back to Germany false information about how accurate the V1 rocket's strikes on London were. The bombs were actually undershooting, falling short of their targets, but Chapman informed them that they were overshooting. In 1946, the pair antagonised the authorities by writing an account of their deception for the French newspaper, *Étoile du Soir*. This brought charges under the Official Secrets Act and each was found guilty and sentenced to a fine of £100 (around £3,500 today) or ten years in prison. Needless to say, Chapman had to pay the eternally penniless Macartney's fine. Alongside Chapman, Macartney partied at the time with politicians such as Michael Foot, future leader of the Labour Party, Aneurin Bevan, Health Minister in Clement Attlee's post-war Labour government and Tony Benn.

The extraordinary life of this minor traitor ended in 1970 and it is probably best to rely on his great friend, the philosopher, AJ Ayer, to sum him up, as he did in his autobiography.

'A remarkable communist, with whom I made friends at this time, was Wilfred Macartney... White-haired and rubicund, with the manner of a hard-drinking journalist, he had a vitality which his years in prison appeared to have done nothing to diminish. He was the most conspicuous example that I have ever come across of those who combine left-wing opinions with an appetite for high-living. I think of him in an expensive hotel suite, which he had the air of having annexed, drinking champagne and surrounded by pretty girls, being still unwilling to deny the possibility that the defendants in the Moscow trials had really been guilty of the charges brought against them. He was not a man whom one could altogether admire but one would have needed to be a greater puritan than I was not to enjoy his company.'

John Herbert King:
The Spy Who Didn't Exist

The Cipher Clerk

The name of John Herbert King had appeared for many years on the Foreign Office List, a directory of all the people working at the Foreign Office, until 1940, when it simply disappeared without any explanation. The reason was that he had been exposed as a Soviet spy and went to prison from 1939 to 1945. Nobody knew until 1956, and even then it was denied.

King was born in Ireland in 1884 and during the First World War served in the Artists' Rifles which attracted mainly recruits from public schools and universities. During the war, he was sent to the Middle East where he worked as a cipher officer, a job that involved the encrypting and decrypting of coded messages. He was good at it and joined the Foreign Office immediately after the war in the same capacity. Posted to Paris, he associated with the so-called 'Ace of Spies' – Sidney Reilly, a Russian-born adventurer who worked as a secret agent for the Foreign Section of the British Secret Service Bureau, which would later become known as MI6. In 1926, King was transferred to Berlin and we learn that he had been married because around this time, he separated from his wife.

From 1932 to 1934, King was in China, working for the Foreign Office and on his return was sent to Geneva to work as a cipher clerk as part of the British Delegation to the League of Nations. At the city's International Club, King was introduced by a Foreign Office official named Raymond Oake to a Dutchman, Henri Pieck. Oake was courting the daughter of Captain Harvey, the Principal British Passport Officer in

Geneva and Pieck made a point of befriending British officials he considered potential spies. King became friendly with Pieck, socialising with him on a number of occasions while in Geneva.

In 1935, the two men's paths crossed again, at Ward's Irish House, a pub in Dartmouth Street in London. Oake, who was present, reintroduced them and after that, King went on to meet Pieck on a number of occasions. The Dutchman had an office in the City and another above an art shop in Buckingham Gate where he had set up a special locked room for photo-reproduction of stolen telegrams and documents. Pieck set his trap, telling King he knew a banker in The Hague who could make them both money if King could obtain for him information passing through the Foreign Office from various embassies. When King demurred, Pieck reassured him, telling him that the banker was simply eager to obtain advance political information that he could exploit in order to make deals on the stock market and in the money exchanges. Pieck offered to share with King any money he made as a result.

At that point in time, John King was certainly fertile ground for an agent of a foreign power who could dangle the prospect of easy money in front of him. His situation was dire – his wages were low, he had no pension and minimal career prospects. Worse still, he was in financial difficulties, with a young son to take care of and an American mistress – Helen Wilkie – who had expensive tastes. He was also disgruntled, believing he was being discriminated against at work because of his Irish background. He was delighted to have found a solution to his financial problems and unhesitatingly agreed to do what Pieck asked. What he did not know, however, was that the information he was providing, the documents and telegrams, would not be going to a Dutch bank that wanted to get ahead of its rivals. Rather, they would be going straight onto the desk of a Soviet intelligence officer in Moscow.

Telegrams and Roneos

John King began to smuggle information out of the Foreign Office, although, in his statement to Special Branch, he attempted to minimise the importance of what he took out:

'I handed to Pieck, from time to time, copies of telegrams coming in from Embassies – for example, reports of conversations between Sir Neville Henderson [then British Ambassador to Germany] or between Kemal Atatürk [President of Turkey] and the Ambassador in Turkey or some such persons. There were sometimes eight or nine pages of roneoed matter – sometimes three or four – never more than ten. They were never of great political importance.'

To effect the handover of information, he met the Dutchman in various places – the Victoria Hotel, the Lancaster Gate Hotel or at Pieck's office in Buckingham Gate. In return for the copy of the telegram or document, Pieck would pay him between £50 and £200, his share, according to Pieck, of the profit made by the non-existent banker from earlier telegrams he had handed over.

In 1936, in danger of being exposed, Pieck was suddenly ordered by Moscow to lie low. Before he did so, however, he introduced King to his replacement, 'a very tall, cadaverous looking man, aged about 40', according to King, called Petersen. He was Eastern European – perhaps Hungarian, King thought. In reality, he was a Soviet agent, Theodore Maly. Born in Timişoara (in present-day Romania) in Austria-Hungary in 1894, he had been ordained as a priest, but, losing his faith during the horrors of the First World War, had joined the Bolsheviks. He was one of the controllers of the Soviet spy ring known as the Cambridge Five. For 18 months, Petersen was King's handler but, in June of 1937, he told him that he had to go away 'for a month or so' and never returned. Maly had actually been revealed as a spy by the British Secret Service in a case in which secret documents were being stolen from Woolwich Arsenal. Fortunately for him, he was tipped off before MI5 could move in but back in Moscow, he became caught up in Stalin's dreadful purges of the late 1930s. He was executed in Moscow in 1938 after confessing under torture to being a German agent.

During those 18 months, King handed Petersen/Maly copies of telegrams, as he had done with Pieck, meeting him once or twice a week at his own flat, in Holbein House in Chelsea, or in a room at the Royal Court Hotel where King stayed for a few weeks. All he knew of Petersen was that he lived somewhere near Marble Arch. What Petersen really wanted from King, however, was a Foreign Office cipher and the re-ciphering tables that were used – basically, the code. Horrified, King adamantly refused to provide what Peterson wanted. In his statement he swore that he had 'never, never taken any ciphers or tables' out of his office. 'In other words,' he said, 'I have never transmitted to any person any cipher or re-cipher tables or in any way been party to such transaction. All the documents I gave to Pieck and Petersen were already decoded.'

King had earned good money from his espionage, estimating that he had received about £1,200 from Petersen and about £1,300 from Pieck. Two years before his arrest, he had given £1,300 to Helen Wilkie to be deposited at the Chancery Lane Safe Deposit where she worked, and he told her that if anything were to happen to him, she was to have it. He later insisted that she knew nothing about how he had come by this money.

The Damage Done

King passed his Soviet handlers documents between 1934 and 1936. They made their way to the Soviet Embassy in London and, on several occasions where they were relevant to Italian interests, they were forwarded to the Italian Embassy. The first instance of this was the 1933 report by a committee headed by Sir John Maffey on British interests in Ethiopia; the second was the briefing paper Lord Privy Seal Anthony Eden took with him on an official visit to Rome in June 1935; and the third was a 1936 dossier of reports and a memorandum written by Eden who was by that time Foreign Secretary. These documents, gathered under the title 'The German Menace', fell into the hands of Count Galeazzo Ciano, Italian Foreign Minister, but also the son-in-law of Benito Mussolini. In October 1936, Ciano showed them to Adolf Hitler at Berchtesgaden. The source of all this material was undoubtedly the Soviet Embassy in London and they must originally have come from the Communications Department of the Foreign Office which was responsible for sending and receiving such documents to and from embassies and legations around the world. There was no possibility that they could have been intercepted in transit or deciphered because they were substantial in size and were transported in diplomatic bags or in the sealed red dispatch cases – 'Red Boxes' – that were used to transport ministerial documents around Whitehall. There was no way, therefore, that the British would be aware of the fact that the Soviets were in possession of such documents. King, it seemed, had nothing to fear.

The Italians received no further leaks after 1936, but between 19 April and 17 August 1939, leaked material began to arrive at the German Embassy in London. It consisted of selected, edited details of telegrams between the British and the Soviets about Russia joining efforts by Britain and France to stop German expansion into Eastern Europe. The Soviet Union signed a non-aggression pact with Hitler's Germany on 24 August 1939, ending the negotiations but it is evident that whoever was leaking material must have been in a position to access the actual texts of the telegrams because they are very accurate.

Only in two parts of the Foreign Office could anyone have such access – the Central Department which worked on the texts, or the Communications Department where John King worked.

The information was also received by the Germans very soon after telegrams had been sent. Thus, the Soviet reply to proposals put forward by the British on 6 May was handed to the British Embassy in Moscow on the evening of 14 May. This reply was dispatched to London shortly after midnight, arriving at 9.30 the following morning. At 9.33 that night, the German Embassy was sending the details of the telegram to Berlin. It is worthy of note, however, that the information was not entirely correct. The information received by the Germans claimed that the Russians were keen to leave out of the negotiations the issue of the Baltic States, Estonia, Latvia and Lithuania, until there was agreement on their proposal for an alliance between the Soviet Union, Britain and France. But, this was, in fact, not the case. The Soviets had insisted on the inclusion of these matters from the start.

The first telegram that was leaked to the Germans by what they described as 'a reliable source' was about the 'so-called pact of mutual assistance' and referred to Soviet proposals. There were also details of discussions between the Soviet ambassador to France, Jakob Suritz, and French officials, and in Moscow between the Soviet deputy Foreign Minister, Vladimir Potemkin, and the French chargé d'affaires, Jean Payart. Some factually incorrect information was given, in that the British at no point proposed a pact of mutual assistance. It was the Russians, rather, who had put forward such a proposal on 17 April. This Russian proposal was received in London at 6.35 in the morning of Tuesday 18 April. By the evening of Friday 21 April, the Germans had a pretty accurate digest of the Russian proposals and these arrived in Berlin at 9.15am on Saturday 22 April. A third, once again slightly incorrect telegram was leaked a few days later, and again on 8 May, the Germans transmitted a summary of British counter-proposals that had been sent on 6 May. By this time the British and French stances on the issue had diverged, the French eager to accept the Soviets in an alliance, the British wary of its effect on parts of the world that were enemies of communism, such as eastern Europe, and Catholic countries such as Spain.

Proposals and counter-proposals continued to be made throughout the next few months but the 'reliable source' chose to pass information to the Germans on just two occasions. On 12 June, he sent them a summary of a new British proposal that had been sent to the French. There was nothing further until 29 June, on the afternoon of which it was reported to Berlin by the London embassy that the British and the French had agreed to a new proposal that was going to be given to the British ambassador in Moscow that day. The telegram presented the main points of a telegram that had been sent two days previously to the British ambassador in Moscow, Sir William Seeds. The Germans noted that the Soviets were negotiating without any real enthusiasm and would probably be quite happy if they were to fail.

The 'reliable source' woke up again on 12 July, delivering Russian demands that had been passed to Seeds on 6 July, and more information was to follow on 17 July, stating that Seeds had received instructions not to make any further concessions on the issues of indirect aggression or a military pact. Britain was demanding that Molotov should sign the political pact and the military pact at the same time, something to which the French objected.

On 10 August, after being silent for a time, their source reported to the Germans that the British had conceded the right of the Russians to enter the Baltic States if they were attacked, even if they were not actually requesting assistance. The source appeared twice more, passing information on negotiations to the Germans on 14 and 17 August.

The question remained as to who the source was and there were really only two possibilities. Firstly, it may have been a British person who was opposed to the idea of Britain negotiating with the Soviets. Or, it may have been a Soviet agent.

Of course, the actual spy was John Herbert King, code-named MAG.

Arrest and Trial

As noted, the material that King provided for his Soviet handlers was very fresh. There were telegrams, weekly summaries of diplomatic communications, documents stolen from the cipher department safe and observations, analysis and reports by him. But it was all brought to an end by the Soviet defector, Walter Krivitsky, Chief of Soviet Military Intelligence for Western Europe. Deciding that Russia was turning into a fascist state and dismayed by Stalin's purges in which four of his agents, including Maly, had been executed, Krivitsky defected.

He revealed, in an interview by Isaac Don Levine for the American *Saturday Evening Post*, that the Soviet Union had a couple of agents working deep within the British government. Levine told the British ambassador in Washington that one of these agents was called King and worked in the Foreign Office Communications Department. In Krivitsky's words, King was 'selling everything to Moscow'. In September 1939, even though it was felt that Krivitsky was of dubious credibility, it was decided that it would be too risky to leave King on duty in the Cipher Department. Fortunately, his health had not been good of late and his eyesight had been giving him problems. He was given leave until 25 September and, in the meantime, would be kept under surveillance, his postal and telephone communications scrutinised for suspicious activity. By then, Pieck's business partner had made a statement that Pieck had had dealings with an unknown man who, Pieck had told him, was one of two cipher officers in the British Delegation to a conference in Brussels. It was quickly ascertained that King was one of the two officers. Surveillance of him yielded nothing of substance and his bank account showed nothing other than his salary. Of great suspicion, however, was the fact that Pieck's organisation had a 'control centre', a flat in West London, the telephone account of which was in the name of Helen Wilkie, King's mistress. He had been seen visiting the property on a number of occasions. This connection between Pieck and King proved to be the turning point in the case and King was picked up *en route* to a meeting with his Russian handler in a teashop in Whitehall. In his possession was a top-secret message.

He was interviewed on 25 September by Colonel Valentine Vivian, the head of Section V of the Special Intelligence Service, but King refused to confess, leaving them without a solid case. 'I have no doubt he is guilty – curse him,' wrote Sir Alexander Cadogan, Permanent Under-Secretary for Foreign Affairs in his diary on 26 September, 'but there is no absolute proof'. During the long interrogation, King maintained that his acquaintance with Pieck amounted to no more than a few chance meetings here and there. Helen Wilkie was interviewed, also giving nothing away.

Leaving the Foreign Office after his interview about 6.30pm, King headed straight for Wilkie's West End flat but, having anticipated that he would do this, Special Branch officers were waiting for him. After refusing to make a voluntary statement, he was charged under Section 2(1)(aa) of the Official Secrets Act of 1911. Finally, four days later, while on remand, he asked to make a statement and in it he confessed to everything in order to exonerate Helen Wilkie. Although she was actually charged under the Official Secrets Act, it was felt that the charge would not stand up in court because of King's statement exonerating her. She was released.

King was committed to the Central Criminal Court for

JOHN HERBERT KING

trial on 9 October 1939, the trial presided over by Mr Justice Hilbery. As the first trial of a spy in Great Britain during World War Two, it was conducted in the utmost secrecy; the MI5 officers who arrested King travelled to the court in a car with the windows curtained and all the corridors in the Old Bailey were cleared. Although in such trials the proceedings are held in camera, the verdict and sentence are normally made public but, in the case of John Herbert King, no details were published. No one even really knows when King was eventually released from prison, although it is believed to have been shortly after the end of the war in 1945.

The first anyone outside official circles knew anything about King's activities and his imprisonment came with the publication in 1956 of an American newspaper article about him. Initially, the government denied that there had even been a spy named King, but it could no longer be denied when it emerged that an MP had knowledge of the case and, using Parliamentary privilege, was about to announce it to the House of Commons.

By that time, King was living quietly in a block of flats in London but the press managed to find him. Confronted by a gaggle of reporters, he denied that he was John King, but eventually confessed that he was the person they were looking for and that he had done 'stupid things'. He remained adamant, however, that he had never given any information to the Russians. He claimed that he had been '… up against the powers that be, the War Office and the Foreign Office. I never knew where the information against me came from. I never really understood the charges. But when you are up against the powers that be, there is nothing you can do. Trial is a formality. I pleaded guilty and the trial took only a matter of minutes.'

'Dave' Springhall: A Political Animal

A Boy Sailor

The beautifully landscaped Babaoshan Revolutionary Cemetery in western Beijing is the last resting place for high-ranking revolutionary heroes, important government officials and those who have made a significant contribution to Chinese society. Amongst the gravestones is a fairly substantial one, marking the last resting place of the English traitor, Douglas Frank Springhall, nickname 'Springie', but more commonly known as 'Dave', one-time National Organiser of the Communist Party of Great Britain (CPGB). 'Douglas Frank Springhall...' it is inscribed, '... Vanguard fighter of the British working class and loyal friend of the Chinese people.' There is little doubt that Springhall would have been proud both to have had that inscription on his headstone, and also to have ended his days in Communist China. After all, this was a man whose first act, when waking up after being shot through the cheek at the Battle of Jarama in the Spanish Civil War, was to ask how the CPGB had done in the London County Council elections.

Born in Willesden on 28 March 1901, Springhall opted for a naval career, serving on the training ship HMS *Arethusa* and from there, aged just fifteen years and three months, enlisting in the Royal Navy as a Boy Second Class on board HMS *Ganges*, a training establishment where he became a Boy Telegraphist. In 1917, he did a year of temporary service in the Royal Australian Navy on the battlecruiser, HMS *Australia* before, in 1918, joining HMS *Indomitable*, serving on her until February 1919. He was discharged to Devonport Barracks – HMS *Vivid II* – and promoted to Ordinary Telegraphist on his 18th birthday. It seems he may have been less than proficient at the job as just a month later he became a stoker, working in the heat of the engine room.

In November 1920, his naval career ended in ignominy when he was discharged 'in disgrace' for 'acting as an agent or distributor of seditious material in the armed forces during or after the First World War'. He was also believed to be using the pseudonym 'H.M.S. *Hunter*' to write articles for *Workers' Dreadnought*, a weekly newspaper published by the suffragette, Sylvia Pankhurst. It bore the slogan 'Socialism, Internationalism, Votes for All' and, in June 1920, was adopted as the official organ of the Communist Party in Britain. Springhall's article carried the headline 'Discontent on the Lower Deck' and laid bare the dreadful conditions under which ordinary seamen worked and lived.

In 1920, he was a founding member of the Communist Party of Great Britain, immediately making himself a surveillance target for the security services. Still in his early twenties, he began to make progress through the ranks of the party with election to the national leadership of the Young Communist League (YCL).

Springhall threw himself into politics with relish, becoming Thames Valley Organiser for the National Unemployed Workers' Committee Movement which involved lobbying the Boards of Guardians in Richmond in Surrey and other neighbouring areas. These were the bodies that administered the Poor Law in the United Kingdom and unemployed workers were, of course, dependent on them. He was elected several times to serve as an unemployed workers' candidate on the Richmond Board. He also became involved in trade union politics, sitting as a delegate on the Richmond Trades and Labour Council, and attempted to enter local politics, standing as a candidate for Richmond Town Council, once as a Labour Party candidate and a second time for the Communist Party. At this time, he worked in the construction industry, but, in 1924, increasingly in trouble for his activism, he began a long career working for the Communist Party.

That same year he travelled to Russia, as a delegate to the Fifth Congress of the Communist International (the Comintern) and the Fourth Congress of the Young Communist International. A couple of years later, he was back in Russia, attending the Plenum meetings of the Comintern and the YCL. Once again, he was in trouble, however. In 1926, he was twice jailed for his activities during the General Strike. The *Times* reported his arrest alongside RW Robson who would later become the Communist Party's National Organiser:

> 'Dave Douglas Frank Springhall, 25, of Alton Road, Richmond and Robert William Robson, 29, clerk of Rothwell Street, Camden, were charged at Bow Street Police Court on Saturday with being in the possession without authority or excuse of documents containing reports the publication of which would be a contravention of the Emergency Regulation Act.'

The two men were arrested outside the YCL office in Great Ormond Street and in their possession at the time were documents such as a mimeographed leaflet with the heading 'Young Striker' which also referred to troops. The court took a dim view of their activities, sentencing Robson to six weeks' imprisonment and Springhall to two months' hard labour. Each was also fined £100, equivalent to about £4,000 today.

Moving Up

Undeterred by prison, Springhall returned to work for the party on his release, while the security services maintained their surveillance. They reported on a meeting of ex-service communists that he addressed at a café in High Holborn in June 1928 and soon after, he was in Moscow, studying at the International Lenin School, a training establishment for communists from around the world.

By 1929, the Communist Party in Britain was changing and Springhall, along with men such as William Rust, was deeply invested in this change. The old leadership was being replaced by leaders who were reluctant to follow the Comintern to the letter and who wanted to create a Communist Party that was more suited to the British experience. It was felt that the many threats they faced – such as the growth of fascism, the increasing popularity of corporatist politics and the failure of the General Strike – all indicated that the party had to adapt and change.

After another trip to Moscow in 1931, Springhall returned to Britain as MI5 noted in its files:

'We know that SPRINGHALL returned to this country as the result of a wire from H. POLLITT [another leading figure in the Communist Party of Great Britain] to Moscow – "Essential Miller [a codename for Springhall] return immediately" – and the inference is that he has been recalled to assist in Communist activity directed against the Navy.'

He did indeed carry out activity aimed at fomenting unrest in the Royal Navy. One MI5 memorandum speaks of the interception of a long letter sent to the *Daily Worker* from someone calling himself 'a naval comrade' which was forwarded to Springhall with a request for him to write an article based on it. The letter was then circulated in pamphlet form amongst the crews of the Atlantic Fleet. The MI5 memorandum speaks of the need for MI5 to find out the identity of the letter-writer and the name of Springhall's contact on the Atlantic Fleet.

That same year, Springhall was sent by the CPGB to the North East of England where he became the party's Regional Secretary for that area. Colonel Sir Vivian Kell immediately made the Chief Constable of Newcastle aware of this fact: 'Dear Mr Crawley, I have recently received information to the effect that the well-known communist D F SPRINGHALL is now in Newcastle. I am at the present moment extremely interested in the activities of this individual and should be most grateful if you could let me know his private address,' Meanwhile, more CPGB promotions followed for Springhall – he became Secretary of the London district, he was elected to the Central Committee and he earned a place on the Political Bureau. As such, he played a large part in ejecting Trotskyists from the party, making his feelings clear to one unfortunate victim: 'I'd rather be shot than expelled from the party.'

When the Spanish Civil War broke out in 1936, Dave Springhall was one of the first senior party officials to be sent. Initially, he was a political Commissar of the British Battalion of the International Brigade, but then became Assistant Commissar to the entire 15th Brigade. One member of the International Brigade, Jason Gurney, was distinctly unimpressed by him, describing him as 'a pleasant but hopelessly obtuse and humourless man'. He went on: 'His principal function at Madrigueras seemed to be the delivery of exceedingly boring homilies at the morning parades... He seemed to be a well-intentioned man who was completely out of his depth in the position in which he found himself.' In February 1937, he had a close shave when a bullet passed through his cheek at the indecisive, but fiercely fought Battle of Jarama that resulted in thousands of casualties on both sides.

Olive Sheehan and an Envelope

On his return from Spain, Springhall resumed his party activities but while he was in Moscow, representing the CPGB at the Comintern in September 1939, the British Prime Minister, Neville Chamberlain, made his declaration of war with Germany. Springhall returned to Britain immediately, to take over the role of National Organiser, sharing the leadership of the party with two other communists, Rajani Palme Dutt and William Rust. Under the Government's emergency powers, the *Daily Worker* was banned. There were fears around this time that a peace would be brokered with Germany that would allow Hitler to turn his attention to defeating the Soviet Union. In June 1941, Germany invaded Russia and the United Kingdom and the Soviet Union united in a military alliance against the Germans. With the Soviet Union now an ally, the popularity of the Communist Party of Great Britain was soaring which made it all the more damaging to party prospects when Springhall, one of its senior officials, was exposed as a Russian spy.

Olive Sheehan, a secretary at the Air Ministry, was cultivated as a contact and a source of information by Dave Springhall. According to her evidence at his trial, Springhall turned up at her door in Prince of Wales Mansions in Battersea, one night in December 1942. The two had never previously met, although she had been told – most likely by her left-leaning father-in-law – that a man would be coming to see her. She knew Springhall only as 'Peter' and had no idea where he lived. 'Peter' showed her his Communist Party membership card and they talked about communism. He told her of his visits to Moscow and shared with her his experiences in Spain. Every few weeks after that, he would visit her, and they often discussed left-wing politics. When, finally, towards the end of 1942, he quizzed her as to the nature of her work at the Air Ministry, she explained that she did general clerical duties. In February 1943, however, she was moved into a new department, Signals 1 RCM (Radio Counter-Measures), in which new role she had to handle files, 90 per cent of which were marked 'Secret' or 'Most Secret'. She told him that she was often able to read the contents of these classified files and he persuaded her to pass information about them to him. She had already told him she had sympathy with the Russians and felt that it was unfair for the Allies to keep valuable information from them.

One of the most important pieces of information Sheehan passed to him concerned a new anti-radar device codenamed WINDOW. Also known as 'chaff', this involved aircraft spreading a cloud of small, thin pieces of aluminium, metallised glass fibre or plastic in the sky, which either appeared on radar screens as a cluster of primary targets or filled the screens, rendering them ineffective.

Unfortunately for Springhall and Sheehan, however, her flatmate, Norah Bond, accidentally overheard them discussing these matters in the next room and saw her flatmate actually hand documents to him. When she gave evidence at Springhall's trial, she stated that she overheard amongst other things, the words 'counter measure', 'jamming', 'RDF' and 'tinfoil blacked at the back'. In May, she heard Sheehan say 'the Americans have got something similar, but it is corrugated and much too bulky for us to use and it's not blacked at the back – it's about this size'. The morning after the first conversation, Bond wrote to a friend, a Squadron Leader Blackie and then, in May, after overhearing a second time, she wrote again. By amazing coincidence, Blackie was visiting Bond at the flat when Sheehan handed her an envelope to give to Springhall when he called, saying that she was unable to hand it over as she was suffering from toothache and was going to bed. Blackie steamed open the envelope and found inside a list of the names of other left-wing sympathisers in the Ministry as well as some fresh information on WINDOW.

Arrest and Trial

Blackie informed the Air Ministry immediately and MI5 were brought in. Springhall was arrested in 1943 and, because of the top-secret nature of the material involved, was tried in camera.

His defence was that the Soviet Union was an ally, not an enemy of Britain and, as such, had every right to the information. To his dismay, however, this was deemed irrelevant by the court. He remained blind to any notion that what he had been engaged in was detrimental to the country's war effort:

'Something has been said about my possible motives. I deny that I had any desire to obtain any information on behalf of any member of the United Nations, and above all I deny and repudiate emphatically that any action on my part could be considered to help the enemy at all deliberately. My energies have always been devoted to fighting the Nazis and it would be impossible for me to do any act that would assist them.'

It mattered not. He was sentenced to seven years' penal servitude for passing classified material to the Soviet Union. On sentencing him, the Judge, Mr Justice Oliver, announced:

'The jury has convicted you on the clearest evidence of the most detestable offence of worming vital secrets for the protection of our fighting men from a Government department by means of a little woman clerk. What your purpose was I do not know. I will sentence you as a man who has infringed one of the most important – vitally important – laws for the protection of the country.'

On examining Springhall's diary, the security service learned that Olive Sheehan – who was sentenced to three months' hard labour – was not the only member of the ministry's staff who was smuggling out material. Captain Ormond Uren, a staff officer in the Special Operations Executive (SOE), had given Springhall the entire operational structure of the SOE. He was arrested four days before he was to be parachuted behind enemy lines in Hungary. An Intelligence Officer, Major Edward

Cussen, visited Springhall in Wormwood Scrubs on 6 October 1943 and noted that when the names of Uren and Ray Milne, a female secretary in Section V of the Special Intelligence Service, were mentioned, Springhall appeared to be 'visibly disturbed'. Cussen said that Uren had told him that on 9 April, he had been introduced to Springhall at the Pop-Inn Café and had met him at various places after that. At one such meeting, he had handed Springhall a typewritten document containing a description of the secret department in which he worked and an account of his daily duties. Cussen was particularly interested in getting his hands on this document and he asked Springhall what he had done with it after receiving it from Uren. He also explained the danger to the United Kingdom in such documents being available to the enemy. After reflecting for a few moments, however, Springhall merely replied: 'I am saying nothing.'

Uren was court-martialled, receiving the same sentence as Springhall, and Ray Milne was also arrested for passing information to Springhall. Guy Liddell, Director of B Division of the SIS, described Milne as being 'right in the middle of ISOS [Abwehr decrypts] and everything else'. Under interrogation by her boss, Major Felix Cowgill, and by Roger Hollis, the future Director-General of MI5, Milne said little, but suggested, like Springhall and Uren, that the Soviet Union was an ally and therefore, no harm was being done in informing them about initiatives like WINDOW. She lost her job but was never charged.

Needless to say, the leaders of the Communist Party of Great Britain were horrified and, inevitably, there were demands for an investigation into the party's activities. Springhall was immediately expelled while the leaders vehemently denied any involvement in espionage. Shortly after Springhall's conviction, its name was changed to the 'British Communist Party', in a further effort to distance itself from Moscow and, at the same time, emphasise its Britishness.

Springhall served five years of his sentence and, on his release in 1948, worked in advertising. As soon as he was able to travel, he went to Moscow and Prague before finding employment for his wife and himself in China as an adviser to the Chinese Information Bureau of the Press Administration. After being diagnosed with throat cancer in 1953, he went to Moscow for treatment but died there on 2 September. His body was returned to Beijing for burial at the Babaoshan Revolutionary Cemetery.

The Second World War

Introduction

Interestingly, in the substantial 2011 collection of Winston Churchill's quotations – *Churchill By Himself: The Definitive Collection of Quotations*, edited by Richard Langworth – the index jumps from 'Moslems and Hindus' to 'Mosquito eradication' without any reference to one of the most divisive figures of pre-war Britain – 'Mosley, Oswald'. Some suggest, and probably correctly, that Churchill actually had better things to do than to talk about Mosley and his Blackshirts in his speeches and, in reality, perhaps this absence is indicative of the relatively small – and increasingly diminishing – role that the British Fascist movement played in 1920s and 1930s Britain. Where Mosley and his ilk did play a part, however, was in acting as a test tube for Nazi sympathies. And that test tube produced some of the nastiest traitors of the Second World War, men so degenerate that even their Nazi overlords found them distasteful.

Oswald Mosley was a mother's boy. Born in 1896, son of Sir Oswald Mosley, later 5th Baronet Mosley of Ancoats, he was the favourite of his mother, Maud, which probably led him to develop a sense of superiority which never left him. During the First World War, he fought on the Western Front, emerging from the conflict with an enduring passion for military life, remembering fondly a camaraderie that overcame all issues of class or status. He also loved the rigid organisation and discipline.

Mosley's determination to ensure that the sacrifices of so many during the war would not be in vain and his resolve that a better world could be fashioned from such tragedy, persuaded him to seek political office and he was elected Conservative MP for Harrow in 1918. In Parliament, he was quickly disabused of the notion that things would be different after the war. The same old men were still in charge and perfectly content with the status quo. He crossed the floor of the Commons in 1926 to join the Labour Party but things proved no different,

In May 1930, realising there was no future for him with Labour, he resigned in a letter that Prime Minister Ramsay MacDonald described as being notable for its 'graceless pompousness'. Nonetheless, Mosley's resignation speech was greeted with great excitement in the House of Commons, and he began to be hailed as a future leader, a man who could bring new ideas and a fresh approach to governing Britain.

Around that time, many British people were suffering terrible privations. The industries that had made Britain great as well as wealthy in the previous century – shipbuilding, coal, steel and cotton – were in serious decline, lagging behind the United States and Japan. Cheap Polish coal and Indian cotton imports forced the closure of pits and factories, leading to around 10 per cent of the population being unemployed throughout the 1920s. Then, in 1929, share prices on the New York Stock Exchange plummeted, heralding the calamity of the Wall Street Crash. In 1931, austerity measures introduced by Ramsay MacDonald's government made life even more intolerable for people. Food became scarce and living conditions were often deplorable. Still, nothing changed.

Mosley started to believe that fascism was the only answer – 'an explosion against intolerable conditions, against remediable wrongs which the old world had failed to remedy. It was a movement to secure national renaissance by people who felt themselves threatened with decline into decadence and death and were determined to live, and live greatly.' He created a fascist movement, uniting all the parties of the far-right under the umbrella of his new organisation, the British Union of

Fascists (BUF). Employing his overblown oratorical style to push his corporatist approach to the economy, he unashamedly used patriotism to appeal to the minds of the young:

> 'Hold high the head of England; lift strong the voice of Empire. Let us to Europe and the world proclaim that the heart of this great people is undaunted and invincible. This flag still challenges the winds of destiny. This flame still burns. This glory shall not die. The soul of Empire is alive, and England again dares to be great.'

He cast himself in the mould of Adolf Hitler and Benito Mussolini and embraced the braggadocio, danger, vigour and even violence that fascism encapsulated. If nothing else, it represented a break with the past and with the old elites, that had prevailed since the war. Membership numbers soared into the thousands and amongst them were some notable people from the ranks of the aristocracy and the military. Success seemed assured as the numbers grew and the 35-year-old Mosley glibly informed an American journalist that he would be in power by the age of 40.

He led marches and protests that became increasingly violent, eventually forcing the government to introduce the Public Order Act 1938, which banned amongst other things, political uniforms and quasi-military-style organisations. When Britain went to war, however, the government began to consider him and his ideas dangerous, especially when he campaigned to have Britain accept Hitler's March 1940 offer of peace. Finally, in May of that year, along with other British fascists, he was interned in Holloway Prison under Defence Regulation 18B until November 1943. The rest of his war was spent under house arrest.

Mosley's political career was ended by the war, but many had been won round by his philosophy. A number of these became traitors to their country and several, as we shall see, paid dearly for their treachery.

Others, as ever, betrayed their country for more mundane reasons – money or stupidity – but they too paid the highest price.

William Joyce: 'Lord Haw-Haw'

The Making of a Fascist

William Brooke Joyce was a strange man, to say the least. Undoubtedly clever, he gained a First from Birkbeck College, London and his knowledge and interests encompassed such disparate subjects as Old Norse poetry, mathematics, physics, chemistry and constitutional law. He could quote extensively from the great poets, but, somewhat incongruously, he could also exude an air of violence and this violence with which he was surrounded at times was made manifest on his face, an angry scar extending from the right corner of his mouth across his cheek and ending just below his ear. He liked to tell people that it had been inflicted on him in 1924, while canvassing in that year's general election. A Jewish communist had assailed him from behind, he claimed, and in the ensuing struggle had slashed Joyce's face. Another story has him being chased and assaulted by a gang of Jews. Yet another version suggests that the scar was caused by a knife thrown by an Irish woman exacting revenge for his activities on the side of the British government in the Irish War of Independence. It certainly attracted attention, however, and a picture of Joyce on his hospital bed appeared in the London *Evening Standard*.

Joyce would become the most notorious British traitor of the Second World War but he was actually born in Brooklyn, New York, in 1906. Michael, his father, had immigrated to the

United States and had taken US citizenship in 1894, something that would become important at Joyce's trial in 1945. Michael married Gertrude Brooke – known as 'Queenie – who was from Lancashire, in May 1905. After the birth of William the following year, they remained in America for only another two years.

William was a spoilt child. To his mother, he was a source of comfort in the alien environment in which she found herself. She told her young son: 'I shall never in my life forget how lonely I have felt in America. Even before you were born you were my only comfort in this atmosphere of strangeness, lack of interest and hostility.' She undoubtedly communicated this to the young William, possibly instilling in him his intense dislike of Americans. Queenie's unhappiness contributed to the family's decision in 1909 to make a fresh start in Ireland. Michael had put aside enough money to start anew and it was not a bad time to return to the old country as the economy was prospering. In 1910, he bought a pub on the main road between Lough Mask and Westport in County Mayo.

In 1912, the family was on the move again, for a brief stop in Tourmakeady, living in a large white house on a hill. A brother for William, named Frank, came along that year and the following spring, the Joyces moved to Galway where William was enrolled in the Convent of Mercy school, Michael calling himself an 'architect' on the enrolment form, although he was in fact only a builder. He had invested wisely, however, in property and the family moved into a house at Rockbarton in Salthill, a very desirable area.

In 1915, William progressed to secondary school, St Ignatius in Galway, by now a very self-assured child, arrogant even, and this did not help in his dealings with the Jesuit teachers. But he was a good pupil, 'a clever sort of lad', as one of his peers described him. He claimed to be a Boy Scout – most likely because of their Britishness – even though there were no Scout troops in Galway at the time, and wore a khaki Scout shirt and a Scout tie and badge. In fact, he was obsessed with anything military, even though it is said that he was never the tidiest or cleanest of individuals.

Loyalist to the Core

The Joyce family – especially Queenie – were ardent loyalists and the young William was brought up to love England and the British Empire. Taught that patriotism was the highest value to which a person could aspire, his pro-British attitude could, on occasion, get him into trouble, but he was becoming increasingly belligerent as he grew older and was happy to stand up for his provocative opinions. He would lecture his schoolmates on the dangers, as he saw it, of communism, and he once received a broken nose after lashing out at another boy who called him an Orangeman. The broken nose would result in him acquiring the particular tone of voice that later became so identifiable. He is also said to have once pulled a gun, somehow obtained from the Royal Irish Constabulary (RIC) barracks, on a boy who had draped an Irish tricolour round his body. When the boy refused to remove it, Joyce threatened him with the gun and that brought an end to his time at St Ignatius. Nonetheless, he left a strong impression on one teacher: 'In one sense, he was beyond his years, but emotionally, he never seemed to grow up. He was a morose and lonely little fellow at all times... For all his brightness, there was something missing in Willie. I cannot precisely define it, but he was not the normal type of healthy schoolboy.'

In 1920, when the Irish War of Independence began, William Joyce was 14. By this time, he had another brother, Quentin, born in 1917 and a sister, Gertrude, followed in 1920. The family was doing well; Michael owned property in Galway, some of which was rented by the RIC. He also had shares in the Galway

Omnibus Company and took over its management in 1920. The lack of stability in his homeland must have been of grave concern to him, however. The RIC were failing to establish control, leading the Westminster government to recruit in Britain for men to reinforce it. This was the notorious unit known as the Black and Tans – named for their khaki army trousers and dark green RIC tunics, caps and belts – an ill-disciplined and often drunk force of around 10,000 men that would be responsible for a great many atrocities during the conflict. This did not stop young William Joyce from becoming a kind of mascot to them and he even seems to have been recruited to work for them, informing on people with Republican tendencies. However, one former Black and Tan man recalls that he was viewed more as a pest:

'He was one of our greatest embarrassments in Galway City. His trouble was fanatical patriotism to England and a burning wish to fight against the Irish "rebels", as he always called them. He often tried to smuggle himself into our lorries… we laughed at him, but we used to chase him fairly fiercely for, if he had been killed or wounded, his ending would have caused the man in charge of the patrol a lot of trouble.'

He recruited other boys into a little gang to support the British forces in Ireland and, as usual, when he adopted a cause or a belief, Joyce took it to extremes. This, of course, resulted in his witnessing a great deal of violence at an early age. On one occasion, he reportedly saw a Sinn Fein activist being chased and murdered by the RIC. He was also linked to the murder of Father Michael Griffin, an Irish Catholic priest who was taken to the Black and Tans' headquarters for questioning, but whose body was later found in an unmarked grave, killed by a bullet to the head. In Berlin, many years later, Joyce suffered from the memory of such incidents.

To England

After the local branch of the IRA decided to eliminate William, his father took steps to get his son away from trouble. He was sent to England, aged 15 and alone.

Although underage, he enlisted in the Worcester Regiment on his arrival, but his real age was discovered after four months and his military career was over. Next, he decided to enrol at London University, hoping he could find a way into the military through its Officer Training Corps. He wrote to that body, informing the recipients that he had been born in America of British parents, but proclaiming his 'pure British descent'. 'I have always been desirous of devoting what little capability and energy I may possess to the country which I love so dearly,' he wrote.

He passed the London University matriculation exam and started at Battersea Polytechnic before progressing to Birkbeck College in September 1923, taking an intermediate BA course in English, History, Latin and French. But, his political sensitivities were being aroused and, as well as being a member of the Conservative Party, he joined the British Fascisti, a radical conservative anti-communist organisation founded by the eccentric Rotha Lintorn-Orman. He was attracted by its militancy, especially when it was employed to steward Conservative Party meetings. In fact, it was at one of those meetings, while providing protection for a Unionist parliamentary candidate, that Joyce received his disfiguring facial wound.

He gained a first-class honours degree in English in 1927, by which time he was married, and took a position as a lecturer at Victoria Tutorial College. A year later, he applied for a job at the Foreign Office but was rejected, claiming afterwards that his rejection was due to snobbery, as ever blaming some external force for his own failure. Nothing was ever his fault and, increasingly, he blamed the Jews. His facial wound, for instance, he ascribed to 'a Jewish communist'. He also claimed not to have completed his Master's degree because 'a Jewish woman tutor' stole his research. Anti-Semitic views were certainly not uncommon amongst the right-wing people with whom he associated but Joyce's were extreme, leading him to resign from the Conservative Party in 1930.

The Blackshirts

Joining Oswald Mosley's BUF in 1933, his intelligence and talent as an orator immediately made him stand out from ordinary adherents to the party. Mosley was, of course, a brilliant speaker, as was 'Mick' Clarke, a rabble-rouser who ran the East End of London – one of its most important constituencies – for the organisation. Joyce quit his teaching job and became West London Area Administration Officer. A year later, he was promoted to Propaganda Director, with the respectable annual salary of £300. Like many other members, he was determined to place more emphasis on anti-Semitism, while Mosley was intent on spouting his theories on corporate fascism. The anti-Semitic faction gained ground as a result of a huge rally that was staged at Olympia in West London on 7 June 1934, one of a series planned by Mosley. It was heartily supported by Lord Rothermere, owner of the *Daily Mail*, who wrote an article in his newspaper in January 1934 adorned with the now notorious headline 'Hurrah for the Blackshirts'. It was full of praise for what he described as Mosley's 'sound commonsense, Conservative doctrine'. This article and others provided invaluable publicity for the BUF, membership numbers soaring as a result. Communist and anti-fascist groups, however, were determined to disrupt the Olympia rally.

On the night of the event, there were 2,000 anti-fascists outside the hall and another 500 inside who had succeeded in infiltrating the audience. At 8.40, Mosley entered the arena, marching dramatically to the dais followed by 56 black-shirted disciples carrying Union flags. No sooner had he started to speak than the anti-fascists in the audience began to chant slogans and jeer. Unable to quiet them, Mosley ordered his men to take action. Although no one died and there were no serious injuries, there was outrage at the level of violence. It led to Lord Rothermere distancing himself and his newspaper from the BUF and many supporters rescinded their membership. The following December, anti-Semitism became official BUF policy and William Joyce, for one, was delighted.

He threw everything into his job but his marriage suffered as a result and, when he met a young fascist woman at a meeting in Dumfries, it was effectively over. Margaret Cairns White worked as a secretary but in her spare time had become a regular speaker on the BUF circuit. Divorced on 8 February 1937, Joyce married Margaret five days later. There was no time for a honeymoon, however, as he was standing as BUF candidate in a London County Council election and, campaigning hard, he performed relatively well, finishing third with more than 2,500 votes.

By this time, he was becoming disenchanted with Oswald Mosley and by his own lack of progress in the party. At the same time, the BUF was leaking funds and cuts had to be made; Joyce and his colleague, former Labour MP John Beckett, were sacked. Another friend and colleague, Angus Macnab, editor of the *Fascist Quarterly*, resigned as a result and the three launched a new right-wing organisation, the National Socialist League, funded by Alec Scrimgeour, a retired stockbroker, and the takings from a bar in the League's small headquarters. Joyce could now freely give vent to his racial hatred, ranting in a National Socialist pamphlet that: 'International Finance is controlled by great Jewish moneylenders and Communism is being propagated by Jewish agitators who are at one fundamentally with the powerful capitalists of their race in desiring an international world order, which would, of course, give universal sovereignty to the only international race in existence'.

In 1938, with international tension growing following the annexation of Austria by Germany, and with continued unrest in the German-speaking border regions of Czechoslovakia known as the Sudetenland, war was beginning to look increasingly inevitable. For Joyce this threw up a terrible dilemma as his politics made it impossible for him to contemplate fighting against National Socialist Germany. He decided that perhaps it would be best for him, Margaret and Macnab to travel to Dublin and from there make their way to Germany. He tried to obtain a British passport, lying about his place of birth but the Munich agreement brought an end to the immediate crisis. However, there was growing hostility at meetings where Joyce spoke supportively of Adolf Hitler and his regime. The summer of 1939 brought increased tension between Britain and Germany and once again Joyce contemplated a move to Berlin. He reached out to Christian Bauer who worked in the German Ministry of Propaganda, and was told that he and Margaret would be made welcome in Germany. In fact, he was told, Josef Goebbels himself was prepared to ensure that the Joyces would have a smooth path to naturalisation. Suddenly, after Germany signed a non-aggression pact with the USSR, Joyce's bête noire, he was less sure. However, he came round eventually to the notion of a Russo-German agreement, reasoning that Germany had to protect itself and Russia was, after all, the biggest threat to its security.

Meanwhile, the British government was contemplating contingency proposals to deal with fascist sympathisers in the event of war. Plans for the detention of such people were drawn up, and William Joyce had little doubt that he would be detained. On 24 August 1939, therefore, he renewed his passport until 1 July 1940. That same night, he learned that Emergency Defence

Regulations were going to be introduced two days later and that he would be interned. Next day, he withdrew what money he had from the bank and on 26 August, he and Margaret set out for Berlin. They sailed through immigration and from the deck of their cross-channel ferry stole a glance back at England. It would be almost six years before they would see it again, although in vastly different circumstances.

Germany Calling

The Joyces arrived in Berlin to disappointment. Bauer had exaggerated his influence and Goebbels was blissfully unaware of this couple newly arrived from England. In fact, it looked like they would suffer the same fate as they would have faced had they remained in England – internment. They contemplated returning home, but, instead, resolved to stay, renting inexpensive accommodation.

They had some contacts in the city, one of whom, Mrs Frances Eckersley, proved invaluable. Mrs Eckersley, a fascist, who was living in Berlin with her son, arranged a meeting for Joyce with a friend, Dr August Schirmer, who worked at the German Foreign Office. Schirmer asked him to translate one of Hitler's speeches, a task that he completed very quickly and for which he was paid.

Meanwhile, on 3 September, the inevitable came to pass when Great Britain and France declared war on Germany in response to the German invasion of Poland. Joyce felt vindicated in coming to Berlin but still he waited for an opportunity to help his adopted homeland. Schirmer had been working on his behalf, though, and a meeting was arranged with Erich Hetzler who worked closely with the German Foreign Minister, Joachim von Ribbentrop. Hetzler was an ardent anglophile, who had been educated at the London School of Economics and he took to Joyce immediately. For his part,

Joyce explained his support for Hitler's anti-Jewish stance and how he was hoping that he could somehow help the German war effort. Hetzler suggested that the best option might be a position as an English language broadcaster with the overseas service of Reichsrundfunk, the German Radio Corporation. Reichsrundfunk broadcast in English to Britain, North America and the Far East. It also broadcast programmes to other countries, all strictly controlled, of course, by Goebbels' Ministry of Propaganda. Joyce auditioned and was thought to have potential as a broadcaster. Later that day, he read a bulletin and the die was cast. The Nazi traitor who came to be known as 'Lord Haw-Haw' was born.

The English language service of Reichsrundfunk was mainly made up of Germans who had been educated in Britain or the United States or had lived in one of those countries for a time, plus a few of mixed British-German parentage. The items broadcast were fairly lacklustre: news and comment that was, of course, very anti-British. There was a great deal of fake news and exaggeration of German successes in the war. The broadcasts in English – entitled 'Germany Calling' but in Joyce's strange accent, 'Jairmany Calling' – became very popular during the early months of the war, the period known as 'the phoney war'. By October 1939, nine programmes in English were being broadcast daily. A news bulletin would be followed by a commentary by one of the station's English speakers. One of the broadcasters was dubbed 'Lord Haw-Haw' by the *Daily Express* journalist, Jonah Barrington, who wrote: 'A gent I'd like to meet is moaning periodically from Zeesen [the location of the English service transmitter]. He speaks English of the haw-haw, dammit-get-out-of-my-way variety, and his strong suit is gentlemanly indignation.' The *Sunday Dispatch* writer, Lord Donegall, suggested that the voice belonged to the erstwhile leader of the National Socialist League but on meeting Angus Macnab and playing him a recording of one such broadcast, he was told by Macnab that the voice did not belong to Joyce. The name would stick to him, though.

As the war heated up, France and the Low Countries falling to the Germans and the British Expeditionary Force making its daring escape from Dunkirk, the broadcasts became ever more sinister, with the British people being lied to and threatened. People were astonished at Haw-Haw's apparently accurate local knowledge, describing, for instance, town hall clocks that were running fast or slow or detailing troop and shipping movements. Much of this was completely without foundation and was symptomatic of the hysteria that gripped Britain in the face of the invasion threat.

In Germany, officials began to realise just how potent a weapon William Joyce was in their propaganda war and, although, like everyone else, they did not know which one of their broadcasters Lord Haw-Haw actually was, they began to introduce Joyce under that sobriquet. A book written by Joyce was published, *Dämmerung Über England* (*Twilight Over England*), with more than 100,000 copies being printed.

Meanwhile, life was good for British traitors in Berlin. The Joyces were given decent wages, an apartment in Charlottenburg and freedom to go where they pleased in Berlin. They had a good social life and were permitted to associate with foreign journalists in the Foreign Press Club. By 1941, however, William's relationship with Margaret was beginning to founder. He was under considerable stress and had a heavy workload, and this often led to him taking out his frustration on her. She began to feel neglected and, in search of companionship, entered into a relationship with a young German officer. The Joyces eventually divorced in August 1941 but were back together again under a year later, remarrying in February 1942. By this time, Joyce had become disenchanted with Germany. He had never taken up membership of the Nazi Party which, to his mind, had become corrupt and had failed to carry out the objectives of the National Socialist revolution. Still, he remained the principal English broadcaster on Reichsrundfunk until the fall of Hamburg in April 1945, also writing many of the scripts that formed the programmes and recruiting prisoners of war to the German broadcasting cause.

Capture

With Berlin being bombed in the early months of 1945, Büro Concordia, the special department at Reichsrundfunk dealing with Britain, was evacuated to Helmstedt, a couple of hundred kilometres west of the capital where it continued to broadcast. A month later, the team that was responsible for 'Germany Calling', including William and Margaret Joyce, was moved to Apen, a town close to the Dutch border where they continued to make programmes. Suddenly, however, it was all over. As the Americans approached Berlin, Hetzler distributed fake identity cards to the staff of Reichsrundfunk still in Helmstedt. To prevent the Joyces from being captured by the Allies, a plan was hatched to smuggle them to Ireland on a U-Boat, but no submarine was available. Even if there had been, there is little likelihood that it would have succeeded, so tight was the grip of the Royal Navy and Royal Air Force on the North Sea. It was decided, therefore, to try to get them to Denmark and from there to Sweden. Joyce was given the fake ID of Wilhelm Hansen, purportedly a schoolteacher from Galway.

He recorded his last broadcast on 30 April 1945 at Radio Hamburg, a drunken ramble ending with the words 'Heil Hitler and farewell', after which the Joyces were driven to Flensburg but the car that was supposed to meet them there never arrived. They continued over the border into Denmark and waited four days for news. Hearing nothing, they returned to Flensburg and from there, on 11 May, travelled to Wassersleben where they found lodgings. On 28 May, after lunch, William went for a walk in some nearby woods where he fell asleep. Realising when he woke up that his wife would be worried about him, he walked on the road instead of through the forest to get home quicker. Before long, he passed a couple of British officers searching for firewood. Approaching them, Joyce said in French: 'Here are a few more pieces.' The officers looked over at him when he spoke and he repeated his words in English. One of the men, Captain Alexander Lickorish, immediately recognised the distinctive voice. 'You wouldn't happen to be William Joyce, would you?' he asked. Joyce immediately reached into his inside pocket to produce his fake identity papers, but thinking that he was reaching for a gun, the British officer drew his .38 revolver and shot him in the buttocks. Joyce fell to the ground and it was all over.

Trial and Execution

William Joyce was loathed in Britain which explains the consternation at the news that, because of his nationality, he might escape the ultimate punishment. There was widespread demand for him to be brought to justice and he appeared at Bow Street Magistrates Court on 18 June where he was remanded in custody on a charge of high treason. Those baying for his blood were satisfied, but the arguments as to Joyce's origins were not yet over.

He appeared at the Old Bailey before Mr Justice Tucker on 17 September 1945, facing three charges of high treason. Surrounded by many of his supporters, he answered 'Not guilty' to the charges, his defence being that he was not a British citizen and could not, therefore, have committed treason. This issue dominated the proceedings.

The prosecuting counsel was the Attorney-General of the recently elected Labour government, Sir Hartley Shawcross, who sought to confirm Joyce's British nationality from his enlistment in the OTC in 1922 and by his renewal of his British passport several times in the 1930s. Against this, Joyce's counsel, Gerald Slade KC, insisted on Joyce's status as a US citizen, because of his birth in New York, until his German naturalisation. Three days into the trial, the judge caused outrage by ruling that the first two charges should be dropped – the counts of broadcasting throughout the war and committing treason by becoming a German citizen during the war. Many began to think that Joyce would be released and an angry crowd gathered outside the court.

The question became one of whether or not Joyce would have received the protection of the Crown because of his passport. Shawcross argued that he would have but Slade reasoned that Joyce could only leave Britain to go to Germany with a passport, even though it was obtained fraudulently, and that he, at no point, intended to seek the protection of the Crown. Mr Justice Turner came down on the side of the prosecution, noting in his summing-up:

'My duty is to tell you what I believe to be the law on the subject, and that you have to accept from me, provided you believe the facts about the passport, going abroad, and so forth. If you do not believe that, you are entitled to reject it and say so, because you are not bound to believe everything, but if you accept the uncontradicted evidence that has been given, then, in my view, that shows that this man at the material time owed allegiance to the British Crown.'

The jury took a mere 23 minutes to reach a guilty verdict and the judge placed the traditional black cap – not a cap at all, but a square of black cloth – on his head and sentenced William Joyce to death by hanging. Following the trial, Joyce was taken to Wandsworth Prison, having been on remand at Wormwood Scrubs. Wandsworth had one of the two gallows in London, the other being at Pentonville.

An appeal was launched immediately and was heard by Lords Jowett, Macmillan, Simonds, Porter and Wright over three days from 30 October at the Court of Criminal Appeal at the Royal Courts of Justice on the Strand. Judgement was handed down on 1 November. The appeal was dismissed and the conviction and death sentence were confirmed. All that remained was an appeal in the House of Lords, heard on 10 December. Again, however, the conviction and sentence were upheld. Joyce's execution was set for 3 January 1946.

By then, Margaret had arrived in London from Germany and was being allowed to stay in Holloway Prison and to meet her husband regularly. On the day before the execution, the pair met for the last time. That night, he wrote an eight-page letter telling her he loved her and that he was sure they would meet again in the afterlife. One biographer has suggested that Joyce had entered into a deal with the prosecution not to bring up at his trial links he had had with MI5 in return for Margaret not being charged and she was the only one of 32 British traitors arrested in Germany at the end of the war who was not charged with treason. Outliving her husband by several decades, she died in London in 1972.

Joyce saw his brother, to whom he had been writing from prison, on the afternoon of the day before his execution and passed to him an anti-Semitic statement that was to be made public after his death. That night he was provided with a sedative by the prison doctor and woke at 6.30 the following morning. After being given communion by the prison chaplain, he wrote another letter to Margaret, noting the time of completion at the bottom – 8.36. He also wrote a brief message to Angus Macnab, with whom he had also been corresponding from prison.

At nine o'clock his cell door swung open, revealing the hangman, Albert Pierrepoint. Joyce's hands were strapped behind his back and he followed the hangman through the door to the gallows, reputedly looking down and smiling at the trembling in his legs. His ankles were strapped together and a white hood was pulled over his head, swiftly followed by the noose. Pierrepoint pulled the lever that released the trapdoor and William Joyce dropped to his death.

John Amery: A Difficult Young Man

Son of an Eminent Man

Albert Pierrepoint described John Amery as the bravest man he ever hanged. 'Mr Pierrepoint, I have always wanted to meet you,' Amery said, standing when the hangman entered his cell on the morning of his execution, 'though not, of course, in these circumstances.'

Amery, the second son of Leo Amery, Member of Parliament for Birmingham South – later Birmingham Sparkbrook – was born on 14 March 1912, a member of a distinguished family, but a somewhat difficult child, so difficult that private tutors arrived and departed on a regular basis from the Amery household, defeated by his intransigence. Even Harrow School, one of the finest educational establishments in the world, found him unmanageable and he left after just one year. 'Without a doubt, the most difficult boy I have ever tried to manage,' opined his frustrated housemaster.

Certainly, he must have found it difficult living up to expectations. His father had enjoyed a glittering career. After first class honours at Balliol College, Oxford in 1896 and a successful career as a journalist and lawyer, he was elected to Parliament in 1911, turning down opportunities to be editor of both *The Observer* and *The Times* in order to concentrate on politics. In 1916, he accepted the role of special adviser on European affairs and he was appointed First Lord of the Admiralty in 1922. From 1924 to 1929, he was Secretary of

State for the Colonies and the Dominions. Such success led his son to try to create a reputation for himself that did not depend on his family name. Withdrawn from Harrow at the age of 15, John tried to launch a career in the film industry, using funds from investors to set up a film company. They lost their money but this did not prevent Amery from continuing with his film career throughout the early 1930s. Nothing worked out for him, however, and he was made bankrupt in 1936. He was also in trouble with the law, having notched up a staggering 74 convictions for motoring offences.

In 1931, at the age of 21, Amery married a former prostitute, Una Wing, who was older than him. His family tried to prevent the marriage, but the couple fled to Athens where they were married in an Orthodox church. By this time, he had become a fervent anti-communist and, like many, believed that the only bulwark in Europe against Bolshevism and Jewish control of the world was Hitler's National Socialism. After his bankruptcy, he left his wife behind in England and moved to Paris where he befriended the French fascist and former communist, Jacques Doriot. Doriot had been the communist mayor of St Denis, in Paris, but his politics swung to the far right in the early 1930s when he formed the fascist Parti Populaire Français (PPF) which by 1939 had 250,000 members. Fascinated by fascism, Amery travelled to Italy, Austria, Czechoslovakia and Germany to see the political philosophy in action, journeys of discovery that cemented his far-right views and encouraged him to blame the Jews for all the ills of the world. His father would later write:

'His failures in the film world, and his unfortunate experience with money lenders… inclined him to accept current Nazi and Fascist doctrine of the Jews as the prime instigators of Communism as well as the evils of international high finance.'

From the Spanish Civil War to Berlin

In 1937, Amery travelled to Spain to join Francisco Franco's Nationalists fighting the Republicans in the Spanish Civil War. He told his family at the time that he was fighting with Italian volunteers as an intelligence officer and that he had been awarded a medal by them for valour. Instead, he was running guns from France to Spain, acting as liaison for Franco with the fascist French terrorist group, La Cagoule, who were supplying them.

At the end of the Civil War, he remained in Spain for a few months, living in San Sebastian and making plans for a return to the film business. Seven months after the Second World War broke out, he travelled to Paris to meet his father and then headed for Nice where he had a contract to produce three short films. Around this time, however, the French army capitulated to the Germans and the armistice was signed, dividing France into two – an Occupied Zone and an area in the south governed by Marshal Philippe Petain's Vichy regime. Amery found himself virtually trapped in the south and, in May 1940, he fell ill with tuberculosis. He received treatment in a sanatorium in Grenoble, rejecting an offer to repatriate him in July.

In June 1941, following the German invasion of the Soviet Union, his political feelings seem to have been aroused once more. He was horrified that Britain was now allied with the Russians. Meanwhile, his extreme views and the suspicion of the Vichy authorities made him increasingly isolated from friends he had made in France and from his family back home. He tried several times to obtain permission to leave but his requests were denied. In November 1941 he was arrested and held for almost a month, before his release was negotiated by Doriot and Amery's French girlfriend, Jeanine Barde. Free again, he applied for repatriation on the grounds of his poor health but once more his application was rejected.

Suddenly, in the summer of 1942, he was provided with a way out. The head of the German Armistice Commission in Savoy suggested that he might be useful to Germany in Berlin. An excited Amery sought reassurance that the offer was genuine, receiving it from Hauptmann Werner Plack who was a member of what was called the England Committee, a German body responsible for propaganda directed against Britain. Amery was given permission to travel to Berlin for meetings with the German Foreign Ministry after receiving assurance that he would be able to return to France following his discussions.

With Jeanine Barde he took up residence at the Kaiserhof Hotel in Berlin and met the chair of the England Committee, Dr Fritz Hesse, explaining to him that what most interested him was Britain and Germany joining forces against the real enemy – Bolshevism and the Jews. He asked to be permitted to host an hour-long radio programme during which he would call for peace negotiations. He also suggested the creation of a British anti-Bolshevik force. He said it would be like the LVF – the Legion of French Volunteers Against Bolshevism – which was a unit of the German army formed by volunteers from Vichy France to take part in the German incursion into Russia in 1941.

Apparently, Hitler himself was informed of Amery's offer which was something of a game-changer for the German propaganda operation aimed at Britain and a few weeks later, Amery was told that the Führer had approved his suggestions. Plans were laid to launch a recruitment campaign.

Amery would make several broadcasts before which the announcer would dissociate the German government from any involvement but the British contingent already in Berlin were less than happy with the news that he was going to start broadcasting. William Joyce was especially concerned at the effect Amery's radio shows would have on his broadcasts. But Amery was of the opinion that Joyce was simply preaching to the converted, to those already of the fascist viewpoint. While he considered Joyce and his ilk to have been converted to the German cause he, on the other hand, was a British patriot, a man who wholeheartedly championed the British Empire and all it stood for. He just happened to disagree with the stance of the current British government.

He gave seven talks, the first, broadcast on 19 November 1942, opening with the words:

'Listeners will wonder what an Englishman is doing on the German radio tonight. You can imagine that before taking this step I hoped that someone better qualified than me would come forward. I dared to believe that some ray of common sense, some appreciation of our priceless civilization would guide the counsels of Mr Churchill's Government. Unfortunately, this has not been the case! For two years living in a neutral country I have been able to see through the haze of propaganda to reach something which my conscience tells me is the truth. That is why I come forward tonight without any political label, without any bias, but just simply as an Englishman to say to you: a crime is being committed against civilization.'

The content of Amery's broadcasts differed slightly from the usual anti-British rants. He was more considered in his approach. He berated Britain for allying with the Soviet Union; he railed against what he saw as Jewish control of the wheels of power in Britain, the USA and Russia; and he championed the notion of a 'Nordic Bloc' under the control of Britain and Germany. He argued that Germany and Britain could co-exist in the world and that the concept of German world domination was no more than a Jewish construct. The German army, he insisted, was all that stood between the world and communism.

The sign off to each broadcast was: 'You have been listening to John Amery, son of the British Secretary for India, the Right Honourable Leopold Stennett Amery. We should like to remind you of the fact that Mr John Amery spoke in his own name and that the German government bears no responsibility for what Mr Amery has said.' Naturally, his family back home – especially his father – was horrified by the publicity generated. The audience for 'Germany Calling' had fallen, however. No one wanted to hear such blatant propaganda and, with the war now raging around the world, it was no longer funny.

The British Legion of St George

Amery continued to broadcast until January 1943 when he requested permission to travel to Paris to meet Jacques Doriot and another prominent collaborator, Marcel Déat. He travelled with Barde and also present was Werner Plack who was effectively his minder on behalf of the England Committee. Doriot and Déat both expressed disappointment at the conduct of the war, seeing no signs of the promised fascist social revolution. They also conceded that, as Germany was the only country fighting against the Soviet Union, they had no choice but to remain committed to the German cause.

In the meantime, Amery was asked to write a book – *England Faces Europe* – as an accompaniment to his radio broadcasts and spent February and March of 1943 engaged in that. Back in Berlin, he was also engaged in having fun, hosting rowdy parties at his hotel and at the Foreign Press Club. On 7 April, he celebrated finishing his book with a particularly riotous session there. After an argument, he and Jeanine left the club and went back to the Kaiserhof Hotel. They were both very drunk and he had to put her to bed. Sometime in the night, she choked on her own vomit and died while he slept soundly beside her.

He returned Jeanine's body to France where she was interred at her home town in Bergerac and afterwards proceeded to Paris with Plack to launch the recruitment campaign for what he called the British Legion of St George. They began at a POW camp at St-Denis in the north of the city where a number of likely candidates from all parts of the British Commonwealth had been selected. A group of them were assembled in the camp theatre and a leaflet entitled 'British National Representation Proclamation to all British Subjects Interned' was distributed before Amery stepped out onto the stage to speak. His hour-long talk was filled with lies, claiming British pilots had crossed the lines to join the German effort and that the British Legion of St George already consisted of several hundred men. The assembled men were promised they would never have to fight against British forces. Unfortunately, however, one attendee stood up at the conclusion of Amery's speech and reminded everyone that what was being asked of them was treasonable and that there would be retribution for it after the war. Amery hurriedly brought the meeting to a close and left the theatre.

After a further two weeks at the camp, distributing material and talking to inmates, just four men were recruited: a professor of Italian ancestry who wanted to join so that he could study Plato on one of the Greek islands that were under the control of the Axis powers; Maurice Tunmer, son of wealthy Parisian retailers; Oswald Job whose parents had been German, although he was born in London and was living in Paris when he was interned; and 17-year-old Kenneth Berry, taken prisoner when he was aged just 14 and serving on the SS *Cymbeline* which was sunk by a German warship off the coast of France.

Although Amery was very proud of his concept of a British legion in the German army -'by far the BIGGEST PROPAGANDA IDEA that anyone has EVER thought out', he claimed in a report – he never really had much more to do with it. The Germans used him to deliver lectures during the first half of 1944 and he travelled to Czechoslovakia, Belgium, France and Norway, speaking to collaborators in those countries. He was well paid for it, receiving around 650 marks a week, considerably more than any other British traitor and when he finally returned to Berlin, he was admonished for straying too far from the Nazi Party line in his lectures and was informed that he should stay away from Paris and keep a low profile. He obliged, making one last trip to the French capital to collect his belongings before retreating to a southwestern suburb of the German capital. By now he had found another woman with whom to share his life – Michèle Thomas, whom he had met at the Foreign Press Club a year after the death of Jeanine. In October 1944, the couple married. In the meantime, Amery had spoken for the last time on the 'Germany Calling' programme in August, to deny that he was, in fact, being held prisoner by the Gestapo in Berlin.

Mussolini, Capture and Execution

Amery was allowed to travel to Italy in October to meet Benito Mussolini, by this time head of the Italian Social Republic in North Italy. Il Duce told him that he wanted to negotiate peace between Germany and the Allies and needed his help to do so. As a result, Amery spent the remaining six months of the war on a lecture tour of northern Italy, giving speeches and making radio broadcasts. His last meeting with Il Duce was on 23 April 1945, just five days before the Italian dictator was captured and killed. At this meeting, Mussolini offered him a commission in his Black Brigades – a fascist paramilitary group that was responsible for a number of atrocities during the latter stages of the war in Italy. Amery rejected the offer, principally because, had he accepted, he would have been fighting against his own country's troops. Nonetheless, he was happy to don the uniform of the fascist paramilitary organisation, the Muti Legion, a uniform he was still wearing on 25 April when he was captured, together with Michèle Thomas, near Como by Italian partisans of the Garibaldi Brigade. The couple were to be executed, but, instead, were reprieved and sent to Milan to be handed over to the Allies. Amery was taken into custody by an officer whose name would become familiar to television viewers after the war – Alan Whicker.

On 28 November 1945, John Amery stood in the dock at the Old Bailey in London, charged with eight counts of treason. At a preliminary hearing, he had argued that he was not a Nazi, merely an anti-communist. His counsel, Gerald Osborne Slade KC, argued that Amery was mentally ill but the judge, Mr Justice Humphreys, would not allow it. Out of the blue, however, on the first day of the trial, Amery announced that he was pleading guilty to all eight charges. Mr Justice Humphreys made it clear to the accused that, if he persisted with a guilty plea, the only sentence open to him was the death penalty. Amery indicated that he did, indeed, understand the consequences but wished to stick to his plea. The judge said:

'John Amery... I am satisfied that you knew what you did and that you did it intentionally and deliberately after you had received warning from... your fellow countrymen that the course you were pursuing amounted to high treason. They called you a traitor and you heard them; but in spite of that you continued in that course. You now stand a self-confessed traitor to your King and country, and you have forfeited your right to live.'

He was sentenced to death after a trial that had lasted a mere eight minutes.

It is suggested that Amery had been warned by his counsel that there was very little likelihood of any other outcome than a guilty one and, to his credit, had decided to spare his family through any more anguish.

Thus, on 19 December 1945, Albert Pierrepoint arrived at the door of John Amery's cell in Wandsworth Prison and led him to his execution. Amery's body was buried in the prison cemetery, but his remains were later exhumed and cremated, his ashes being scattered in France.

George Armstrong: A Traitor Alone

The press reports of the execution were sketchy, merely regurgitating the facts included in a press release issued by the Home Office. They reflected the secretive nature of George Johnson Armstrong's arrest and trial. Little was known about what he had done to deserve this, the most extreme of punishments. The *Daily Herald* attempted to fill in some of the background to Armstrong's life and to his crime:

> 'George Johnson Armstrong, a 39-year-old British engineer who was executed for treachery at Wandsworth Jail yesterday, carried his family secrets with him to the grave. If he had any relatives living, he never spoke of them from the time he was arrested until the warm sunlit morning when he walked to the gallows. Nobody made application to see him during that time. Nobody wrote to him… This Home Office statement, issued yesterday, threw a little more light on Armstrong's crime. "A few months ago, he offered his services to the German espionage organisation operating against Britain, through the intermediary of one of the German consuls in the United States. On his subsequent return to this country he was arrested and put up for trial."'

George Armstrong had a record for petty crime by the time he reached his mid-twenties. Born in 1902, he had been arrested while still young for the theft of a bicycle and a coat and for obtaining money by false pretences and for forgery. He was 37 years old on 1 February 1940 when he was sentenced to three years and three months for another conviction of obtaining money by false pretences.

Somehow, Armstrong managed to avoid prison because, by July of that same year, he was in New York, staying at the Chelsea Hotel on West 23rd Street. He had crossed the Atlantic on the MV *Britannic* and in two weeks was due to join the merchant steam tanker, the *La Brea*, as an engineer. He claimed later that while drinking in a bar near his hotel, he met a German woman named Alice Hahn. She was working with a German agent, Carl Klein, whom Armstrong had already met in London. Hahn was ingratiating herself with merchant navy personnel in order to glean information about the Atlantic Convoys that were keeping Britain supplied.

The *La Brea* never arrived, having been sunk by a Nazi torpedo in the North Atlantic, but by that time, Armstrong was no longer in New York. He had travelled to Boston where he was arrested and interned by US Immigration in a holding centre in Massachusetts. Coincidentally, Carl Klein who had been arrested and charged with spying for Germany as well as with being an illegal alien, was a fellow inmate, awaiting deportation. Armstrong would later state that he took the opportunity to try to learn more about Klein's activities. Klein, he claimed, was operating British agents and he was trying to identify them. Klein admitted to Armstrong that he was an agent of the Third Reich, but denied spying in America. Armstrong claimed not to have believed him.

Klein told him that Dr Herbert Scholz, German Consul in Boston, controlled a Nazi spy network that stretched not only across the United States but also across the Atlantic. He showed Armstrong documents, one of which was a list of names. One of the names he remembered was that of a man who had worked at Buckingham Palace and now worked on the staff of the Earl of Athlone. Armstrong wrote to Scholz on 19 November. He told British intelligence that it was merely a ruse to try to discover the names of agents in Britain but it was, ultimately, a letter that put a noose around his neck:

'I am an officer of the British Service, an engineer at recent date attached to the Inspection of Aircraft Dept. (AID) in England. Latterly I was transferred to the Marine Dept. under control of the British Admiralty. My intention is to make German contacts here in the US which may be beneficially used on my return to England. Naturally in the various capacities in which I was employed in England, I have information which would be very valuable in the proper sources. You will no doubt agree with me that it is not advisable to enter into any written discussion upon this subject here at this time, but if you could have someone contact me who was reliable then the matter could be more fully gone into. I was detained by the US Immigration authorities before I could make any such contacts here in the US and have been transferred from East Boston Immigration Station to Deer Island to be held pending deportation proceedings. I feel that the information which I have and the value of someone so placed in England in these times would be greatly appreciated by yourself or those who you would put in contact with me.'

Scholtz never read his words because the letter was intercepted by officials of US Immigration and immediately forwarded to MI5 in London. Armstrong was himself returned to London shortly afterwards and was interrogated at New Scotland Yard by MI5's chief spycatcher, Colonel William Hinchley-Cooke. Initially, he failed to mention Scholz but, when confronted by the letter he had written to the German, he came up with his story of trying to glean information about German agents operating in Britain. Damning him further, however, were notes he had made about the port of Halifax in Canada that had been found when he had been searched by police. They concerned

Merchant Navy ships that assembled there before heading off in convoy across the Atlantic and it had been feared for some time that details of these voyages were being passed to the Germans. Once again, however, Armstrong claimed that this was all part of his efforts to penetrate the German spy network in America and Britain, and to find out who was leaking information about the convoys.

He was not believed, especially as his story about trying to infiltrate the spy network only emerged when he was confronted with evidence of his spying. On 5 March, he was charged at Cannon Row police station with breaching Defence Regulations. A charge under the Treachery Act was added to his charge sheet five days later.

George Armstrong's trial lasted just two days and was conducted in camera. He insisted from the witness box that he was not a spy but the jury, failing to believe a word of it, took just 15 minutes to find him guilty as charged. Wearing the customary black cloth on top of his wig, Mr. Justice Lewis pronounced the only sentence open to him – the death penalty.

On 9 July 1941, 16 days after his appeal was dismissed at the Court of Criminal Appeal, 39 year-old George Armstrong was hanged at HM Prison Wandsworth in London.

Duncan Scott-Ford:
The Traitor Who Died for Love

An Unpleasant Man

By all accounts, Duncan Alexander Croall Scott-Ford was not a very nice man, a thief with a liking for strong drink and foreign prostitutes. He was born in Devonport in 1921 as Duncan Alexander Croall Smith, but, believing it would enhance his social standing, he later changed his surname to Scott-Ford. His father, a medical orderly in the Royal Navy, died of pneumonia after overdosing on morphine in a suicide attempt in 1933 when his son was 11. Not long after, Scott-Ford enrolled as a boarder at the Royal Hospital School in Holbrook, remaining there until 1937. Aged 16, he enlisted in the Royal Navy as a Boy Seaman, First Class, and for the next two years, he sailed the world's oceans.

In June 1939, just a few months before the outbreak of war, while Scott-Ford's ship, HMS *Gloucester*, was paying a goodwill visit to Dar-es-Salaam in what was then Tanganyika and is now Tanzania, he met and became infatuated with a pretty 17-year-old German girl, Ingeborg Richter. Richter's father was manager of a car company in the town, but he was also a Nazi Party official and Ingeborg was an enthusiastic member of the Hitler Youth. The two agreed to stay in touch by letter, but she told him that her father must never know. Following this liaison, HMS *Gloucester* left port and made for Egypt where the 21-year-old sailor began to consort with a local prostitute, Nahid Mohamed. Mohamed might have been a German spy, which is attested to by a note in Scott-Ford's MI5 file that suggests that she obtained information from him. He had been lavishing a great deal of money on her and on a number of occasions had manually altered the balance shown in his Post Office savings account which allowed him to withdraw more money than was actually in the account. His crime was discovered and he was convicted of embezzlement on 3 March 1941, jailed for two years and given a dishonourable discharge. Following an emotional appeal by his mother, his sentence was reduced to six months and he was given an honourable discharge. Scott-Ford had little option but to go back to sea, enlisting in the Merchant Navy. By September 1941, he was serving on the SS *Finland* on convoys across the Atlantic and in the Mediterranean. In May 1942, his ship arrived in Lisbon, capital of neutral Portugal, at the time a hotbed of espionage.

He had changed little since Egypt and, on 15 May, he picked up a prostitute and spent the night with her in a cheap hotel. The next night, he was drinking alone in a sailors' bar when he was approached by a German named Rithman who claimed to be a businessman. The two got talking and the conversation came round to East Africa. Scott-Ford told the German of the girl he had met in Dar-es-Salaam and the German drew the conversation round to a new convoy that he had heard was being assembled. He said the date of 28 June had been mentioned and that, if Scott-Ford could provide him with any information or confirm that date, he would not only pay him 1,000 Escudos (around £350 in today's money) but would also help him to get into Germany to reunite with Ingeborg. Scott-Ford agreed to meet with Rithman's associates and did so five times between 17 and 21 May, being interrogated by a 'Captain Henley' about various matters including shipbuilding in Britain. Henley promised him a great deal of money if he could provide maps that showed the positions of British minefields. Scott-Ford was given 1,000 Escudos in exchange for a promise to obtain the required information as well as up-to-date copies of *Jane's Fighting Ships* and *Jane's All the World's Aircraft*.

A few days later, he met Henley again in a flat above a wine shop. They gave him 'plenty to drink', as Scott-Ford put it and, once again, Henley pressed him for information about minefields and about the arrival of US troops in Britain. As Scott-Ford later admitted:

'Henley asked me if I could confirm any places where there were American troops in Britain and the extent of their training and efficiency, also their numbers. He asked me to try and find out the American naval base in Britain and about the three new battleships which were being built and the approximate date of completion. I told him I would try and he gave me two hundred Escudos.'

Information about British warships that were moored at Gibraltar was also on the agenda. Scott-Ford mentioned a battleship and a light cruiser that he knew to be there and said that they were waiting to provide protection for the next convoy. He also passed to Henley details of the plans to defend Gibraltar in the event of a gas attack. He promised to gather other material such as ration books and identity cards once he returned to shore. These were to be copied and given to Nazi agents in Britain. Henley requested that Scott-Ford sign a receipt for the money he had been paid for his information. Foolishly, Scott-Ford signed it, even using his own name.

When ships returned to dock in Britain, the crews were routinely quizzed as to whether they had been in contact with enemy agents while in Lisbon and, after the *Finland* docked in Liverpool on 20 June, and crew members were quizzed about approaches from enemy agents, Scott-Ford nonchalantly replied that he had indeed been approached, but had sent them packing.

The *Finland* once more sailed for Lisbon, arriving on 26 July, and Scott-Ford was almost immediately summoned to a meeting with Henley who was furious when he learned that the sailor had brought none of the requested items – information about bases, ship manuals or ration books. Henley explained to Scott-Ford how serious his position was. He reminded him how much he had been paid so far – around 1,800 Escudos – and that he had signed a receipt for it. Unless he did better next time, he threatened, the receipt would find its way into the hands of the British Consul in Lisbon. Henley stuck the knife in a little bit deeper, suggesting that if he did not do as he was asked, there might also be trouble for his old flame, Ingeborg Richter, back in Germany. Panicking, Scott-Ford provided Henley with classified information regarding five British ships that had been sunk but it was not enough for Henley. He was told to bring the *Jane's* books and the ration books next time and it does appear that he provided some of the material when they next got together. Satisfied with that, Henley gave the Englishman another mission. He was given £50 (equivalent to around £2,000 today) that was to be handed over to a Nazi agent operating in Scotland.

A Welcoming Committee

The money never found its way into the agent's hands because what Scott-Ford did not know was that while in Lisbon he had been under surveillance by an MI6 agent and when his ship docked in Salford, therefore, a welcoming committee awaited him. When they began interrogating him, he tried to brush it off, but gradually it became clear to him that they knew everything. They had even found notes about the convoy in his quarters on board the *Finland*. For a moment, he was terrified, according to the MI5 report, but then began to confess nearly everything, although still holding back on certain details:

'At this point, and this point only, Scott-Ford was completely nonplussed. For a very brief space he showed terror and soon after this confessed to taking money from Enemy Agents in Lisbon... [But] he steadfastly refused to give the name or description of this man... and gave the impression, almost, that in confessing to his traitorous activities he was hoodwinking the interrogator or rather turning him away from the really dangerous part of his story.'

It was decided to send him for further questioning to Camp 020, a British interrogation centre at Latchmere House in southwest London, used for quizzing German agents. The officer who ran the centre, Captain Robin 'Tin Eye' Stephens, found him a difficult subject. He noted his lying and his bragging about his prowess as an agent. Eventually, however, Scott-Ford broke down and cried, complaining about the threats that had been made to him in Lisbon. Ominously, the record ends with:

'Scott-Ford is frankly terrified of the Germans and is now equally terrified of the authorities in this country. As he has stated, he does not know where to turn. In addition, he states that if he were at liberty, and returned to Lisbon, he is quite certain that the Germans would liquidate him. On the other hand, he knows that he faces a traitor's death in this country.'

His trial, at the Old Bailey on 16 October 1942, was short and not very sweet, held entirely in camera, and lasting just one day. Duncan Scott-Ford pleaded not guilty and appeared in his own defence but his counsel chose not to call any witnesses. He told the court that he had not intended to help the enemy and that he had been physically threatened and blackmailed by them. The reason, he claimed, that he had had anything to do with them was simply so that he might be able to communicate with Ingeborg Richter. His claims fell on deaf ears, however, the jury taking no more than a few minutes to reach its guilty verdict. He was sentenced to hang by Mr Justice Birkett.

The officers at Camp 020 were asked whether Scott-Ford should be reprieved but 'Tin Eye' Stephens could find no reason why. 'Indeed, there may well be many,' he wrote, 'who will agree that death by hanging is almost too good for a sailor who will encompass the death of thousands of his shipmates without qualm.'

Eighteen days later, Duncan Scott-Ford was hanged, aged 21.

Theodore Schurch: A Gullible Traitor

Woolwich 2424. Extn. 1.
Subject:- General Court Martial
   No. T/61711 Pte. Schurch, Theodore John William
To:- Commander
   R.A.S.C.
   Woolwich

Sir,
On 17th Sept, 1945 I was tried by General Court
Martial in London on nine charges under Section
1 of the Treachery Act 1940, and on one charge of
desertion under Section 12(1) of the Army Act. I was
found guilty on all charges and sentenced to death.
The Court made no recommendation to mercy. I now
respectfully submit this appeal against the sentence
on the grounds of severity and respectfully draw
attention to the following points, namely:-

(1) Ever since I can remember I have been looked at
    askance by my fellows at school, and later when
    I went to work. This was on account of my foreign
    name. The result was that my mind became warped
    and distorted at an early age.
(2) At the age of 16 I was introduced to the British
    Union of Fascists and readily believed their
    high-sounding doctrines.
(3) While completely under their influence I joined
    the Army at the age of 18, and supplied them
    with information which I regarded as being of an
    innocent nature; information which was ostensibly
    required for an innocent purpose.
(4) When I realised the nature and gravity of my
    actions, I endeavoured to extricate myself from
    my position, even to the extent of attempting to

commit suicide early in 1942. I was thereafter warned that reprisals would be taken against my parents unless I continued to help the enemy.

(5) In spite of this, I did, when possible, supply false information. Lieut. Bromage, R.N. confirms this.

(6) When I came into Allied hands in La Spezia in March 1945, I made a voluntary confession to the Americans, and later to the British Authorities. It was principally on these statements that I was convicted.

(7) In my statement to the Americans, I disclosed the names of 60-70 enemy agents operating in Italy and the Austrian Tyrol. In a statement made to British Military Intelligence on 14th Sept 45 I made further disclosures. In view of the presence of the press at my trial, I instructed my defending officer to remain silent on these points.

In view of the foregoing, I appeal against the sentence of the Court, and beg that it be commuted.

    I have the honour to be, Sir
        Your obedient servant

(Signed) Theodore J.W. Schurch

The desperation in the above appeal, taken from the National Archives, is almost palpable, as if Theodore Schurch has finally realised the gravity of his situation. It came after he was sentenced to death following his conviction at a court martial on nine counts of treachery and one of desertion with intent to join the enemy. How did it come to that?

Born in Marylebone in London in 1918, Theodore John William Schurch was a Swiss national through his father who worked as head porter at the Savoy Hotel. His army career began in 1936 when he joined the Royal Army Service Corps as a driver and then a clerk, serving in Palestine and Egypt.

By this time, however, his head had been turned by the British Union of Fascists with its poisonous messages about Jews and its commitment to a social revolution. It is almost certain that Schurch had been ordered to join the army by the BUF so that they could glean information from him.

On the outbreak of war in September 1939, Schurch was serving in the Middle East, remaining there until his capture when Tobruk fell to German and Italian forces in June 1942. The normal procedure in this event was for his name to be notified to the Red Cross and for him to spend the remainder of the war in captivity. The Red Cross had the responsibility of visiting and monitoring prisoner of war camps and of exchanging messages regarding prisoners and missing persons. But Theodore Schurch simply vanished and there was no record of him being in any POW camp anywhere.

The suspicions of British intelligence were aroused in 1943 by a report that was collected by MI9, the intelligence department responsible for dealing with escapes, evasion and the debriefing of POWs who had somehow made it back to Britain. One such former POW, a Sub-Lieutenant Roberts of the Royal Navy, reported on a man named 'Captain Richards' who he said was widely known to be operating as an informant in POW camps in Italy. It did not take the Secret Service long to work out that Captain Richards was, in actual fact, the missing Theodore Schurch, a fact confirmed by another former POW who had had dealings with Richards and recognised Schurch as the same man from a photograph. Schurch's name was added to the arrest list of all those British subjects who were believed to be aiding the enemy.

In April 1945, Schurch finally surfaced, wearing the uniform of a British officer, in La Spezia, a northern Italian naval port. La Spezia had been used as a base by the ultra-loyal Italian Fascist Decima MAS Special Forces unit and was also a hub of Italian and German intelligence operations. Arousing suspicion, Schurch was arrested by agents of SCI/Z, the counter-intelligence branch of the Office of Strategic Services (OSS), America's intelligence agency during the Second World War.

Interrogation

He was taken to Rome where the head of SCI/Z, James Angleton, interrogated him. Angleton, who would later be chief of counter-intelligence at the CIA, the OSS's successor agency, quickly realised that Schurch was of limited education, but he was wily and had a natural intelligence. He concluded in his 75-page report that, although Schurch claimed to have behaved as he did purely because of his fascist ideals, in reality it had provided him with a lifestyle that he could not now do without.

The formal arrest of Theodore Schurch by the British Army's Special Investigation Branch (SIB) took place on 28 May 1945. He was initially held on a charge of impersonating an officer to gain military information for the use of the enemy. Angleton's report listed Schurch's espionage history, stretching back over nine years. It had begun with his time as a member of the BUF, continued in the Army before the war and then in Palestine and Egypt during the war. He had worked for the Italian Servizio Informazioni Militare (SIM) and the Abwehr, German military intelligence. When the Abwehr was abolished by Hitler in February 1944, he began working for the SS's intelligence service, the Sicherheitsdienst (SD). Angleton described him as a paid asset who frequently met his handlers to obtain instructions. He recommended that Schurch should be subject to legal proceedings.

Back in Britain, Schurch was interviewed at Gibraltar Barracks in Leeds by Percy Edwards who was a civilian official from the General Staff at the War Office. It was a stressed and exhausted man that Edwards saw. Schurch pleaded with him:

'I don't want to be treated as a soldier and put into battledress. I want to be dealt with as a civilian. Why are they prolonging the agony instead of shooting me right away? My world has been shattered and everything I stood for is now in the dust, so I have no desire to live.'

Schurch had very obviously been thinking about how to escape a charge of treason, saying to Edwards as he left: 'Still, you've got to prove I owe allegiance to your king as I am really Swiss and never took any oath.'

Moved to Connaught Barracks in Woolwich, London, where the RASC was based, Schurch began to tell the investigators all he knew about Italian and German intelligence, naming officers and agents who had crossed his path while he had been masquerading as 'Captain Richards'. These ultimately were of great help to the prosecution case, proving he was up to his eyes in espionage.

Court Martial

Schurch was to be tried as a soldier, under military law, and his court martial was held in September 1945 at Chelsea Barracks, presided over by Judge Advocate General, Major Melford Stevenson, who later became a High Court judge. Prosecuting was Major RAL Hillard KC and the defence was led by Lieutenant AC Brands of the Royal Artillery. The defendant faced nine charges under Section 40 of the Army Act as well as a charge of treachery as defined in Section 1 of the Treason Act 1940:

'If, with intent to help the enemy, any person does, or attempts or conspires with any other person to do any act which is designed or likely to give assistance to the naval, military or air operations of the enemy, to impede such operations of

His Majesty's forces, or to endanger life, he shall be guilty of
felony and shall on conviction suffer death.'

There was an additional charge of desertion.

Schurch betrayed his fascist leanings at the start of the
proceedings. Members of the board – equivalent to the jury in
a civil trial – were asked to state their religion and when Major
FA Holland of the RAOC said he was Jewish, Schurch objected.
The case commenced with five men who had been prisoners of
war taking the board through their encounters with 'Captain
Richards' in various camps. Lieutenant John Bromage, for
instance, who ran into 'Richards' at Camp 50 in Rome in April
1943, reported that he seemed to be 'highly nervous' and 'seedy'
and he even warned the POWs to beware of 'stool pigeons'
and that, for all they knew, he might even be one. Another
statement was provided by Lieutenant-Colonel David Stirling
of the Scots Guards, now famous as the founder of the Special
Air Service (SAS). Captured in North Africa, Stirling also met
'Richards' in Rome, but had already been warned that he was
an informant. Schurch had attempted to discover the name of
the officer who would have succeeded Stirling and although
Stirling could not remember if he had given the information to
'Richards', Schurch maintained that he had. Schurch claimed
that two SAS patrols had been captured in autumn 1942 as a
result of captured documents, but also from information from
prisoners obtained by Schurch in his officer's disguise.

Schurch's nationality was never an issue during the court
martial and nor was the initial statement that he had given
Angleton in Rome challenged. The defence argued instead that
Schurch was an uneducated man of low mentality who had
been exploited by the Germans and Italians. Schurch claimed
that the information he provided was already known to them or
had been made up by him. Melford Stevenson pointed out the
length of time during which Schurch was active, saying that he

would certainly have been well aware of the consequences of his actions. He also reminded the panel that Schurch constantly used 'we' and 'our department' in referring to his fascist masters. Thus, he aligned himself closely with them.

As had been inevitable from the start, Theodore Schurch was found guilty and sentenced to death by hanging. Two appeals failed, including one to the King. The information he gave to investigators did not bring him any mercy, one Special Investigation Branch officer brushing aside his appeal to the King: 'This man's history shows that he has no loyalties to anyone and I do not feel that I am justified in suggesting that the information which he gave was of such value as to affect any recommendation which may be made to the King regarding confirmation.'

Meanwhile, Schurch had appended a handwritten note to his appeal which pleaded for him to be treated as a soldier:

'Very Important.

Please arrange with the Secretary of War that if the final decision is still one of death that, as all my charges were military ones, whilst England was at War, and that I was given a Military Court Martial and not a Civilian Trial, and also that I am a British Soldier, that I may therefore be entitled to a soldier's death by being SHOT not hung. This I ask as a last request, and if refused please submit me the name and position of the one who does so.'

Theodore Schurch did not get his wish. He was hanged by Albert Pierrepoint at Pentonville Prison on 4 January 1946. It was just one day after the execution of William Joyce across London at Wandsworth Prison. Schurch was 27 years old.

The Cambridge Spies

Introduction

The failure of the General Strike to incite revolution in Britain and events such as those surrounding the trial of Wilfred Macartney and his handler, Georg Hansen, persuaded Moscow towards the end of the 1920s that it was time to change tactics. Instead of infiltrating the Communist Party of Great Britain and other organisations, they created a new system involving what they termed 'illegals' that they had tentatively trialled with some success in the United States in the 1920s. The Deuxième Bureau – the French security service – provided MI5 with an agent's report detailing the new approach to the recruitment and management of spies:

'In 1927 the authorities in Moscow decided to change their methods which they judged to be no longer sufficiently secret and which constantly threatened to bring about diplomatic complication. The sections of the G.P.U. were shorn of a part of their power which was handed over to illegal organisations, the chief or 'resident' of which was of superior rank to any of the other G. P. U. agents left in the Embassy. For the purposes of cover the illegal agents usually pose as business men or proceed to set up commercial companies, the business activities of which usually remain nebulous. Contact is kept up between the Embassy section and the secret section by means of one or more skilful agents... The secret agents or 'residents' of the G.P.U. are almost invariably recruited amongst the citizens of foreign countries so that the Soviet authorities may, should any awkward incidents occur, disclaim all responsibility. Should Russian citizens be employed in these capacities they are always provided with false passports of other nationalities. In addition to the aboved [sic] described organisms there is also a mobile section of well-tried agents mostly consisting of Germans, Hungarians, Letts [Latvians] and Austrians.'

Although fully aware of this new development, MI5 and SIS found it almost impossible to identify the actual illegals. The security services were still of the misguided opinion that the most fertile ground for recruitment of spies lay within the CPGB or with the working class – trade unionists, for example. But the Soviets were thinking more creatively, looking towards the great universities of Britain.

There had been a change in the attitudes of students as the 1930s began. There was a great deal of anger about the legacy of the First World War and the many broken promises made to the men who had survived the horrors. There was also grave concern about the rise of fascism across Europe, with Mussolini in power in Italy and Adolf Hitler on the verge of power in Germany. The British government, as well as others, appeared to be taking no stand against the wave of authoritarianism sweeping across Europe and it seemed obvious to many students that Soviet Russia was the only power that could and would act as a bulwark against it. Soviet illegals, therefore, began to target idealistic young students, many of them from elite families, studying at the pre-eminent institutions of learning in the country. The plan was that, once recruited and their education complete, these young men would find themselves in positions of power and influence and be of the utmost use to the Soviet Union. The highly effective Soviet illegal, Arnold Deutsch, was responsible for the recruitment of some 20 agents, the most successful of whom were the ones discussed in this chapter – Kim Philby, Donald Maclean, Guy Burgess, Anthony Blunt and John Cairncross – all recruited while at

Cambridge University and known to us now as the Cambridge Five.

One source lists four typical motivations for spying. These are money, ideology, compromise and ego. In the case of the Cambridge Five, there is little doubt that ideology was the main reason they became spies. They may have thought only Russia would take a stand against fascism, but primarily they were unswerving ideological spies. They believed wholeheartedly in the image promulgated of Russia as a workers' state where social justice and equality were available to all. The reality, as has been noted previously, was just the opposite. Stalin's Russia was a brutal dictatorship where opposition to the government inevitably resulted in imprisonment in the gulag or worse. Their handler, Deutsch, shared their idealistic view of the Soviet Union and their desire to see the ultimate defeat of capitalism. These men could already be said to be rebels, anyway; Burgess and Blunt were homosexual, Maclean was bisexual and Cairncross and Philby bore a great deal of antipathy to Britain's antiquated class system and the status quo.

At this time, it should be noted that MI5 and SIS had no idea that the Russians were targeting universities. And British intelligence certainly was not. University men were viewed as vapid, effete intellectuals. The mentality in the service was strictly colonial or military and that did not always produce the people with the best brains or with the greatest experience of the world. They liked to recruit people similar to themselves, from prominent families they knew or from the social circles in which they operated. The 'Old Boys' Network' was very much in play which made it all the more complicated later when traitors began to be exposed in their midst. They were slow to act and sometimes failed entirely to do what was required.

The exposure of the Cambridge spies over the years was a long slow nightmare for British intelligence and for the British government. Harold Macmillan, for instance, was convinced his government would fall on the sword of espionage. Occasionally, the embarrassment was so intense that it seemed better to give the traitor immunity rather than reveal all in court. The legacy was deep distrust from Britain's greatest ally, the United States and a reluctance to share secrets in quite the same way as before.

The individual stories of these extraordinary men read like film scripts but their treachery is unmatched in British history.

Guy Burgess: 'The Genius in the Network'

'Clearly a clever boy'

It is tempting to view the Cambridge spy, Guy Burgess, as something of a buffoon – a clever one, of course, but a buffoon nonetheless. After all, he spent a great deal of his time drunk and he dressed like a tramp, with stained jackets and frayed shirts albeit with an omnipresent Eton tie. It is remarkable how many people noted his filthy fingernails and generally scruffy appearance. A young woman colleague in the Foreign Office described him as 'extremely repulsive. He was rather greasy and dirty. He was always telling awful, dirty jokes.' But even more people describe his wit, his sense of fun and his deep knowledge of a wide range of subjects, especially politics. MI5's Arthur Martin described him as '... clearly a clever boy. But it was more than that. He had a magnetic personality.' Some would say, if asked who the major figure in the Cambridge spy ring was, that Burgess was the mainstay of the group. The KGB controller of the Cambridge spies, Yuri Modin, wrote:

'… the real leader was Burgess. He held the group together, infused it with his energy and led it into battle, so to speak. In the 1930s, at the very start, it was he who took the initiatives and the risks, dragging the others along in his wake. He was the moral leader of the group.'

Leading spy writer, Nigel West, has reported that:

'Anthony [Blunt] told me that Guy Burgess was the genius in the network, the key man. He was the person everybody had to go to for instruction, help and advice. Guy was always in touch with the Russians and could make decisions and could counsel other people.'

Guy Burgess pined for England in his Moscow exile, had luxuries sent from London and clung like a limpet to any English person who happened to be visiting the city. Why, therefore, did he betray this nation he loved, endanger all that he held dear, and end up in the capital of the Soviet Union? The truth is probably that he had an urge to change the world, to do something, rather than just theorise about it. It was partly a result of his growing up in the 1930s, part of a generation that wanted to take action to change things. He failed at most of the jobs he took on and was never going to scale the heights that many of his contemporaries did, but he was eager to be someone. Moreover, fascism was an existential threat that many of this generation believed could only be defeated by communism. Guy Burgess was one of those, believing the great choice to be made was between the United States and the Soviet Union and for him America was anathema. There could, therefore, be only one choice. There is little doubt, too that he also relished the opportunity not only to scandalise the class from which he came – and he did that daily – but also to live a life of secrecy and adventure. There is also the fact that the Russians would not let him stop.

A Military Family

His immediate family had a military background, his grandfather on his father's side spending most of his military career in foreign fields in the service of the Royal Artillery. His father joined the HMS *Britannia* training ship at Dartmouth aged 14 but his career as a junior officer was not notable until he was found guilty in 1902 of causing a collision between his vessel, HMS *Thrasher*, and another ship near Malta. A court martial for the loss of a signal book from the battleship HMS *Prince George* followed two years later. By 1907, he was training at Devonport for the reserve. That year he married Evelyn Gillman, daughter of a wealthy former banker and Guy Francis de Moncy Burgess came into the world on 16 April 1911. He was brought up in a female household, his father being away at sea much of the time, and, as a result, he developed a close relationship with his mother. Malcolm Burgess retired from the Royal Navy and moved his family to West Meon in Hampshire.

The young Guy was schooled at Lockers Park, in Hemel Hempstead, the most expensive prep school in England, before going to Eton in 1923 where he was to spend a year before, like his father, attending the Britannia Royal Naval College at Dartmouth. Tragedy struck in September of that year, however, when Malcolm died, aged just 43.

A few months later, Guy Burgess arrived at Dartmouth, aged 13. At the time, the school instilled rigid discipline into its students; corporal punishment was frequently used, and cold baths were the order of the day. Often top of his class, Burgess was regarded as 'excellent officer material' and his talent as an artist led to his work appearing in the school magazine. He left the school in 1927, purportedly because of his poor eyesight, but some have suggested this was an excuse often used to cover up dishonesty or homosexuality. Others say he was simply a misfit. 'He was not popular and had no close friends. He was left-wing,' said one fellow student. He returned to Eton, very happy to do so.

Burgess would later tell the Soviets that he had first realised he was homosexual at Eton and, certainly, homosexuality was common at England's premier public school. The good-looking Burgess would certainly have attracted admirers, but uncharacteristically, given his behaviour in the future, he was very discreet. At Eton, some loved him, admiring his intelligence and wit, while others described him as a loner and unpopular. He became a voracious reader, the books becoming increasingly political in content.

Winning a scholarship to Trinity College, Cambridge, he arrived there in October 1930. He was elected at the end of his first term to the Trinity Historical Society whose membership consisted of the 25 most promising undergraduates and postgraduates including Kim Philby, a year ahead of him. He found a lover in his first year – Jack Hunter, son of the Hollywood director, T Hayes Hunter. He also met future fellow-traitor, Anthony Blunt, who was now a graduate student. Blunt took an initial dislike to Burgess, but soon came to recognise 'the liveliness and quality of his mind and the range of his interests'. Both homosexuals, it is unknown whether they were actually lovers at any point, but it is said that Burgess introduced Blunt to the pleasures of 'rough trade'.

The Apostles

The country was beset by crises in 1931. There were three million unemployed; around a thousand sailors of the Royal Navy openly mutinied in September at the naval base at Invergordon, causing a run on the pound which forced Britain off the Gold Standard; and Labour Prime Minister Ramsay MacDonald was forced to form a National Government. In Europe, Mussolini's Fascists ruled Italy and Adolf Hitler's National Socialists were attempting the same in Germany. In response, the Cambridge University Socialist Party became a fulcrum for left-wing thought and activity at the university. It was also viewed as a recruitment vehicle by the Soviets. Burgess had, himself, become increasingly interested in Marxism and it showed in his work at university.

Trinity don, Steven Runciman, took a shine to Burgess, attributing his wild behaviour and his drinking to the young man's lack of confidence. 'Drink,' he said, 'gave him the confidence to behave badly.' Nonetheless, Burgess continued to perform well, winning the Earl of Derby Studentship, awarded for distinction in the Historical Tripos.

In November 1932, Burgess was elected to one of Cambridge's most exclusive societies – the Apostles, a secret society founded in 1820. This group championed the intellect for its own sake, believed in freedom of thought and expression, and the refusal to be held back by moral restraints. He was sponsored by Anthony Blunt. Each Saturday evening, a member had to deliver a paper on a philosophical question which was then debated. There were some illustrious members at the time, including the Regius Professor of History, G. M. Trevelyan; the writer E. M. Forster; Edward Marsh, who became private secretary to a number of prime ministers, including Winston Churchill; the philosopher, Ludwig Wittgenstein; and the economist, John Maynard Keynes. His election spoke highly of Burgess's powerful intellect. He and Blunt brought in fellow communists to the Apostles, as they did for some of the other important Cambridge societies.

In his third year, Burgess failed, through illness, to complete Part II of the Tripos, instead being awarded an *aegrotat*, an ungraded degree that was awarded to students who were ill at the time of an exam. It is uncertain whether, as one source suggests, he suffered a nervous breakdown, or whether he simply failed to put in the necessary work. A contemporary, Lord Thurlow, claimed that Burgess had taken amphetamines before the exam and had to be carried out halfway through.

Back at Trinity in autumn 1933 as a research student, his Marxist views were being reinforced by the influence of two men – John Cornford and James Klugmann. Cornford, a poet and a passionate and effective recruiting officer for communism, who would die aged twenty-one in the Spanish Civil War, led a communist takeover of the Cambridge University Socialist Society which at the time had a membership of around 200. While Cornford was already an experienced activist, Klugmann was a theorist who made communism accessible. They both championed resistance to war and opposition to fascism and under their undoubted influence, Burgess completed his political journey, joining CUSS. Amongst campaigns he joined were those in support of striking sewage workers and bus drivers and he protested against high council house rents. The Communist Party supported the hunger marches that took place at this time and Burgess was amongst the Cambridge University communists who joined the marchers as they proceeded through Cambridge on their way to London.

But he received a devastating blow in March 1934, when he learned that the subject of his doctoral dissertation – 'Bourgeois Revolution in Seventeenth-Century England' – had been covered in a newly published book. At that moment, any prospects of an academic career were over, leaving him to devote his life to communism. In fact, he visited the Soviet Union in the summer of 1934 with a communist friend from Oxford University, Derek Blaikie. *En route*, they stopped in Germany and saw the developing European political situation first-hand.

Recruitment to the Cause

Burgess returned to Trinity for a fifth year and, around this time, his name was on a list of potential recruits supplied by

Kim Philby to his handler, Arnold Deutsch. Moscow was told that 'Burgess is the son of very well-off parents. For two years he has been a party member, very clever and reliable (ideologically speaking), but in [Philby's] opinion, somewhat superficial and can occasionally make a slip of the tongue.' According to Philby, Burgess was questionable, his flamboyance and homosexuality being problematic. The Soviets, on the other hand, believed that his homosexuality could be an asset, could open the door to contacts in that tight-knit world whose members already had to lead secretive lives, ever in fear of exposure and even prosecution.

Donald Maclean, who had also already been recruited, let slip to Burgess that he was working for Soviet intelligence, leaving the Russians little option but to bring Burgess into the fold. Deutsch met him in late December 1934 and Burgess was immediately thrilled at the prospect of an adventure and delighted to be of service to the Communist Party. He told Deutsch that he was honoured by the invitation and would sacrifice everything in order to serve the party. And so, with the codename 'Mädchen' – German for 'Girl' – he joined Kim Philby and Donald Maclean in the Cambridge spy ring.

There was some debate amongst the Soviets about Burgess's recruitment. For a start the decision to do so had to be made by Deutsch without their say-so because of a temporary breakdown in communications with Moscow. Secondly, it was strictly against the rules for agents to know each other, and, of course, Philby, Maclean and Burgess were all friends. Deutsch vigorously defended him: 'Though I rate him lower than SÖNCHEN [Philby] and WAISE [Maclean], I think he will come in useful.' Moscow gave in and Burgess began his training to be a spy. He completed the first task that was normally given to a novice agent – to provide a list of personal contacts – by supplying no less than 200 names. There was also a separate list of the names of prominent homosexuals with whom he was acquainted. From the NKVD files of this time, it is evident that there were still lingering doubts about Burgess's suitability to the role:

> 'Mädchen' has imagination and is full of plans and initiative, but he has no internal brakes. He is, therefore, prone to panic easily and he is also prone to desperation. He takes up any task willingly, but he is too unstable to take it to its conclusion. His will is often paralysed by the most insignificant of difficulties. Sometimes he lies, not maliciously, but because of fear of admitting some minor error on his part. In relations with us he is honest and does everything without objections and sometimes produces an impression of a person who is too readily subdued. Though he dresses very scruffily, he still likes to attract attention. This is a generally characteristic feature of his. He craves to be liked and only reluctantly acknowledges his weaknesses.'

Leaving Cambridge

To the disgust and surprise of his friends, in the spring of 1935, Burgess resigned his membership of the Communist Party and quit Cambridge, moving to a flat at 38 Chester Square in London which he paid for from his family trust and from the frequent payments he received from the Soviets. He decorated it in red, white and blue and would often spend entire weekends reading in bed, drinking red wine and eating from a saucepan that he filled with kippers, porridge, bacon, garlic and onions. He reviewed history books for the *New Statesman*, had various affairs and occasionally socialised with Kim Philby and his wife Litzi.

The Soviets ordered him to apply to study Russian at the School of Slavonic Studies in order to form acquaintances with fellow students who could possibly be MI6 operatives learning Russian. They also wanted him to get to know one of the teachers, Elizabeth Hill, who was related to General Yevgeny Miller, leader of the anti-communist Russian General Military Union in Paris. Burgess was lucky enough to be assigned to Elizabeth Hill and learned from her that there were indeed MI6 officers being taught at the school. Furthermore, he learned that the director's secretary was a communist. Burgess was starting to prove to his Russian masters that he could deliver useful intelligence to them.

In 1935, he was given a job by John Macnamara, Conservative MP for Chelmsford, acting as secretary, personal assistant and travelling companion. Macnamara was a member of the Anglo-German Fellowship which contained amongst its followers many who were pro-Nazi. Burgess's association with Macnamara and the Fellowship was useful on several counts. Importantly, it helped him to distance himself in others' eyes from his communist past. It also enabled him to meet highly placed homosexuals such as Edouard Pfeiffer, a sado-masochist and leading light of the French Boy Scout movement, who was also secretary-general of the French Radical Socialist Party and *chef de cabinet* of Edouard Daladier who would be prime minister of France three times between 1933 and 1940. Pfeiffer was also an agent of the French Deuxieme Bureau – the external military intelligence agency – as well as MI6.

Burgess was writing for a number of publications at this time, work that frequently took him abroad and introduced him to interesting people such as Willi Münzenberg, an important propagandist for the Comintern. He continued to display his right-wing credentials to friends, telling one that 'the only way that collectivism is likely to come to Europe is through the Conservative Party'. To the journalist, Goronwy Rees, he explained that, 'The only people who really believed in holding India, and had the will to do so, were the Right of the Conservative Party, led by Mr Churchill... Their only hope of success was in alliance with the extreme Right in Europe, as represented by the German National Socialists and the Italian Fascists, who had no objection to a strengthening of British rule in India, so long as they were given a free hand in Europe.' The agony such statements must have put him through demonstrates the sacrifice he was prepared to make for the cause in which he believed with all his heart.

The BBC and Anthony Blunt

In January 1937, Burgess landed a job as assistant producer in the Talks Department of the BBC, finding speakers for BBC current affairs and cultural programmes. Naturally, his huge number of personal contacts came in handy in this role but his relationship with the management of the corporation was often sorely tested, especially when he argued with them about his pay. Meanwhile, his colleagues struggled with his arrogance and untidiness.

Anthony Blunt benefited greatly from Burgess's new job, recruited by him to give a number of talks that contributed to his growing reputation as an authority on modern art. Burgess believed Blunt had the requisite skills to become a spotter of potential spies and approached him at an opportune moment, when democracy and fascism confronted each other in the Spanish Civil War. Like many others, Blunt was convinced that 'the Communist Party and Russia constituted the only bulwark against fascism, since the Western democracies were taking an uncertain and compromising attitude towards Germany'. A wealthy American and fellow Apostle, Michael Straight, and John Cairncross, an employee at the Foreign Office, were the first of Blunt's and Burgess's recruits.

Burgess's love life had been given a boost in autumn 1936 when he met a dancer from Gateshead, Jack Hewit, who for 14 years would be his lover and general dogsbody. Burgess liked to show off his working-class paramour, to the extent that

Hewit claimed 'He wore me like a badge'. Of course, this did not put an end to Burgess's promiscuity. As Hewit said, 'He was the most promiscuous person who ever lived. He slept with anything that was going… If anyone invented homosexuality, it was Guy Burgess.'

Eventually, his promiscuity got him into trouble, when he was arrested for soliciting in the toilets at Paddington Station. He was acquitted but the incident brought on a nervous breakdown. It was felt he should leave the country for a while and he went with his mother and Anthony Blunt to France. In Paris during his 'convalescence', he spent time in the company of Edouard Pfeiffer, gleaning information from him about the French attitude to the *Anschluss*, the annexation of Austria by Germany, information which, of course, was immediately fed to his Soviet handler. It was also fed to British intelligence for whom he was now also working.

MI6 Agent

Burgess was becoming increasingly frustrated with the interference of the government in the BBC's programming and the censorship it imposed. Eventually, he resigned, the reason given in his personnel file being 'To undertake MI activities for the War Office'. Recruited by his friend, Major George Ball, who was involved in the reorganisation of the Secret Service after the dismissal of Vernon Kell, the Director of MI5, in the summer of 1940, he was appointed to Section D, a clandestine new organisation within the British Secret Service tasked with investigating non-military ways of attacking the enemy. With his BBC experience in mind, Burgess was made Section D's representative on the Joint Broadcasting Committee (JBC) which had been set up in April 1938 to work with the BBC to transmit anti-Hitler broadcasts to Germany. Naturally, this work gave him access to a considerable amount of information regarding Britain's preparations for war. He was able to pass to Moscow Central the fact that the British reckoned they could defeat the Nazis on their own and saw no need for a pact with the Soviets. This must have served to increase Stalin's suspicion of Britain and might conceivably have encouraged him to opt for the Soviet-German pact that was signed in August 1939.

By 1940, Burgess was working in the Ministry of Information's Foreign Division Directorate, as part of the Foreign Publicity Division, liaising between the Ministry of Information and the JCB. In May 1940, he became Temporary Civil Servant, Civilian Assistant, War Office, MI6, with access to the names of agents working abroad. Around this time, he succeeded in getting his friend and fellow spy, Kim Philby, into Section D. The Soviets were delighted to have two of their agents at the heart of British intelligence but the purges in Moscow had weakened their strength in London and the *rezidentura* – the base for Soviet espionage operations in London – had effectively closed. The defection of Walter Krivitsky just before the outbreak of war had also exposed elements of the Soviet Western European network.

Burgess's private life continued unabated. He picked up young soldiers, airmen and sailors in pubs and took them to seedy boarding houses or brought them home. Goronwy Rees wrote:

'… to spend an evening at Guy's flat was rather like watching a French farce which had been injected with all the elements of a political drama. Bedroom doors opened and shut; strange faces appeared and disappeared down the stairs, where they passed some new visitor on his way up; civil servants, politicians, visitors to London, friends and colleagues of Guy's, popped in and out of bed and then continued some absorbing discussion of political intrigue, the progress of the war and the future possibilities of the peace.'

Burgess was out of a job at the end of 1940 when Section D ceased operations. This made him liable for call-up but he avoided it by returning to the BBC Home Talks Department. However, after he had saved Anthony Blunt from losing his position with British intelligence when his communism had come to light, Blunt returned the favour and had Burgess recruited as an agent by MI5, operating under the codename 'Vauxhall'. He was given the job of running agents and was now in the remarkable position of running agents for both the British and the Soviet Secret Services.

Back in action, the London *rezidentura* was delighted to receive information from Burgess, via his Cambridge friend Dennis Proctor who worked at the Treasury, about the secret talks between Churchill and US President Roosevelt at the 1943 Allied Conference in Casablanca. They learned from Burgess that there would be an invasion of Sicily in June 1943, but that the invasion of France would not be staged until the following year.

However, in Moscow there was still suspicion about the Cambridge spies. How could several of them be working for British intelligence, they wondered, given their left-wing sympathies as students? One NKVD analyst, Elena Modrzhinskya, chief of the British department in Moscow, had a deep mistrust of them. She found it hard to believe that these men, who had been communists in their pasts, were so easily able to find positions in the British Secret Service. Soviet agents were sent to investigate but found nothing incriminating. Burgess continued to work at the BBC, and, on the whole, his career was flourishing. In June 1944, however, he left to take up a position in the News Department of the Foreign Office.

New Roles

Burgess's new job was to explain government policy to foreign newspaper editors and London representatives of the foreign press, and to react to events as they happened. He had access to everything produced by the Foreign Office, including telegraphic communications, both decoded and encoded. He was perfect for the job, but it was also the ideal position for someone who was passing information to Moscow. He worked Saturdays when no one else did and could take documents home at night which, of course, made it easier for them to be shared with his Soviet handlers. Now the most productive source of material, much of it marked 'Top Secret', he was given financial rewards by Moscow for his industriousness. He reported on, amongst other things, the parliamentary debates on Poland; shared telegrams regarding the conference in San Francisco that set up the United Nations; and British thoughts on how Germany should be divided after the war. He even gave the Russians a Chiefs of Staff report on Operation Unthinkable – war between Britain and the Soviet Union.

In the general election following the war, the Labour Party's landslide victory brought Burgess a new job, as private secretary to Hector McNeil, Minister of State in the Foreign Office. Burgess had cultivated McNeil during the war and it had paid off, providing him with a direct link to government. The Foreign Office was less than happy with the appointment of an 'outsider', but the new government had intimated that it wanted to do things differently; therefore, they were forced to accept Burgess. His role was to act as personal assistant, write speeches and do anything else that the minister required of him.

McNeil was pretty lazy and, while he went out to restaurants, cinemas and theatres, Burgess did a great deal of his work for him, dealing with classified documents and reports that he fed straight to Moscow Central. He had access to the minutes of cabinet meetings, the Defence Committee and meetings involving the Chiefs of the Imperial Staff. Britain's military strategy was available to him as well as all the gossip around the Foreign Office. Naturally, Moscow was delighted. He and his colleague, Fred Warner, wielded huge influence over McNeil's decisions and McNeil was in awe of him.

New Handler

A new handler arrived in the autumn of 1947. This was Yuri Modin's first overseas posting and he would work with Burgess for the following three years, the pair sometimes meeting every day when there was a crisis. Burgess would dial a number and the Russian agent who answered would take a code number from him and then end the call. The code told Modin or a colleague named Korovin to meet him at a prearranged rendezvous. They gave Burgess money to buy a car because they thought that would make it easier to stay in touch with him but Burgess splashed out on a second-hand, convertible, two-seater gold Rolls-Royce. Needless to say, his driving was terrible. Meanwhile, the documents continued to flow from him to Moscow, more than three hundred in a five-week period towards the end of 1947.

In 1948, he worked for a brief spell at the innocuously named Information and Research Department – closely linked to MI6 and established to seize the propaganda initiative from the Soviet Union – but he was soon back working with Hector McNeil, having been kicked out of the department. The flood of leaked documents continued and, between November 1947 and May 1948, he handed over 2,000. On 1 November 1948, he was on the move again to the Far East Department, gaining him a view of Britain's reaction to the final months of the civil war raging between Mao Zedong's communists and Chiang Kai-shek's nationalists. He was then able to feed to Moscow information on the British attitude towards the People's Republic of China after Mao's victory. As the Korean War approached, he was also able to keep the Russians up-to-date on British policy towards Korea. Around this time, the amount of material he was passing to Moscow became so large that he asked them to buy him a suitcase to transport it all.

His life continued to be chaotic. On holiday with his mother in Dublin in 1949, after falling down some stairs and banging his head at the Reform Club in London while drunk, he was arrested for driving while drunk and for dangerous driving. He claimed that the tomato juice he had been drinking must have been tampered with and the case was dismissed.

Washington

After complaints about incidents in Tangier and Gibraltar while on another holiday and a suspicion that he had passed material to an American journalist who had links with Soviet intelligence, the Foreign Office personnel department summoned Burgess to a meeting. It was possible that he would either be dismissed or be forced to resign but MI5's Deputy Director General, Guy Liddell, protected him. Instead, he was severely reprimanded and warned about his future behaviour.

The arrest of Dr Klaus Fuchs in February 1950 for passing information about the Manhattan Project to the Russians unnerved Burgess and all his fellow spies. A scientist codenamed 'Charles' had been named in decryptions that formed part of a project known as Venona. US codebreakers had managed to break what had been thought to be an unbreakable code used by the Soviets, enabling them to decipher 3,000 Soviet intelligence telegrams that had been sent from the United States to Moscow. Information was revealed about hundreds of Americans who had become Soviet spies during the war, about spies in the US Treasury, the Manhattan Project, the State Department and the OSS itself. Venona was so secret that the President was not told about it for three years. Burgess had been informed of the uncovering of Charles – suspected to be Klaus Fuchs – by Kim Philby but had forgotten to pass the information to his handler, Yuri Modin. His warning might have allowed Moscow to extract Fuchs to safety instead of being sentenced to 14 years in prison.

On 9 May, Burgess was given the news that he was to be posted to Washington as a second secretary. It was not a decision that was universally applauded. MI5 were appalled but it was thought that he could be more easily controlled there and, if he had to be dismissed, it would attract less attention if it occurred across the Atlantic. Burgess himself accepted the posting reluctantly, but he was heavily in debt, despite his Foreign Office salary and the money he received from Moscow, and in the end he had no choice. If he resigned, his job prospects were low and, anyway, the Russians were keen for him to go.

On arrival in the United States, he stayed with Kim Philby and his family, living in the basement, not an arrangement relished by Aileen, Philby's second wife, but her husband insisted, mainly because he could use Burgess as a courier. Needless to say, Burgess proved a social disaster, upsetting dinner parties at the Philby house and regularly insulting people. Not long after starting work, he was in trouble, reported for leaving classified documents out in his office instead of returning them to the registry. He was given a warning. No one really wanted to work with him and he was tasked instead with gathering information during his constant socialising and writing reports about what was happening in America. Several committees on which he sat gave him some access to classified material.

The Venona project continued to divulge invaluable information. One nugget was that in 1945, a Soviet agent codenamed 'Homer' had been working in the British Embassy in Washington. This information was passed to Philby who immediately told Burgess. The net began to close in on Donald Maclean – 'Homer' – until it became evident that the culprit was either him or one other man. Maclean would have to be exfiltrated.

Meanwhile, Burgess's behaviour and his drinking was getting worse. In February 1951, he was stopped a couple of times on the same day for speeding. Claiming diplomatic immunity, he was let off but, when his car was stopped a third time, his travelling companion – a young black gay man named James Turck – was driving and the officer who stopped him rejected the claim of diplomatic immunity. This time bail of $55 had to be paid. After the story of Burgess's day landed on the desk of the Governor of Virginia, it was forwarded to the British ambassador in Washington who interviewed Burgess and suspended him. A disciplinary board was lined up at which he would either be dismissed or asked to resign. Burgess was apparently furious, although it has since been suggested that he engineered this situation so that he could get back to London. Whatever the truth, he left the United States on Saturday 28 April.

'Don't you go, too!'

As Kim Philby drove Burgess to Union Station a few days before his departure, Burgess was morose. Philby had something of a presentiment. 'Don't you go, too!' he told his old colleague.

On arrival in London, Burgess informed Anthony Blunt that Maclean was about to be exposed. Blunt told Modin and he passed it on to his bosses in Moscow who agreed almost immediately to get Maclean out. As Burgess frequently met with Maclean on his return, he came under suspicion and MI5 started watching him. But matters were swiftly progressing. Moscow advised Burgess to accompany Maclean part of the way during his escape. It was decided that they would leave Britain on a ship often used by men entertaining their lady friends as it cruised along the French coast. It would occasionally put into ports such as Saint-Malo to allow passengers off to do some shopping. The advantage of this method of escape was that passengers did not have to show their passports.

Meanwhile, the decision was made to bring Maclean in for questioning on Monday 28 May, and this was communicated to Kim Philby so that he could keep the Americans informed. Philby was also keeping Burgess informed. On Friday 25 May, Burgess booked a cabin on the cruise ship for him and a visiting American friend, Bernard Miller. He hired an Austin A-40 before meeting Blunt at the Courtauld Institute and lunching at the Reform Club. There he produced maps of the Lake District and Scotland, making out that he was going touring in the north.

Donald Maclean, meanwhile, had enjoyed a lunch to celebrate his 38th birthday with a couple of friends. As he was leaving the Foreign Office that evening, he bumped into Roger Makins, Deputy Under-Secretary of State, and informed him that he would not be at work the following day. He then made his way to Charing Cross station and caught his usual train to Tatsfield in Surrey where he lived with his pregnant American wife, Melinda. Not long after he arrived home, Guy Burgess turned up in his hired car. He and Maclean had supper before leaving around nine o'clock. Arriving at Southampton just before midnight, they abandoned the Austin on the dock and ran up the gangplank. Their flight had not gone unnoticed, however. Maclean's name was on a watch list that had been distributed to ports and an eagle-eyed immigration official noticed it and contacted MI5. British intelligence operatives were informed but the French police were not told as there was a fear that the news would be leaked. At nine the following morning, abandoning their luggage on board, Burgess and Maclean jumped into a taxi to Rennes where they boarded a train to Paris. After that, they simply vanished.

It would be five years before anyone from the West would see them again.

The Aftermath

Later, it was revealed that the pair travelled from Paris to Berne in Switzerland where they were issued with documentation at the Soviet Embassy. Zurich was next and from there they caught a flight to Prague. Protected by the Iron Curtain, they completed their trip to Moscow.

Back in London, it became evident to his friends on Saturday that Burgess had failed to return. On Monday 28th, Melinda Maclean phoned the Foreign Office to report that Donald had left on Friday night with a colleague named 'Roger Styles' and had not come home. She was wondering if they knew where he might be. On the Tuesday, as concern ratcheted up at MI5 and in Whitehall, Anthony Blunt went to Burgess's flat and removed anything incriminating but later, when Special Branch searched it, they discovered a 14-page handwritten document relating to the Foreign Office and a number of officials, dating back to 1940 and written by another MI5 Soviet spy, John Cairncross.

Meanwhile, news of the spies' flight was greeted with horror in Washington. Philby, under immediate suspicion, returned home to grab his copying camera and other accessories he used in his espionage. He drove to Great Falls, outside Washington, and buried them in woodland. Soon after, he was summoned to London and interrogated by MI6 over several days. No evidence was found to suggest he had warned Maclean.

The British government worked hard to prevent the news getting out but it was splashed across the front page of the *Daily Express* on 7 July – 'Yard Hunts Two Britons' was the headline. Trying to downplay the story, the Foreign Office issued a statement: 'Two members of the Foreign Service have been missing from their homes since May 25. One is Mr D.D. Maclean, the other Mr G.F. de M. Burgess. All possible enquiries are being made. It is known that they went to France a few days ago. Mr Maclean had a breakdown a year ago owing to overstrain, but was believed to have fully recovered. Owing to their being absent without leave, both have been suspended with effect from June 1.'

Naturally, the press went crazy, besieging the homes of Burgess's mother and Melinda Maclean. They also visited Burgess's old friend, Goronwy Rees, to whom Burgess had confessed years previously to being a spy, creating an enduring fear that Rees would one day expose him. On 8 June, the frenzy was heightened when Burgess's mother received a telegram from Rome, purportedly from her son: Terribly sorry for my silence,' it said. 'Am embarking on long Mediterranean holiday. Do Forgive. Guy.' A telegram also arrived at the Maclean house, signed 'Teeno' which had been the nickname given to Donald as a child.

The government continued to be resolutely tight-lipped but, in the meantime, Burgess's friends, Christopher Isherwood, Victor Rothschild, and John Lehmann were all interviewed, and questions were asked in the House of Commons. There were serious implications for cooperation between the British and American intelligence services and the Americans broke off liaison on atomic energy. A committee of enquiry, headed by Lord Cadogan, was set up. It recommended more positive vetting, especially for all who had access to classified information but failed to recommend the type of background checks that might have uncovered the communist associations of the Cambridge spies.

Life in Moscow

In February 1956, almost five years after Burgess and Maclean's vanishing act, *Sunday Times* journalist, Richard Hughes, was in Moscow to interview the Soviet Foreign Minister, Vyacheslav Molotov, when he received a phone call asking him to come to Room 101 of the National Hotel where he was staying. Entering the room, he found five men seated at a table covered with a white cloth. One of them, a tall man in a blue suit and red bow tie stood up and reached out his hand. 'I am Donald Maclean,' he said to Hughes's astonishment. A man beside him also stood up. He wore a blue suit and an Old Etonian tie. It was, of course, Guy Burgess. Hughes and the several other reporters already there were handed a 3,000-word statement by the two men. One section of it read:

'We both of us came to the Soviet Union to work for the aim of better understanding between the Soviet Union and the West, having both of us become convinced from official knowledge in our possession that neither the British nor, still more, the American government was at that time seriously working for this aim... We neither of us have ever been communist agents... As the result of living in the USSR we both of us are convinced that we were right in doing what we did.'

In Britain, of course, the pair were roundly condemned. Goronwy Rees wrote a series of articles for the Sunday newspaper, *The People*, in which he described Burgess as 'the greatest traitor in history'.

A short while after arriving in Moscow, Burgess and Maclean had been sent to Kuybyshev, an industrial city now known as Samara, about a thousand kilometres southwest of the capital. In characteristic style, Burgess described it as 'permanently like Glasgow on a Saturday night'. The October after they arrived, they were granted Soviet citizenship and were given new names, Burgess becoming 'Jim Andreyevitch'. True to form, he slipped into something approaching his old ways, drinking and reading. He was also vociferous in his complaints to the authorities about the way he was being treated. In fact, he fully expected to be able to go back to England, believing that he could bluff his way through any interrogation that the security services threw at him. One thing that did cause him problems was the total intolerance of the Soviet authorities towards homosexuality. Eventually, he met Tolya Chisekov, a good-looking electrician in his twenties with an interest in music, in the large underground urinal behind the Hotel Metropol. Tolya stuck with him until his death, acting as his lover, servant, secretary and fixer. Unfortunately, he was also informing on him.

By early 1956, Burgess was working at the Foreign Languages Publishing House, promoting translations of classic British novels for publication. He also worked for the Anti-Fascist Committee that gathered information on fascist trends around the world. He missed London but, above all, his friends, terribly.

His mother was allowed to visit him in July 1956 and around that time, he was interviewed by the Labour Party MP, Tom Driberg, for his largely sympathetic biography of him, *Guy Burgess: A Portrait with Background*. Other visitors to Moscow met up with him. The actor Michael Redgrave, an old friend from Cambridge, visited with the Shakespeare Memorial Theatre Company. This tour also brought his meeting with the actress, Coral Browne, who would feature, with Alan Bates as Burgess, in Alan Bennett's 1983 television drama, *An Englishman Abroad*.

When Prime Minister Harold Macmillan visited Moscow in 1959, Burgess seized the opportunity to lobby officials for permission to return to England to visit his mother who was very ill. The government realised that it was far from a certainty that should Burgess land on British soil and be arrested, he would be successfully prosecuted. In the end, Burgess decided not to pursue the idea.

His excessive lifestyle had, of course, pushed his body to the limit for years and eventually, it took its toll. In 1960 and 1961 he spent time in hospital receiving treatment for arteriosclerosis and stomach ulcers. He died of arteriosclerosis and liver failure on 30 August 1963, a few months after Kim Philby finally defected to the Soviet Union, and was cremated five days later. His brother Nigel represented the Burgess family and his fellow defector Donald Maclean delivered a eulogy, describing Burgess as 'a gifted and courageous man who devoted his life to the cause of a better world'.

On 5 October that year, Burgess's ashes were returned to his beloved England where they were interred in the Burgess family plot at St John the Evangelist in West Meon where he had grown up.

Donald Maclean:
The Spy Named 'Homer'

Recruiting a Spy

It was as much the spectre of unemployment and poverty as it was Hitler and fascism that drove many young men into the welcoming arms of the Communist Party in the 1930s. The hunger marchers shambling through Royston, close to Cambridge, in February 1934 made a huge impression on many young students and drove them to the writings of Karl Marx and others. As the writer Arthur Koestler said: 'I began to read Marx, Engels and Lenin in earnest. By the time I had finished... something had clicked in my brain which shook me like a mental explosion.' In the still lengthy shadow of the Great War, Marxism provided answers to the issues that particularly exercised the minds of the young at that time – the class struggle and imperialism. Some joined the party and dealt with such matters that way. But for some that was not enough. They wanted to actually do something. Donald Maclean was one such man.

He was born in Marylebone, London on 25 May 1913, the son of the Liberal Party politician Sir Donald Maclean and his wife Gwendolyn. Five years after Donald's birth, with the Labour Party lacking a leader and Sinn Fein refusing to attend Parliament, his father became in effect leader of Her Majesty's Opposition. At school, the young Donald was successful both as a scholar and in sports and games. It may be that his communism began to flourish at this time. His friend, James Klugmann, a regular visitor to the Maclean house in London, became a communist while still at school. And there were others, such as Brian and Roger Simon, the sons of Lord Simon of Wythenshawe, who would later join the party.

In 1931, he won a place at Trinity Hall, Cambridge – not to be confused with Trinity College – reading modern languages. He had grown into a good-looking man by the time he arrived in Cambridge, six feet four inches tall, slightly built, debonair and with an able wit. He had a degree of arrogance about him and was convinced of his ultimate success at university. Almost immediately, he began to flex his communist muscles, taking part in a demonstration by the unemployed in London at which demonstrators clashed with the police. He was arrested but not prosecuted. Being the son of a Cabinet minister brought certain advantages.

In June 1932, his father died following a heart attack, leaving Donald free to air his political views at home, much to the bemusement of his mother. At Trinity Hall there was a great deal of interest in communism and Maclean took part in debates and discussions. Like many at the time, he had an idealised version of the USSR, in his mind a country full of happy, fulfilled peasants who gathered in the harvest to feed the equally happy new republics that constituted the Soviet Union. Some such as Malcolm Muggeridge actually managed to make the journey to Russia and returned seriously disillusioned. Maclean did not and persisted in viewing the Soviet Union through rose-tinted spectacles. The truth was, of course, that there was resistance to the collectivisation of agriculture and it was the cause of devastating famines that affected tens of millions of people. In fact, Maclean and his friends of the same persuasion dismissed such reports in the press as propaganda dreamed up by right-wing newspaper proprietors.

It appeared clear to many at the time and especially to Maclean and men like him that capitalism was about to fall. Economic catastrophe had blighted the world in recent times and poverty and hunger were on the rise in Europe. They thought that before long the proletariat would rise up and throw off its capitalist shackles. The threat of fascism oiled the revolutionary wheels. The West was not rising to the threat that Hitler and his Nazis posed; only communism, in the form of the Soviet Union, would stand up to them.

Maclean was recruited by an illegal, the ubiquitous Soviet intelligence operative, Theodore Maly. As with the other Cambridge spies, Maclean was ordered to give up all of his political ties and, once he had left Cambridge, he was to enter the Diplomatic Service. His handlers would then pick the right time for him to start providing them with information. No money or inducements of any kind were offered. Maclean was a spy because of what he believed, not so that he could be rewarded for it.

He put his energy into the study of economics and modern history that were part of the examinations to get into the service. To do this, he spent a year at a college that specifically prepared candidates for the Civil Service examinations. He sat those in 1935, but a year earlier had to undertake a preliminary interview. When he told his mother, who would have to provide financial support during the next year, she asked him about his communist beliefs. '... I've rather gone off all that lately,' he replied. He had his final year at Cambridge still to finish and he used his studies as a cover for withdrawing from all political activity. It paid off when he was awarded a BA degree with first-class honours.

Maclean passed the exams and started work at the Foreign Office in October 1935. He had, of course, been asked about his political opinions at the interview part of the entrance exam and was careful not to deny that he had been politically active at Cambridge. He even admitted that he was not entirely free of his strong political sentiments. It now seems a disingenuous response, but he was playing a heavily nuanced game and it worked, backed up as it was by his college giving him an excellent reference that failed to mention his left-wing views.

He started out in the League of Nations and Western Department, the 'Western' part referring to Spain, Portugal, the Netherlands and Switzerland and he would remain there for three years. He was disappointed in the men for whom he worked, the leaders of government who were indecisive in their approach to fascism. Indeed, he feared that they would formulate some kind of pact with Hitler. And he was also concerned about Britain's military spending and lack of enthusiasm for the League of Nations. This was in contrast to the Soviet Union's membership of the League and treaties it had signed with France and Czechoslovakia.

When Neville Chamberlain became Prime Minister 1 May 1937, his policy of appeasement of Nazi Germany began to be applied, to the great disappointment of the Foreign Office and tensions with Downing Street grew. Maclean would write 30 years later that Chamberlain's policy to 'use Germany as a military counterforce to the Soviet Union' was a bad one. At this time, Stalin's purges were underway in Moscow and there was something of a hiatus in espionage activity by the NKVD as a result. Against all advice, Theodore Maly decided to return to Moscow and fell victim to the purges.

Paris

Maclean's next posting was a prestigious one – Paris – which suggests that he must have been viewed as a loyal and dedicated civil servant. Now Third Secretary at the British Embassy in the French capital, he began to report to Moscow on embassy activities. When he arrived, the Munich Conference was taking place, the meeting at which it became clear that Chamberlain and the French Prime Minister, Edouard Daladier, were happy to let Hitler have Czechoslovakia, instead of stopping him, perhaps in alliance with the Soviet Union. Indeed, Maclean was reporting back to Moscow on the absence of the will to fight that he was finding in France. Perhaps he would have joined several other civil servants in resigning in protest at the Munich Agreement, but, of course, the game he was playing did not allow for that.

He must have been surprised and dismayed to learn that Stalin had made discreet approaches to Adolf Hitler, with a view to negotiating a pact. When France and Britain later tried to negotiate with Moscow he saw the telegrams sent by the British Embassy in Moscow and the Foreign Office. He informed his control of their contents, keeping Stalin up-to-date on the British response to the negotiations. Towards the end of August 1939, the Hitler-Stalin pact was signed. It looked certain there was no other course but war and soon it came to pass. This made Maclean's position even more perilous. He was now helping an enemy and the only word for that was treason, a crime punishable by death.

Death was also a possibility at the hands of the NKVD. Several men died mysteriously in Paris in 1938 – Trotsky's son, Leon Sedov, went into a clinic for treatment of an ailment that was far from serious and died there. The headless body of Sedov's friend, Rudolf Klement, was found in the Seine several months later. Maclean could be sure that the NKVD would brook no doubts from him. His offer to work for them was one that he could not withdraw without probably fatal consequences.

In his role as Third Secretary, Maclean saw just about everything coming into and going out of the embassy. He would have seen that the Allies had been very close to intervening in the Winter War fought from 1939 to 1940 between the Soviet Union and Finland. He will have shared Allied plans to block Russian oil flowing to Germany by attacking Baku. But around this time, something else was going on in Donald Maclean's life. He had fallen in love with an attractive 23-year-old woman named Melinda Marling who was taking a course in French at the Sorbonne University. As the Germans moved closer to Paris in the spring of 1940, Maclean proposed to Melinda. She asked for time to think it over, but she was already pregnant and the decision was made for her.

The two were hastily married before they had to flee south from Paris. They ended up in Bordeaux with the rest of the embassy staff before embarking on a ship for England. As Melinda's pregnancy progressed, they decided the baby should be born in the United States and she flew to New York. Their baby boy was born on 22 December 1940 but survived only a few days and she remained in the city until the autumn of the following year. In the meantime, Kim Philby, freshly recruited by the British Secret Service, had met twice with Maclean whom he had not seen in a number of years. He had fallen out of touch with Moscow control after leaving France with the British Expeditionary Force, and wanted Maclean's help in re-establishing contact.

Walter Krivitsky's defection to the West in October 1937 must have been a terrifying moment for Maclean who was very nearly identified by the Russian. Krivitsky described 'a spy who was Scotsman of good family' who had been educated at Eton, and Oxford. He sometimes wore a cape, which Maclean did, and mixed with artists, which Maclean also did. Maclean probably escaped scrutiny because he had gone to neither Eton nor Oxford. His distress must have played a part in Moscow's efforts to assassinate Krivitsky and eventually the defector was found with a bullet in his head in a Washington hotel room, a death that was ascribed to suicide but was more likely to have been the work of a Soviet agent.

After returning from France, Maclean, now promoted to Second Secretary, worked in the General Department, a new section dealing with the Ministry of Shipping, Supply and Economic Welfare. He was also having to get used to a new control – Anatoli Gromov, codenamed 'Henry', a Second Secretary at the Soviet Embassy. Things had changed in the NKVD and Gromov insisted on copies of documents which, of course, introduced new dangers for Maclean.

It can only be imagined how relieved he and his fellow Cambridge spies must have felt in June 1941 when Hitler invaded the USSR. They would now no longer be supplying an enemy with secrets, but an ally. And so what if they were handing over information that Britain did not want to share with the Russians? As a loyal friend, Russia should be party to everything, they reasoned. That was a rather simplistic view of things, because, although the Russians and the British were now on the same side, they did not really see eye to eye on how the war should proceed. Stalin was anxious for Churchill to open a second front in Western Europe to take some of the pressure off the Soviet Union. Instead, on 7 November 1941, British and American troops landed in French North Africa. Two weeks before the landings – codenamed Operation Torch – the Russian ambassador, anxious to let everyone know that this was not to Stalin's liking, told the editor of the *News Chronicle* about it, endangering the entire operation and, of course, many thousands of lives. The information is likely to have come at least partly from Donald Maclean.

Washington

In April 1944, with a second child due, the Macleans set sail for Donald's latest posting in the United States. He was promoted to First Secretary and by 1946 was working at the Chancery in the embassy in Washington, on matters connected with the development of the atom bomb – codenamed 'Tube Alloys' by the British and the 'Manhattan Project' by the Americans.

In February 1947, he was appointed joint secretary of the Combined Policy Committee (CPC), set up after a meeting in Quebec between Churchill and Roosevelt. After the atom bomb was dropped on Hiroshima and Nagasaki, ending the Second World War, Stalin began to focus on the production of Russia's bomb. For this, information was required about the American bomb and Maclean was a prime source.

Meanwhile, Maclean's star was on the rise in the Diplomatic Service. He worked long hours and showed an innate ability to grapple with complex issues. This helped him to operate at full capacity for his Soviet masters. He started to provide information about bases from which American missiles or planes could reach Soviet territory. They were particularly interested in bases at which the US bomber, the B-29, capable of delivering an atomic bomb, could land and take off. Around this time, Maclean was meeting with Alger Hiss, Director of Special Political Affairs at the State Department regarding a resolution placed on the agenda of the United Nations that would require member states to declare the number and location of forces in non-enemy states. This gave Maclean plausible reasons to visit New York where he could liaise with his handlers. Maclean and Hiss would have exchanged figures for the number of British and US personnel in foreign territories, the information about US troops abroad being very useful to the Soviets. In 1948, Hiss was alleged to be a Soviet agent but the Statute of Limitations had expired and he was only found guilty of perjury.

When Melinda went into hospital to deliver her and Donald's second son by caesarean, a vital clue that contributed to his exposure as a spy was inadvertently created. Later, in 1949, American crypto-analysts discovered from fragments of a cipher telegram that came from the NKVD in New York that five years previously, an agent who enjoyed the codename 'Homer' had access to communications between Roosevelt and Churchill. And another fragment, deciphered in April 1951, suggested that Homer had been in New York for the birth of his baby. It did not take British agents long to work out that Homer was, in fact, Donald Maclean.

Maclean's role as joint secretary of the CPC gave him greater access to documentary materials, vital to the NKVD because Maclean was, obviously, not an atomic expert and needed to provide them with actual materials rather than conversations he had heard in meetings. He was now able to extend his contacts to American officials involved in the atomic programme and ask sensitive questions without arousing any suspicion as to his motives and he attended meetings and conferences at which atomic weapons were discussed. In 1956, long after Maclean had defected, the Senate Internal Security Western Department admitted that Maclean would have had:

'... access to information relating to the estimates made at that time (January 1948) of ore supply available to the three governments, requirements of uranium for the atomic energy programmes of the three governments for the period 1948-1952, and the definition of the scientific areas in which the three governments deemed technical co-operation could be accomplished with mutual benefit.'

What the Russians really wanted to know was how many atomic bombs the Americans had stockpiled and how they would use them if war broke out. What the Russians probably learned from Maclean was that US military might was something of a myth. Post-war demobilisation had greatly reduced US forces while the USSR had never demobilised. Moreover, America's atomic weapons were far from ready to use. They had to be assembled first and the people who knew how to do it were no longer in the military. Therefore, only around a dozen or so were ready for immediate use. Even if there had been more, there would not have been enough B-29 bombers to deliver them to targets and the only bases from which they could have operated against the Soviet Union were in Britain and Egypt. Knowing America was unprepared for war would undoubtedly have given Stalin the confidence to undertake the blockade of Berlin. And Maclean gained even more access when he was provided with a pass that gave him entry to the United States Atomic Energy Commission building at any time, something he used on numerous occasions, often at night when few staff were present. There is little doubt that he engaged in conversations with employees who would divulge all kind of information to this very trusted man.

As the Macleans prepared to leave Washington in August 1948, Melinda Maclean confided to other embassy wives that her husband was often moody and preoccupied and that he had been working long hours and at weekends. He was also drinking heavily. Many have suggested that she was aware all along that her husband was a spy, but in light of such complaints to others, it seems unlikely that she knew.

His next move was to Cairo, as head of Chancery at the British Embassy, a promotion that made him the youngest Counsellor in the Diplomatic Service. Cairo was a prestigious and important posting. It was the hub of British power in the Middle East and Britain had a large presence there. There were troops in the Canal Zone and in Palestine and from the air bases in the Canal Zone, B-29s with their atomic bombs could reach the Soviet Union. Maclean's job was to liaise with the

United States and try to maintain the status quo in the Middle East where Britain was the major power. Maclean was irritated by the blatant corruption that surrounded the Egyptian King Farouk and he believed Britain should support reform of the country and its politics. But, not to put too fine a point on it, British policy was to keep the oil flowing and keep the Soviet Union out of the Middle East. There was also a constant threat of violence towards British soldiers and officials as the Muslim Brotherhood had declared *jihad* – holy war – against the British. The USSR, meanwhile, had voted for partition and had been happy to see Czechoslovakia supply Israel with arms. Maclean was something of a Zionist and secretly, of course, was in favour of the Soviet approach to Israel.

He and Melinda arrived in Cairo in 1948 and found life to be very amenable but Maclean was acutely aware of the social problems not far from the glamorous hotels, clubs and the lovely house in Gezira where they lived with a nurse for the boys and four servants. He was drinking even more, much to Melinda's chagrin. The drinking made him violent and also brought out his latent homosexuality. There were several violent incidents as well as other drunken episodes. One night, when he failed to come home, he was found drunk and asleep on a bench in one of Cairo's parks.

He was in a dire situation which only served to increase his intake of alcohol. Kim Philby, now working in Washington, became privy to information that the spy named 'Homer' was likely to be Donald Maclean. Of course, if Maclean was brought in for interrogation, there was no knowing where it could lead – possibly to the exposure of both Philby and Guy Burgess. Philby let Maclean know that he had two options; he could either face a long prison sentence in a British jail, or he could opt to defect to the Soviet Union. The arrest and 14-year sentence of atomic scientist, Klaus Fuchs, could only have increased his anxiety. More violent episodes ensued, including the destruction of a couple of flats – one of which was occupied by a couple of American women employed by the US Embassy – which resulted in him being sent home to England for treatment in order to avoid official protests being made. Melinda Maclean was the one who took the decision to send her husband back home which adds to the evidence that she was not party to his spying and was not under the control of the NKVD, unlike him. They did not want him to leave his post and would never have sanctioned his departure.

As for Maclean, the question has been asked as to whether he engineered being sent home so that he could make good his escape to Moscow. Perhaps, it is suggested, that is why he smashed up the flat of people connected to the US Embassy. Had it been occupied by a British official, it could easily have been covered up and he would have got off with a warning. Or, maybe it was just his antipathy to the United States manifesting itself.

Preparing to Flee

In London, he underwent tests and started a course of treatment with a psychiatrist who reported that his condition was due to overwork, marital troubles and suppressed homosexuality, but amazingly, this raised no alarm bells at the Foreign Office. Meanwhile, Melinda had accepted the offer of a well-off Egyptian admirer for her, her boys and her mother, who was visiting, to have a holiday with him in Spain. The writing looked to be well and truly on the wall for their marriage but the Foreign Office did not like the bad press such splits could generate and a mediator, George Middleton, was found to help them patch up their relationship. In London, Donald was still drinking heavily, even as friends rallied round, trying to help him. He became paranoid at times, possibly as a result of the excess of alcohol. On one occasion, while staying with friends in the country, he had an attack of *delirium tremens* that made him keep jumping to his feet and shouting 'They're after me!' When asked who was after him, he said 'The Russians!' On another occasion, he wrote to a friend that there were two men waiting in a car and they had been there for four hours. 'Are they after me?' he asked.

In September, with Maclean in despair about his marriage, Melinda, encouraged by the Foreign Office, came to London and they made the decision to stay together. In fact, Melinda soon fell pregnant again and on 1 November Maclean returned to work as head of the American department. This was, of course, good news for the NKVD who gave him Yuri Modin as his control.

As a head of department, the world was Maclean's oyster. He now had access to telegrams between the Foreign Office and embassies abroad and he saw Cabinet papers. He would have had access to secret information regarding the Korean War. He seemed to be behaving and one official who had been asked to keep an eye on him said: 'I never noticed him the worse for drink. I thought him a good head of Department; he was never fussed or flustered.' For her part, Melinda noted that he had not had any drinking bouts since she had come back into his life, but she was wary because 'the root of the trouble is still not cleared away'. Nonetheless, they moved into a house called 'Beaconshaw' in the village of Tatsfield in Surrey.

By mid-April 1951, it had become clear that 'Homer' was definitely Donald Maclean. At that point, the Foreign Office ensured that he did not receive any documents with the highest level of clearance but it was decided to wait until a date had been set for Maclean's interrogation to inform the FBI, primarily to reduce the chance of leaks. In the meantime, he was to be watched so that a case could be built up against him. Maclean, however, soon became aware he was under surveillance. Fatally, MI5 agreed that it would send a telegram, through Kim Philby, in an effort to deal with a technical issue they had about the original telegram that had mentioned 'Homer'. They requested an interview with a cipher officer who had been on duty in the British Embassy in 1944. Their request gave the deadline of 23 May as the information was required for a meeting to be held the following day. Philby was horrified, reasoning that this might be a meeting in preparation for bringing in Maclean for interrogation. He sent an urgent airmail letter to Guy Burgess that was ostensibly about the car Burgess had left in the airport car park when he left the United States. The postscript was all that mattered, however. 'It's getting *very* hot here,' he wrote.

Maclean was due to be interrogated on Monday 28 May, although that date was not set in stone. And, in fact, a delay was advantageous. Hoover at the FBI had to be informed, for a start, and the Director General of MI5, Sir Percy Sillitoe, wanted to fly to Washington in early June to do that personally. Furthermore, Melinda Maclean was due to go into hospital for a caesarean in the second week of June which would provide an opportunity for the empty Maclean house to be searched for incriminating evidence.

Guy Burgess had reappeared in London, and, as we have seen, with Maclean's interrogation looming on Monday 28 May, engineered the defection of Donald Maclean via a cruise to the French coast on Friday 25 May, coincidentally Maclean's 38th birthday. The Soviets were very anxious to get him out because they feared what he might say under interrogation. Maclean is said to have asked Melinda if she thought they were right to want him to defect and, according to Yuri Modin, she had no hesitation: 'They're quite right – get out as soon as you can, don't waste a single moment.' As we have already seen, Burgess and Maclean vanished and were not seen or heard of again for five years.

Melinda played it very coolly, telephoning the American

Department first on the Monday wondering if her husband was around. She then called George Carey-Foster, Head of the Foreign Office Security Department and explained that her husband had left on Friday night with a man named 'Roger Styles' – the name Burgess had used.

And so, the furore began.

Life in Moscow

As noted earlier, the two defectors were sent for debriefing to Samara (the former Kuybyshev) where they remained for two years, out of the sight of Western journalists and diplomats. They were probably kept under wraps in case Stalin decided on a whim that they should be eliminated – he was not particularly fond of his foreign agents. It was also feared that the Americans might hunt them down, especially Maclean, because of his involvement in handing over their atomic secrets. The two assumed new names, and Maclean became Mark Petrovitch Frazer. But he was desperately lonely in Kuybyshev.

While his fellow defector, Burgess, learned just enough of the Russian language to get by – 'kitchen Russian' was how he described it – Donald Maclean became fluent. He studied and earned a doctorate and, after teaching English at a school in Kuybyshev, he started work in 1961 at the Institute of World Economics and Industrial Relations. He also worked for a journal called *International Affairs*, specialising in British matters and NATO.

In 1953, the NKVD informed Melinda that Maclean had tried to commit suicide. By then, she was living in Geneva and talking about divorce but Maclean wanted her and the children to come and join him in Moscow. On Friday 7 September 1953, Melinda told her mother that she had been invited to spend a weekend with an old friend from Cairo. She and the boys were supposed to go to Montreux, but instead drove to Lausanne.

From there they took a train to Zurich and then another train heading east. A car met them the following morning at Schwarzach St Veit in Austria and presumably took them into what was then still the Austrian Russian zone. For six weeks nothing was heard of them but, at the end of October, Melinda's mother received a letter from her daughter, postmarked 'Cairo'. 'Please believe darling,' it said, 'in my heart I could not have done otherwise than I have done.' It ended 'Goodbye – but not forever'.

Life in Moscow was not bad. As members of the Soviet elite, the Macleans had access to special shops and they enjoyed a dacha about two hours from Moscow. Things really picked up when, in 1956, they were able to communicate with the outside world but, unlike Burgess who latched onto anyone from Britain that he could find, they saw no one from the West and refused to do interviews. Unfortunately, Donald's drinking continued and his anger and violence would rise to the surface when he drank, inevitably creating distance between him and Melinda. Meanwhile, the USSR, under Khrushchev, was changing. The Comintern was dissolved and, to Maclean's delight, Khrushchev even denounced the cult of personality that had surrounded Stalin. When the Red Army marched into Hungary in 1956, however, to extinguish the brave new dawn of Imre Nagy's short-lived government, it suddenly seemed that not a great deal had changed after all.

When Guy Burgess died in August 1963, Kim Philby was not permitted to attend the funeral and it fell to Maclean to deliver the eulogy. The pair had seen little of each other in Moscow in the previous ten years, even though their names were irredeemably linked in perpetuity. The Macleans socialised with Eleanor and Kim Philby, and Philby and Melinda started an affair that intensified when Eleanor returned to America to renew her passport in 1964. Melinda had simply had enough of her husband and sought comfort in the arms of his fellow spy.

Eleanor left Moscow for good in May 1964 and died three years later in California. By then Melinda's affair with Philby was over and he had transferred his affections to a much younger woman whom he married. Maclean allowed Melinda to move back into the flat.

His book, *British Foreign Policy Since Suez 1956-68* was published in Britain in 1970, showcasing all the policies that he had been against in the past 14 years. But his health was suffering and he had an operation and underwent radiation treatment for bladder tumours in November 1971. He was in hospital again in 1978 and 1981. Melinda returned to the United States in 1979 where, until her death in 2010 at the age of 84, she remained tight-lipped about what she had known about her husband's spying. Donald died on 6 March 1983 and was cremated five days later in the grounds of the deconsecrated Donskoi monastery. His family was not represented as his son, Fergus, arrived from Britain too late.

Neither Philby, nor another spy living in Moscow, George Blake, attended. Fergus brought the ashes back to Britain and they were buried at Trinity Church at Penn in Buckinghamshire where his parents had once owned a country retreat.

Kim Philby: The True Believer

A Charming Man

The first thing most of his associates would have said of Harold Adrian Russell 'Kim' Philby was that he was a charming man. He oozed the kind of languid charm that only a certain type of Englishman can carry off. They might have added that his manners were impeccable. He ran to open doors for women, remembered your children's names and drank in what you were saying to him as if you were the only person in the world worth speaking to. He was loved, admired and even worshipped by friends and acquaintances who fell into those soft blue eyes beneath the disobedient forelock that inevitably fell down over his forehead.

Charming he may have been, but he was also a spy, a man who, from 1940 to 1949, rose through the ranks of the British Secret Intelligence Service until he was the British liaison officer to the Central Intelligence Agency (CIA) and the Federal Bureau of Investigation (FBI) in Washington, a job at the very core of the West's intelligence struggle with the Soviet Union at the start of the Cold War. Philby's rise might even, it has been suggested, have been leading to the top of the British intelligence tree – the position of 'C', head of the British Secret Service – had his tower of lies and deception not come crashing down around him in 1953.

Philby was a serving KGB officer who had been recruited when he came down from Cambridge, his mission to penetrate the British Intelligence Service and to feed back information to his handler and onwards to Moscow. For many years, as a trusted intelligence officer, Philby had access to the most classified British and American secrets and the damage he did, therefore, to the interests of the West was substantial.

His father was Harry St John Philby, also known as 'Jack' or Sheikh Abdullah, an Arabist, author, explorer and Colonial Office Intelligence officer, his mother, Dora, the daughter of a senior railway engineer in the Punjab Provincial Engineering Service. St John Philby was an exotic character who studied Oriental Languages at Cambridge before being posted to Lahore in the Punjab in 1908. In 1930, he converted to Islam and took a second wife, a Saudi woman. He became an adviser to Ibn Saud, the founder of Saudi Arabia and its king until his death in 1953, advising him in negotiations with the United Kingdom and the United States after the discovery of petroleum in Saudi in 1938. He was an outspoken character who, in his own mind, was never wrong, a trait that won few popularity contests. Kim, as he nicknamed his only son with his first wife, after the character in Rudyard Kipling's novel of the same name, was born in Ambala in the Punjab on New Year's Day, 1912.

Kim was a quiet little boy with a slight stammer that remained with him throughout his life. At Westminster School as a King's Scholar, like his father he did well, achieving good results through hard work rather than academic brilliance. It is thought that while at the school he underwent some kind of breakdown, perhaps caused by a sexual encounter, most probably of a homosexual nature, as was not unusual in all-male boarding schools of the time. He would later claim rather vulgarly that at Westminster, he had 'buggered and been buggered'. It has also been suggested, however, that his 'breakdown' was caused by religion. The school insisted that he be confirmed and he went through with it, despite having been encouraged by his father to develop a firm agnosticism. He may have felt he had betrayed his principles. Certainly, he was not bothered by a person's sexual preferences and had many friends in the gay and lesbian communities. As an adult, however, he was steadfastly and busily heterosexual.

Trinity

In October 1928, aged 16, he won a scholarship to Trinity College, Cambridge. Cambridge, at the time, was something of a finishing school for the ruling classes, a place of punting, strawberry teas and parties, where the main topic of conversation and debate was more likely to be poetry than politics. It was about to undergo a change, however, with the rise of fascism and the collapse of capitalism following the onset in 1929 of the Great Depression. At Cambridge, Philby was diligent, keeping very much to himself. He did not join any clubs and the only people with whom he mixed were a couple of coal miners – Jim Lees and Harry Dawes – who had been sponsored at Cambridge by the Workers' Educational Association. They tried to politicise him, but found him a tough nut to crack. He neither seemed to cling to his privileged upbringing nor did he display any fellow feeling for the working class. He took people as they came, regardless of their class.

He slowly began to change, however, claiming later that the Labour Party's disastrous performance in the 1931 General Election made him ponder what would be an effective alternative, when Labour, in his opinion, had abandoned the working class and the unemployed. As the United Kingdom and the world moved from one economic disaster to another, and incidents such as the mutiny in the British Atlantic Fleet at Invergordon and the Japanese invasion of Manchuria made the world seem a far less stable place, Cambridge was turning into a febrile political hotbed.

Philby entered the political fray, acting as treasurer from 1932 to 1933 of the Cambridge University Socialist Society (CUSS), founded by Harry Dawes, but it would take him two years of reading, listening and debating to finally become a communist. Economics lecturer and Marxist, Maurice Dobb, was the man who promulgated communism at Cambridge, a man with an undying commitment to the creed whose house in Cambridge became known as 'The Red Household', so frequently were meetings and debates held there. The communist cell created by Dobbs was taken over by David Haden-Guest who had been convinced while studying at Göttingen in Germany that only communism could provide an effective opposition to the Nazis. His cell expanded to include two undergraduates, Donald Maclean and James Klugmann.

Meanwhile, Kim Philby remained hesitant about the step from socialism to communism. He campaigned for Labour in 1931 and organised meals and accommodation for the hunger marchers who passed through Cambridge in October 1932. He felt sympathy for the plight of the poor who were struggling to find enough to eat at the time. Disappointed with the Labour leader Ramsay MacDonald, he travelled to Germany, Hungary and France with a friend, Tom Milne, to see how things were in other countries. In Germany, they encountered an anti-Jewish demonstration and were almost attacked when they remonstrated with those taking part. He came to the conclusion that nothing was any better in other countries – fascism was on the rise, unemployment was bad and the working class had it just as bad as in Britain. He concluded that the world was experiencing the collapse of the capitalist system and on his last day at university finally decided that he was a communist.

Meeting Otto

For many years the Russian intelligence service had wanted to penetrate the British intelligence establishment, and the prevailing environment in English universities finally provided them with an opportunity to recruit young men who would dedicate themselves to the communist cause and who would serve Russian interests no matter where their careers took them. Of course, the requirements for the job were daunting. He or she would have to display a talent for duplicity, would have to deceive friends, family and colleagues at work, but most of all would have to be prepared to betray their country. The Russians knew that the time would never be as propitious for finding such individuals.

In 1933, Kim Philby emerged from Cambridge with a 2:1 degree in economics. He also won a prize with which he purchased the collected works of Karl Marx. He bought a motorbike, from payment for proofreading a book written by his father and claiming he wanted to brush up on his German with a view to landing a job in the Foreign Office, he rode off to Austria.

The address he had been given was the home of a Pole, Israel Kolman, who had lived in Vienna since the First World War, working as a civil servant but also heavily involved with his wife in Jewish welfare work. Their daughter, 23-year-old Litzi Friedmann, was an attractive divorcee who was a communist. Philby fell in love with her and she inducted him into the communist underground, initially working as a courier, while posing as a British freelance journalist. In 1934, however, the Austrian Chancellor, Engelbert Dollfuss, took his country even further to the right, arresting socialists, shutting down their organisations and declaring a state of emergency and martial law. Philby and Litzi helped imperilled people to flee the country, displaying physical courage on many occasions. Eventually, however, the police began to close in on Litzi and, in order to save her, Philby married her on 24 February 1934. The couple were already lovers and, although the marriage was to some extent one of convenience, they were also in love, as Philby indicated later: 'Even though the basis of our relationship was political to some extent, I truly loved her and she loved me.' Three months later, they left Vienna for London, living with Philby's mother in West Hampstead.

Shortly after his return to London, Litzi arranged for him to meet a man in Regent's Park. The man, short and stout and in his early thirties, and with a pronounced Eastern European accent, introduced himself as 'Otto'. Philby quickly realised that he was a man 'of considerable cultural background' and liked him almost immediately. The two talked of communism, of Marx and Lenin, and Philby described his activities in Cambridge and in Vienna. He expressed his desire to join the Communist Party while Otto suggested that he could put important and interesting work in his direction. Having hit it off, they arranged another meeting.

Otto was, in fact, Arnold Deutsch, an illegal. As noted earlier, he was the Soviet Union's chief recruiter in Britain and famously, the creator of the Cambridge spy ring. Variously described as Austrian, Hungarian or Czech, Deutsch graduated from the University of Vienna and by the 1920s he was working for the Comintern, travelling the world with his wife as a courier. In 1933, he was arrested by the Nazis in Germany but regained his freedom with the help of a Soviet agent who had penetrated the Gestapo. He then travelled to Britain where he enrolled at the University of London, studying psychology. In reality, of course, he was in Britain to recruit university students for Russian intelligence. Once the recruits were on board, the plan was for them to distance themselves from communism. Then, from their positions within government or intelligence, they would channel British secrets to Russia. Kim Philby was perfect for the Russians – well-educated, well-connected, ambitious but also absolutely dedicated to communism. He was also keen to find employment in diplomacy, the civil service or journalism which all lent themselves admirably to espionage. At their second assignation, Otto asked Philby if he would like to join the Soviet intelligence service, an offer that the Englishman readily accepted. Philby later wrote:

'Otto spoke at great length, arguing that a person with my family background and possibilities could do far more for Communism than the run-of-the-mill party member or sympathiser… I accepted. His first instructions were that both Litzi and I should break off as quickly as possible all personal contact with our Communist friends.'

He was told that he must now dispense with all his communist contacts and that he should endeavour, outwardly at least, to become a proponent of right-wing views. Even better if he could appear to be a supporter of the Nazis. He was given a codename – 'Sonny'. The Soviets were delighted to have such a man as a spy, the son, after all, of a man they believed to be a

British agent but who was also an adviser to Ibn Saud.

Deutsch instructed Philby to make a list of acquaintances from university who might also join the cause and he was also given his first assignment – to photograph anything interesting that he might find amongst his father's documents at home. This was, of course, something of a test of Philby's commitment, but he performed it without hesitation and so began a series of meetings with his handler in London's parks.

Spying On Franco

Encouraged by Deutsch to find a job in journalism, as a jumping-off point for his future career, Philby took a sub-editing job at *World Review of Reviews* before moving on to a magazine partly funded by the German government. To further enhance his right-wing credentials, he joined the Anglo-German Fellowship, an organisation that was formed in 1935 by several Conservative politicians to foster a closer relationship with Nazi Germany. Members included politicians, aristocrats and businessmen. Of course, Philby was able to glean information from this group about the links between the Nazis and their supporters in Britain. He also travelled frequently to Berlin and on one occasion had a meeting with the German Foreign Minister, Joachim von Ribbentrop. Naturally, many of his old friends were horrified by his conversion from socialist to Nazi sympathiser, but it was a price he was prepared to pay.

Meanwhile, his relationship with Litzi had deteriorated and they separated, Litzi moving to Paris. Deutsch now handed Philby over to Theodore Maly, who would manage the Englishman on a day-to-day basis.

When the Spanish Civil War broke out in 1936, Philby was ordered by Maly to go there as a freelance journalist to spy on the Nationalists of General Francisco Franco, all expenses paid by Moscow. The Soviets were keen to know about the nature of the support being provided to the Nationalists by Germany and Italy, and Philby was soon sending back informed pieces that appeared in several British papers, especially *The Times* which made him its special correspondent in Spain. Of course, at the same time he was supplying his Soviet masters with military intelligence. A brief affair with Frances Doble, Lady Lindsay-Hogg – a former actress who was ten years older than him and a right-wing royalist – gained him an entrée to the people close to the Generalissimo himself.

On one occasion when he was back in London, Philby lunched with Flora Solomon, a Marks and Spencer executive and an inveterate left-winger. Indiscreetly, he told her that he was engaged in 'a very dangerous job for peace' and needed help. He invited her to join the cause. She immediately knew what he was talking about but declined his offer. It was a lunch she would not forget.

Moscow now began to conceive more ambitious plans for its young agent, deciding, somewhat ridiculously, that he should assassinate Franco. Maly, however, realised how difficult and dangerous this would be and, to his credit, said as much to Moscow Centre. 'Even if he had been able to get close to Franco,' he said, '… then he, despite his willingness, would not be able to do what is expected of him. For all his loyalty and willingness to sacrifice himself, he does not have the physical courage and other qualities necessary.' Fortunately for Philby, the plan was quietly forgotten. Not long after, on 31 December 1937, the eve of his 26th birthday, a Republican shell almost killed him while he was covering the Battle of Teruel. The Nationalists rewarded his bravery with a medal.

Following Franco's victory in 1938, Philby returned to London, but by this time Stalin's paranoia had ensured that all the Soviets with whom he had been working were dead or had disappeared into the Gulag. Many died in Stalin's purges but, interestingly, Kim Philby never uttered a word of criticism of the Soviet Union. However, British communists were horrified when, in 1939, Russia signed a non-aggression pact with Germany. Communism was, to their minds, the bulwark against fascism and now the two nations were allies. Philby was confused, asking his new controller: 'What's going to happen to the single-front struggle against capitalism now?' It was a difficult time all round and trust between him and Moscow seems to have faded. For some time, there was no contact.

MI5

By now, despite the assertion by the head of MI5 that there was no Soviet espionage activity in England, Guy Burgess was working for MI6 and would be followed not long after by Anthony Blunt. The Cambridge spy ring was starting to position itself for greater effectiveness. Philby, too, began to consider the British Secret Service as a prospective employer. His contact with Moscow had been re-established early in 1940 when he was sent by *The Times* to France with the British Expeditionary Force as the paper's war correspondent. From there, he was able to inform Moscow about British and French troop strength. Of course, this information would be invaluable to the Germans and with the Soviet Union and Germany now allies, there was every chance it would find its way to Berlin. Philby seemed unconcerned, however.

In July 1940, he took the medical required for call-up into the army but a phone call from Captain Leslie Sheridan of the War Office to *The Times* to enquire if he was available for 'war work' changed everything. He resigned and began working for MI6. Sent to Brickendonbury Hall for training in covert operations and to Beaulieu for training in demolition, wireless communication and subversion, he dressed now in a tweed jacket with patches at the elbows, a cravat and suede shoes and often wore a Homburg hat and a green coat lined with red fox fur. An ebony-handled umbrella completed his outfit. His off-duty hours were often spent at the home of Tomás Harris, another MI5 operative who worked as an art dealer. Harris's Chelsea home was usually filled with officers of the British Secret Service, including Guy Burgess, Anthony Blunt, Victor Rothschild, the chief of counter-sabotage, and Guy Liddell, the head of counter-intelligence. Tim Milne of MI6, another Westminster alumnus, would turn up as would Richard Brooman-White, head of MI6's Iberian operations and Philby's great friend, Nicholas Elliott, also an MI6 operative. A huge amount of alcohol was consumed at these soirées, and Philby certainly proved himself no slouch when it came to drinking.

He quickly became popular at MI6, sharing secrets with fellow officers over drinks and when he was on night duty, scanning incoming telegrams for anything that would be of value to his Soviet masters. When not working nights, he often took home a briefcase filled with documents that he laboriously copied. His work for the Russians was often dull and tiring, and, of course, it was also very stressful. All it would take to expose him would be the defection to the West of one Soviet intelligence operative who could identify him as a spy.

Such a defection had occurred in 1937 when the intelligence officer, Walter Krivitsky, came to the West, handing over the identities of 70 Soviet spies working abroad. As we have seen, it was as a result of this defection that the Foreign Office cipher clerk, John King, was caught. Krivitsky also spoke of a plan for a Soviet agent to assassinate General Franco. Although he did not have the agent's name, he described him as 'a young Englishman, a journalist of good family, an idealist and fanatical anti-Nazi'. One would have thought the ensuing investigation would have uncovered Philby, but there were a number of well-bred journalists in Spain during the Civil War and his name never came up.

Philby and his friend Elliott worked in Section V of MI6. Section V used spies and defectors to gather intelligence about threats from abroad, as its operational brief said, to 'negate, confuse, deceive, subvert, monitor or control the clandestine intelligence collection operations and agents of foreign governments or agencies'. Prior to the war, it devoted itself to battling against the Soviet Union and the spread of communism but, during the war, it focused on the Axis powers. Neutral Spain and Portugal became the base for many operations aimed at Britain, making Section V's Iberian section extremely important. Philby was put in charge of it, working out of a large Victorian house in St Albans. By this time, he was living with Aileen Furse, a store detective for Marks and Spencer, and he moved with her to a cottage in the town. The couple had a daughter in 1941 and a son the following year.

Philby was a popular boss, described by the writer Graham Greene, at the time one of his deputies, as having '... something about him – an aura of loveable authority like some romantic platoon commander – which made people want to appear at their best in front of him'. He worked hard and seemed very happy. He threw parties at which, along with the alcohol, he hoovered up as much information as possible. The enemy was the Abwehr in Spain, headed by Wilhelm Leissner who recruited and sent spies to Great Britain, bugged the British Embassy, bribed compliant Spanish officials and made strenuous efforts to gather intelligence on Allied shipping and sabotage it. On his side, Philby had a distinct advantage – the decoding station at Bletchley Park where German wireless communications were intercepted and decoded.

Philby had not given up his other work, however, and on one occasion delivered a file to his NKVD contact in London containing a description of how his department worked, the names and biographies of those working there, its objectives, operations, successes and failures. It had all been handwritten.

At another time, Moscow Centre decided to test Philby's loyalty, requesting the identities of all British spies working in the Soviet Union. Philby protested that another department in intelligence ran the agents but, when they insisted, he hatched a plan to befriend the librarian, Captain William Woodfield, who was in charge of the Central Registry where all the personal files of British agents around the world were collated. Woodfield liked a drink and Philby became his drinking companion in the local pub. Firstly, he requested the source books for his area – Iberia, before casually requesting the ones for the Soviet Union. By now Woodfield was his bosom buddy and thought there was nothing untoward when Philby requested the Russian source books. Philby discovered that MI6 had not recruited a single major spy in the Soviet Union, principally because British intelligence was focused exclusively on Nazi Germany. The officers in Moscow found this hard to believe and there was even a suggestion that he must be lying; Philby must be a double agent, they insisted. Soviet personnel were detailed to undertake surveillance on the Cambridge spies to try and catch them out, but came up with nothing incriminating.

When the Americans entered the war after Pearl Harbour, Philby was used to teach the officers of X-2, the OSS counter-intelligence section, the tricks of the espionage trade. It was at this point that he first encountered James Jesus Angleton who would go on to be chief of counter-intelligence for the CIA from 1954 to 1975. He was also given more power, adding counter-intelligence operations in North Africa to his portfolio. Working in London again, he was asked to act as deputy to Felix Cowgill, head of the Iberian section of Counter-Intelligence. It was yet another example of his growing influence within the British Secret Service.

Unfailing Belief in the Cause

It cannot be underestimated how many people died as a result of Philby's duplicity but for him it did not seem to matter. His belief in his cause enabled him to justify anything. One example is the defection of the German anti-Nazi, Erich Vermehren. Vermehren had been assigned to the Abwehr and worked as a personal assistant to Paul Leverkuhn, head of Abwehr operations in Istanbul. He was part of a group that wished to oust Hitler and replace his regime with a democratic, anti-communist, Christian state. He and his wife defected and passed on all their contacts in Germany's Catholic underground. These were the people who, in the post-war world, would help the Allies install an anti-communist government in Germany. This invaluable list was obviously not for Soviet eyes, especially as the Russian army was at that point about to invade Germany from the east. Philby, of course, made sure it made its way to Moscow Central. Thus, when the Allies sought out these people after the war, with a view to creating a conservative Christian post-war leadership, they discovered that they had all been killed or deported. No one knows exactly how many died. Philby indicated later that he had been 'responsible for the deaths of a considerable number of Germans'. Sometimes, unfortunately, they were the wrong Germans.

Philby's spying during the war had divulged many secrets, amongst which was classified information concerning the 'Manhattan Project' that developed the atomic bomb; the Allies' plans for D-Day; the British policy regarding Poland; the activities of the Office for Strategic Services (OSS) in Italy; and MI6 operations in Istanbul. The quantity of documents that were handed over was astonishing. Almost in recognition of the work he had done, his code name was changed from 'Sonny' to the more grown-up sounding 'Stanley'.

As the Allies advanced on Berlin, the spies began to look to the future and what they would do when Germany was defeated. British and US focus began to shift towards the communist threat. They were about to embark on the Cold War and this required a rethink. In a move of some genius and undeniable chutzpah, Philby suggested to Sir Stewart Menzies, the current C, that the fight against communist spies could be best fought by a new department, Section IX. He described it as being dedicated to 'the professional handling of any cases coming to our notice involving communists or people concerned in Soviet espionage'. Felix Cowgill was in line to lead this section, but Philby cleverly inveigled his way into running it instead. Therefore, a Soviet spy was now in charge of intelligence operations against the Soviet bloc and, of course, Moscow would be constantly kept informed of all British efforts to counter Soviet espionage.

Yet another defector turned up who was even more dangerous for Philby than Vermehren. Konstantin Dmitrievich Volkov was a Soviet consular official in Istanbul who arrived at the British consulate on 4 September 1944 with his wife to inform the consul that he was, in fact, deputy chief of Soviet intelligence in Turkey but had previously worked for years on the British desk in Moscow. In return for the protection of the West, he was offering details of 314 Soviet operatives in Turkey and 250 in Britain as well as documents that were secreted in an apartment in Moscow, the address of which he would reveal when he and his wife arrived safely in the West. He asked for £50,000 and a new identity in Britain. Importantly, he suggested that there were seven Soviet spies working in the British intelligence services and in the Foreign Office. The matter was passed immediately to MI6 and, ultimately, landed on Philby's desk. Guy Burgess, Donald Maclean and Philby himself were in imminent danger of being revealed as Soviet spies. Philby made sure that he was chosen to go to Istanbul to debrief Volkov, delaying his journey just long enough for two Soviet agents to arrive and spirit Volkov and his wife out of the Turkish capital. They were taken to Moscow where they were tortured and executed. It had been a close shave, but Philby characteristically felt nothing for Volkov, describing him later as 'a nasty piece of work'.

Philby was awarded the Order of the British Empire for his intelligence work during the war but was undoubtedly prouder of his Soviet Order of the Red Banner, awarded secretly in Moscow a few months previously. Having obtained a divorce from Litzi, he also married Aileen Furse, which was a surprise to everyone who thought the couple were already married. Aileen, of course, knew nothing of her husband's double life. She simply knew he worked for the Foreign Office.

In February 1947, in order to round out his experience, he was sent out into the field, as MI6 station chief in Turkey. It was a critical moment to be arriving there. Tension between East and West was high and Turkey was the fulcrum for much of this. Incredibly, before he left London, Philby was given permission to become a double agent, if necessary. Now, if he was caught in communication with the Soviets, he had an excuse. But, in the two years he worked there, he had no contact with Soviet intelligence. He merely sent his information to Guy Burgess in London who passed it on. Meanwhile, his wife Aileen, convinced he was having an affair with his secretary, became seriously ill. Philby learned of a history of self-harm that had started when she was a teenager and was horrified that she had kept such a thing secret. In September 1949, however, she was healthy enough to travel with Philby to a new posting, as MI6 chief in Washington DC.

Washington

His new role was to maintain the intelligence relationship between Britain and the United States, working with the FBI and the CIA. Before he left for Washington, however, he was let into one of Western intelligence's greatest secrets – the Venona decryptions. As we have seen, Venona had uncovered the fact that the Soviets had an agent code-named 'Homer' working in the British Embassy in Washington. They did not yet know his identity, but Philby knew it was Donald Maclean, first secretary at the embassy from 1944 to 1948.

Philby had a grand time in Washington, welcomed as the quintessential English gentleman, and soon involved in a social whirl with colleagues and new US contacts. Huge amounts of alcohol were consumed, and he lunched regularly with James Angleton, now in charge of the CIA's foreign intelligence operations. The two of them played cat-and-mouse games with each other over wine and brandy, each trying to prise as much information out of the other as possible. Angleton would return to his office after these lunches and compile a detailed report on what he had found out, as did Philby. Only later would he write another report that was for his real masters. The result was that operations run by US intelligence around the world invariably went awry, a matter of great bemusement to Angleton and his colleagues. Often these operations ended in bloody disaster, as in Operation Valuable, an attempt to send insurgents into Albania. A number of them were killed on landing by parachute in the country and others were intercepted at the border. The families of the insurgents suffered too, and it is reckoned that for every guerrilla, up to 40 family members and associates were either shot or imprisoned. Philby must bear responsibility for much of the carnage, but, as usual, he was not fazed.

'The agents we sent into Albania were armed men intent on murder, sabotage and assassination. They were quite as ready as I was to contemplate bloodshed in the service of a political ideal. They knew the risks they were running. I was serving the interests of the Soviet Union and those interests required that these men were defeated. To the extent that I helped defeat them, even if it caused their deaths, I have no regrets.'

The Beginning of the End

In 1950, the nuclear arms race was heating up. The Soviets had acquired the technology to stage a nuclear test in 1949, thanks partly to a spy at the heart of the Los Alamos project – Klaus Fuchs. Philby had alerted Moscow to the fact that Fuchs's cover had been blown by Venona, but it was too late and the German-born British scientist now languished in a British prison, serving a 14-year sentence. Venona had not only caught Fuchs and uncovered that there was a spy in the British Embassy, name as yet unknown, but it had also revealed that a network of spies was operating in Britain, and that the codename of one of them was 'Stanley'.

By this time, his marriage to Aileen was under great strain. They now had five children and she was drinking heavily. A dark cloud fell over her when she learned that Guy Burgess had been posted to Washington and that her husband had invited him to live in their basement while he looked for a place of his own. Chaos ensued, as was customary when Burgess was involved.

When it was finally realised that Homer was actually Donald Maclean, MI5 decided not to strike immediately, in the hope of finding further evidence. Venona remained top secret and they worried that a court case would expose it. This, of course, gave Philby time. He contacted his handler, insisting that Maclean be extracted from Britain before he could be arrested and interrogated. But contacting Maclean would be a tricky business. Around that time, however, Guy Burgess was ordered back to Britain because of his customarily bad behaviour and that provided an opportunity to put a plan in motion for Maclean's extraction.

On Friday 28 May 1951, three days before Maclean was going to be arrested, as we have seen, he and Burgess travelled to France and then disappeared. It would be five years before Soviet premier Khrushchev confirmed that the two spies were actually in the Soviet Union. Philby, however, was horrified to learn that Burgess had fled with Maclean. He was directly connected with him and it could be only a matter of time before his colleagues began investigating him. He could, of course, have defected but decided to stay and see what happened, to bluff it out if necessary. After all, he had not been linked with 'Stanley' and no one seemed to suspect him of anything even though the clues were there – the British spy who had worked in Spain as a journalist, for instance, and Volkov's mention of a spy who was a British counter-intelligence officer. The evidence – even if they did put it all together – was not strong enough to nail a prosecution, however, and Philby knew that.

As anticipated, he was summoned to London to discuss the disappearance of Burgess and Maclean, while, in Washington, the CIA were beginning to investigate Philby's links with the two vanished spies. One report, by CIA officer Bill Harvey, was highly critical of Philby, noting his involvement in operations that had, ultimately, failed. Another, by Philby's friend, James Angleton, rejected the idea that Philby knew about Burgess and insisted that he would be cleared by any investigation.

Philby's interview began on 12 June. He was accompanied by Jack Easton, his immediate superior, and the questions were put to him by the head of MI5 counter-intelligence, Dick White. At the end of the day, it was inconclusive, although White had not found Philby's answers to be 'wholly convincing'. Another interrogation was conducted two days later, by which time the CIA had told MI6 that on no account would Philby be permitted to return to Washington. There was even an implicit threat that, if Philby was not fired, the intelligence relationship between Washington and London would be endangered.

The evidence against Philby was becoming undeniable, leading Guy Liddell to write that: 'While all the points against him are capable of another explanation, their cumulative effect is certainly impressive.' The second interview was less amicable than the first, especially when Philby was caught out by a question about how he had financed his trip to Spain. The truth was, of course, that the trip had been financed by the Soviet Union, but Philby, visibly flustered, said he had sold gramophone records and books to raise money for it. By the end of the interview, Philby knew that White believed him to be a spy. White, for his part, told Stewart Menzies – C – that they urgently needed to take action. Philby was summoned to C's office and was asked for his resignation. He was given a payoff of £4,000, a quite substantial sum in those times, which allowed him to leave with honour. Unbelievably, Menzies actually told White that Philby could not possibly be a traitor.

Unemployed

In July 1951, the unemployed Philby and his family moved to a rented cottage in Heronsgate in Hertfordshire. He knew he was likely to be under surveillance; his telephone would be bugged and his post intercepted. He was once again summoned to MI5 headquarters in London to answer more questions from Helenus Patrick Joseph Milmo who went by the nickname 'Buster'. Milmo was an indomitable interrogator, as Philby knew from when the two had worked together during the war. He tore into Philby, accusing him of being a Soviet spy since the 1930s and, amongst other things, of letting Maclean know that he was about to be arrested. But as the questions rained in, Philby gave as good as he got. For instance, when asked about the Soviets giving the order for a young English journalist in Spain to assassinate General Franco, he parried that it would seem stupid to use a Cambridge graduate who had never fired a gun to undertake such a task when all it would take would be the services of a professional hitman. He agreed that he had indeed married a communist, Litzi, but if he had not, she would have ended up in a concentration camp. As Philby dealt with each accusation, Milmo became increasingly angry and after four hours he was getting nowhere. Nonetheless, Philby was ordered to hand over his passport before leaving. This did not bother him at all because, if he had to leave Britain, he would not be using his British passport.

Milmo concluded that Philby was, indeed, a spy, but it was obvious there would never be a confession. MI5 next employed the services of William 'Jim' Skardon, head of surveillance, and reputed to be the best interrogator in the service. He visited Philby at Heronsgate several times but found the charges 'unproven'. Philby's passport was returned to him.

The Third Man

As the years passed and conclusive evidence of his guilt remained elusive, the case became a source of discord in the Secret Service. Most of MI5's senior officers believed him to be guilty, while the men he had worked with in MI6 were convinced of his innocence. Meanwhile, Philby found a job with an ex-colleague's import-export firm and moved the family to Crowborough in Sussex. He was drinking heavily and often reliant on loans from friends. Aileen found work in the kitchen of a large house in London. In effect, however, Philby was trapped. He could not even defect because any contact with his handler would alert MI5. Worried about him, his Moscow bosses used Anthony Blunt to get £5,000 to him which lifted his spirits, especially as the defection of KGB colonel Vladimir Petrov, in Australia, represented another threat to his liberty. Petrov revealed that Burgess and Maclean were, indeed, in Russia, and that they had been recruited at Cambridge. There was a scandal when it was suggested in the media that Harold Macmillan's government had hidden the truth from the British people. There was also renewed speculation about Philby being the 'Third Man'.

Meanwhile, moves were afoot to restore his reputation.

Officers such as Nicholas Elliott argued his case and it was suggested that 'Buster' Milmo's interrogation had been biased. With a concerted effort now being made to exonerate him, he was called to another meeting. Naturally, he was worried that he was about to be confronted with new evidence from Petrov, but the meeting turned out to be an internal review of the situation. It was carried out by two colleagues from his old job, one of them probably Elliott, and it was far removed from his previous grilling. They declared him innocent.

His troubles were far from over, of course, a fact brought home the following week, on Sunday 23 October 1955, when a story appeared in the *New York Sunday News* declaring him to be the so-called Third Man. J. Edgar Hoover, long-time head of the FBI, had tipped off a journalist. Reporters flocked to Philby's house and two days later, Colonel Marcus Lipton MP stood up in the House of Commons and, invoking Parliamentary Privilege, named Philby as the Third Man. A media frenzy broke out immediately and, to avoid it, Aileen and the children went to stay with a relative while Philby moved in with his mother. The government announced that it would make a statement and hold a debate on the matter on 7 November. Foreign Minister Harold Macmillan's statement read:

'Mr Philby had communist associates during and after his university days [but] no evidence has been found to show that he was responsible for warning Burgess or Maclean. While in Government service he carried out his duties ably and conscientiously. I have no reason to conclude that Mr Philby has at any time betrayed the interests of this country, or to identify him with the so-called 'third man', if, indeed, there was one.'

In the debate, Lipton was repeatedly told to make his accusation outside Parliament, where he would not be protected by Parliamentary privilege and the accusation could be tested in a court of law. But Philby went on the attack, calling a remarkable press conference at his mother's flat, at which he displayed all the charm that he had deployed to dazzle and deceive people his entire life. He denied being the third man and said he had to resign because of his friendship with Guy Burgess. He requested that Marcus Lipton repeat his accusation in public. Lipton never did.

Reinstatement

The Suez Canal was likely to provide the British government, headed by Anthony Eden, with its next crisis and reporters were flocking to the region. Nick Elliott found Philby work as a freelance Middle East correspondent with *The Observer* newspaper, his services being shared with *The Economist*. He would be based in Beirut and paid £3,000 a year plus expenses. Elliott also arranged for Philby to work as an agent for MI6. By this time, his marriage to Aileen was effectively over and the Beirut posting put the final nail in the coffin. He travelled to the Lebanese capital alone.

He immediately began making contacts, helped by the fact that his well-connected father was living in the city. Soon, he had begun an affair with an American woman, Eleanor Brewer, a former architect, married to Sam Pope Brewer, the *New York Times* correspondent in Beirut. She said of Philby that on first meeting him: 'What touched me first about Kim Philby was his loneliness. A certain old-fashioned reserve set him apart from the easy familiarity of the other journalists.'

His life in Beirut took off and he was busy, but, of course, he was also waiting to hear from his Moscow masters. Eventually, he was contacted by a man named Petukhov, who worked for the Soviet Trade Mission to Lebanon and told him he was interested in his articles on the Middle Eastern economy. At that moment, Kim Philby could have walked away from it, but his commitment to the Soviet Union was unshakeable. Not even the horrors that had been disclosed about Stalin's time in power made any difference to his faith.

The rules of the game were established. If Philby wanted to have a rendezvous with Petukhov, he would stand on his balcony at an arranged time holding a newspaper. If he was holding a book, that meant he needed an urgent meeting. Meetings would be after sunset in a quiet part of Beirut. Philby was ordered to find out about British and American plans for the Middle East.

Eleanor Brewer left her husband and returned to America to obtain a divorce. The plan was for them to get married, but, of course, Philby would have to deal with his marriage to Aileen first. Her life had virtually imploded after she left Philby and she had spent a great deal of time in psychiatric hospitals. Eventually, on 12 December 1957, she died of heart failure and a host of other ailments, leaving Philby free to marry Eleanor. They tied the knot in January 1959 at Holborn Registry office and moved into a flat in Beirut big enough for his children to visit in the holidays. Life was good: a round of parties and picnics, a bit of writing, some discreet information-gathering for MI6, and, of course, some dirty work for his Russian handler. This seemed to be impressing some at Moscow Centre while others thought it was too opinionated. His work for MI6 was also drawing criticism. 'You could have read it all in *The Economist* last week' was the opinion of one analyst in London.

In 1960, Nick Elliott was posted to Beirut as station chief, a welcome reunion of the two old friends. Elliott resolved to get the best out of Philby, sending him on intelligence-gathering missions to all parts of the Middle East. They met several times a week for debriefing sessions and Philby became a different man. Of course, it was all being passed on to the Soviets as well. He was able to provide them with the names of MI6 agents in the Middle East as well as the identities of sympathetic or malleable Arab officials and politicians.

In the summer of 1960, St John Philby's exotic life ended with a heart attack in Beirut, his last words reported as, 'God, I'm bored'. Eleanor reported that after his father's death, Philby 'drank himself senseless'.

When the Soviet spy, MI6 officer George Blake, was arrested and sentenced to 42 years in 1961, Kim Philby was, naturally, very concerned. He had never met Blake, but his espionage had been carried on for a much longer period and at a higher level than Blake's. He started to worry that, if discovered, he would never breathe fresh air again. Then another Soviet defector appeared on the scene – Major Anatoly Golitsyn of the KGB's strategic planning department. After being debriefed in Washington, he was flown to London to tell British intelligence about a 'very important spy network in the United Kingdom called the Ring of Five'. Recruited at university, they had provided information for years. He did not identify Philby, but interest in him was once again awakened. To make matters worse, Nick Elliott was given a new posting, leaving Philby isolated, scared and drinking even more heavily.

The End of the Game

Flora Solomon had never forgotten the lunch with Kim Philby back in the mid-1930s when he had practically confessed to being a spy. Attending a conference in Israel, she mentioned it to Lord Rothschild who, in turn, passed it onto MI5. They interviewed Solomon but she insisted that she would never give public evidence, being fearful of a Soviet hit squad. Nonetheless, they finally had the evidence they needed.

Arthur Martin, an officer who had been working on the Philby case for more than a decade, was chosen as the person to deal with it. The problem was, of course, that Philby would simply persist in his denial and the embarrassment of a court case, especially when it emerged that he was still working for MI6, would be excruciating, especially if he was not convicted. The government might even fall. If they tried to summon him to London, as they had done with George Blake, he would immediately smell a rat. The plan, agreed with the Prime Minister, Harold Macmillan, was for Arthur Martin to fly to Beirut, present Philby with the overwhelming evidence against him and offer him immunity from prosecution if he would tell them everything. When Nick Elliott was told, he insisted immediately that he should be the one to confront his friend which seemed like a good idea, given Elliott's support for Philby over the years. His moral indignation at his friend's betrayal might make him the ideal man for the job. Dick White hinted to him that Golitsyn had identified Philby, even though he had not. Of course, the officers of MI5 were horrified at the notion of Philby's friend carrying out this task.

Elliott arrived in Beirut on 10 January 1963 but no one knew he was there except MI6 operative, Peter Lunn. He prepared a room in Lunn's secretary's apartment for his showdown with his old friend. The sitting room was bugged and a bottle of brandy was purchased. It was all presented to Philby as a meeting to discuss future plans. However, Philby told his wife that 'The minute that call came through, I knew the balloon was up'. When Elliott opened the door to him, he said, 'I rather thought it would be you'.

At the end of the meeting, Philby stormed off, having been given 24 hours to make up his mind. Next day, he turned up with something of a confession, but claimed that he had stopped working for Moscow after the war. He admitted tipping off Maclean, but it was only out of loyalty to a friend. Elliott reiterated that they wanted all the details – his handlers, his associates, what he had divulged over the years and the interrogation continued for four days. On the fourth, Elliott told Philby he had to leave for Africa the next day but back in a jubilant MI5 headquarters in London, they felt sure that, having agreed the deal, Philby would see it through.

It was a mistake, however. Or perhaps it was not. A prosecution of Philby would be a disaster for British intelligence, especially following the arrest of George Blake. The political fallout would be cataclysmic. Philby was not put under surveillance in Beirut and the Lebanese security service was not informed. He immediately got in touch with Petukhov and was told to wait; his extraction would take a little time to organise. Astonishingly, Peter Lunn, the agent who was keeping an eye on him, went skiing.

Philby and Eleanor had been invited to a party on the evening of 23 January 1963, thrown by the first secretary at the British Embassy. That afternoon, Philby said he had to meet someone but would be home in time to get ready for the party. Later, he phoned Eleanor to say he would be late and would meet her at the party. Still later, there was no sign of him and the dinner went ahead without him. As they were passing the port, he was boarding a Soviet freighter, the *Dolmatova*, using the identity of Villi Maris, a sailor from Riga.

The Aftermath

Philby's defection provoked a tidal wave of shock, embarrassment and anger amongst the various agencies on each side of the Atlantic. Those in MI5 who had believed him guilty were outraged while his MI6 supporters were appalled at how the wool had been pulled over their eyes for so long. Within British intelligence circles there was a suspicion that Philby had been tipped off by one of them, launching a mole-hunt that went on for years. Paranoia and distrust were rampant and even Nick Elliott came under suspicion. James Angleton was furious at being duped by Philby, whom he considered a friend, but took steps to make it appear that he had always suspected him. So eager was he to make this seem the case that he had all the typed records of his meetings with Philby burned. It took until March 1963 for the British government to publicly acknowledge that Philby had, indeed, defected, the Lord Privy Seal and future Prime Minister, Edward Heath, claiming in a statement that, since his resignation 12 years previously, Philby had had no access to official information.

There were mutterings, however, that Philby's flight was perhaps not quite all it seemed. Some suggested that he had, quite simply, been allowed to escape, that to bring him back to Britain would have been far too embarrassing for the British establishment. And, of course, there was the distinct possibility that he could have received the ultimate penalty for being a traitor: the death penalty. Would they really have hanged him? Nick Elliott never divulged whether this theory was true, sometimes saying that Philby's escape had shocked him as much as everybody else; at others that he had indeed made it happen by leaving Philby in Beirut. Philby, of course, did not want to admit that his flight was politically engineered. For many years he was intent on maintaining his image as a master spy who outmanoeuvred everyone with his brilliance. But in the end, he came to accept that he had been allowed to flee.

In Moscow, he was given Soviet citizenship, a flat, a minder and about £200 a month. They promised him that his children would receive financial support. He had no rank in the KGB and, indeed, as an agent who was no longer of any practical use to them, he had nothing to do. Meanwhile, he lived the life of the quintessential Englishman, reading *The Times* – albeit a few weeks late – wearing a tweed jacket and listening to the BBC World Service.

He was desperate to see Eleanor and, despite Elliott and his wife trying to dissuade her, she arrived in the Soviet capital on 26 September 1963. In 1964, however, when she returned to the

United States to renew her passport, Philby started an affair with Melinda, wife of his fellow defector, Donald Maclean. Learning of the affair on her return, Eleanor left Philby for good.

He published his memoirs in 1968, the book entitled *My Silent War*. It was, in essence, a work of Soviet propaganda, presenting his life in Moscow as wonderful. In 1971, he married a Russian writer, Rufina Ivanovna Pukhova but, in time, he became disillusioned with the Soviet Union, although he remained true to his communist ideals. He argued that 'the ideals were right but the way they were carried out was wrong. The fault lay with the people in charge.' He was still drinking heavily and suffered from loneliness and depression to the extent that he is reported to have attempted suicide sometime in the 1960s. The Soviets finally gave him some work in the KGB's Active Measures Department, fabricating secret documents detailing American plans.

In 1988, the duplicitous life of Kim Philby ended when he died of heart failure, aged 76. He was given an extravagant funeral with an honour guard of KGB officers and buried at Kuntsevo cemetery outside Moscow. He was even commemorated on a Soviet postage stamp. The Russian foreign intelligence marked his life with a plaque displaying two images of his profile facing each other. An apt memorial for a man who lived his life with two faces.

Anthony Blunt:
The Spy with No Shame

Early Life and Cambridge

His long, lugubrious face would become tiresomely familiar in the late 1970s, popping up on our television screens and on the front pages of our newspapers, making apologies for his actions, trying to explain them. The world had been stunned in November 1979 to learn from Prime Minister Margaret Thatcher in the House of Commons that the Keeper of the Queen's Pictures, the director of the prestigious Courtauld Institute of Art and knight of the realm, Sir Anthony Blunt KCVO, was actually a *bona fide* Russian spy. Indeed, he was the so-called 'fourth man', the latest in a line of traitors – Guy Burgess, Donald Maclean and Kim Philby – who were educated and recruited at Cambridge University in the early 1930s. To say the world was stunned does not, of course, tell the whole story, because the British Secret Service had known the identity of the fourth man since 1964 when he had confessed everything. Unlike his partners in treachery, Philby, Burgess and Maclean, however, Blunt had not ended up in a dowdy Moscow apartment, drinking too much vodka and longing for the Home Counties. Instead, he was granted immunity from prosecution and became a revered figure in the world of art, heading the prestigious art institution, the Courtauld Institute, and taking on the royal role. And for his work in this field, this arch-traitor was rewarded with a knighthood.

Anthony Frederick Blunt was born in 1907, in the genteel south coast seaside resort of Bournemouth, the youngest of three sons of the Reverend Stanley Blunt and his wife, Hilda. The Blunt family were well-connected and Anthony was a third cousin of Queen Elizabeth, the Queen Mother, through his mother who was a second cousin of her father, Claude Bowes-Lyon, 14th Earl of Strathmore and Kinghorne.

For a few years in his childhood, the Blunt family lived in Paris where his father was appointed chaplain to the British Embassy chapel. The young Anthony learned to speak French and would have undoubtedly assimilated some of the culture of France, creating the groundwork for his later career as an art historian. His interest in art developed even further when he went to school at Marlborough College, a public school in Wiltshire, founded in 1843 for the education of the sons of Church of England clergy. Among his contemporaries at the school were the poets Louis MacNeice and John Betjeman and the illustrator and cartoonist, Graham Shepard. Even then, along with a group of like-minded aesthetes, he was championing modern art and artists in an institution that was a bastion of conservatism. His homosexuality was well-known at school.

Aged 18, Blunt won a scholarship to Trinity College, Cambridge, to study mathematics. It was 1926 and, with the General Strike paralysing the nation, Blunt sympathised with the miners. He was probably alerted to communism by his lecturer, the economist Maurice Dobb, who became an important influence on Blunt's thinking as well as that of other students such as Kim Philby, as we have seen. Dobb had joined the Communist Party of Great Britain in 1920 and Blunt would later say of the growth of communism that Dobb promulgated in the 1930s: 'Cambridge had literally been transformed overnight by the wave of Marxism.'

As was the case with Guy Burgess and other Cambridge communists in the early 1930s, John Cornford and James Klugmann were of great significance in Blunt's political development. For Blunt, Klugmann was 'an extremely good political theorist' and he 'ran the administration of the party with great skill and energy and it was primarily he who decided what organisations and societies in Cambridge were worth penetrating'. Most importantly, Blunt was invited to join the exclusive Cambridge club, the Apostles, of which, as we have seen, Burgess, Philby and a number of other Cambridge communists became members. A fellow Apostle, Julian Bell – son of the painter, interior designer and member of the Bloomsbury Group, Vanessa Bell – became Blunt's lover around this time but he and Burgess also became very close. John Costello, author of the 1988 book about Blunt, *Mask of Treachery* writes:

'Blunt was intensely fond of Burgess, and his personal loyalty never wavered... Burgess and Blunt did not share a lifelong sexual passion for each other, according to other bedmates... Such evidence as there is confirms that their intimacy quickly outgrew the bedroom. This was in keeping with the character of Burgess and his insatiable sexual appetite... Burgess had a peculiar talent for transforming his former lovers into close friends. To many of them, including Blunt, he became both father confessor and pimp who could be relied on to procure partners.'

Blunt spent four years at Trinity, changing his course to Modern Languages and graduating in 1930 with a first-class degree. He started teaching French at the university and in 1932 became a Fellow of Trinity College following a dissertation he wrote on artistic theory in Italy and France during the Renaissance and seventeenth century. This necessitated frequent travel to Europe to pursue his research. At this time, he was also the art critic for the *Cambridge Review* and he took on the same role at *The Spectator* magazine in 1933.

Recruitment

It was Guy Burgess who suggested the recruitment of Blunt to Arnold Deutsch. Blunt could not remember the actual date that it happened, but John Costello has noted that American intelligence was of the opinion that it took place abroad and that would have placed it sometime in the spring of 1934 when Blunt was travelling to Italy through France and Austria, for his research. The water is muddied, however, by the fact that Blunt became active in the spring of 1936 with communist-backed organisations. One would have imagined that, if Burgess or someone else had approached him with the suggestion that he spy for the Soviet Union, like the others, he would have been told to remove himself from all connection with communism. He has himself suggested late 1935 or early 1936 as the time at which Burgess approached him. Almost certainly, however, it *was* Burgess who was behind his recruitment, especially as Blunt barely knew Maclean or Philby. But why Blunt? After all, he was not seeking a career in the Foreign Office and, unlike Burgess, he did not have a list of contacts that the Soviets could exploit. Rather, he was thought to have great potential as a talent spotter. He was not identified with the communist cause too closely, but was a don who made a point of socialising with bright students with leftist tendencies. He was also ideally suited to the secretive life, being homosexual, and he was an unemotional man. He would be able to live the double life that was required of an agent.

The Spanish Civil War was undoubtedly the catalyst for his decision. As we have seen with many others, the Soviet Union was viewed as providing the only defence against the advance of fascism and Nazi expansionism. Working for Russia, therefore, was the best way to fight against these, especially as the Western democracies seemed at the time to be intent on merely appeasing Hitler and Germany. As Blunt later wrote:

'The Spanish war raised the issue of Fascism versus Democracy to a different plane, it brought it to Western Europe, and it gave it the form of an armed conflict instead of the persecution of a minority. Even for the most ivory-tower intellectual it meant that the time of not taking sides was past; the conflict was too near and involved too many of one's personal friends.'

So, he joined Philby, Burgess, Maclean and Cairncross, as well as a few others, such as the American Michael Straight, as a committed ideological spy codenamed 'Tony'. Like them, he believed the mythology that had been created about Stalin's

Soviet Union, that it was a state based on the worker-peasant ethos that dispensed social justice for all. The reality was, of course, that the USSR was a brutal dictatorship that was responsible for the death and imprisonment of millions. Only communism, the Cambridge spies believed, could replace capitalism with all its inequalities and injustices. Of course, they were all already rebels and this made Stalin's message of liberation even more powerful to them. They were against the prevailing rigid sexual mores and the inflexible British class system. It should be remembered that Burgess and Blunt were gay and Maclean was bisexual, and at that time homosexual relations were a criminal offence and would remain so until 1967.

Blunt was undeterred by criticism of his stance. Like many academics, he was dogmatic. To his mind, what he said was the way it was. The Apostles bolstered this feeling of superiority and he also brought it to his work, repudiating medieval Gothic and expressing his boredom with the Renaissance. He wanted to go against suffocating convention, fight against a state that he felt was often wrong and, quite simply, enjoy a taste of danger. His very homosexuality was a statement of opposition to the state that made his very identity illegal. Probably for this reason, after the war, he often sought out relationships with small-time crooks and thieves, egged on, no doubt, by Guy Burgess.

The NKVD were pleased with his recruitment, Deutsch telling them:

'Tony is a typical English intellectual. Speaks very high-flown English. Looks very feminine. A pederast. Mädchen [Burgess] says that with Tony it is congenital. He is very educated and clever. Communism for him is based on theory. Has several works on Marxism in the history of art. Is considerably steadier and more rational than Mädchen. He is a simple person and without big pretensions. Can control himself, is cold and a little mannered. Is to a lesser degree connected to the Communist Party than Mädchen. He would hardly give up his career for the sake of our work. He understands well the tasks he is to do for us and is ready to help us. He has a large influence on students.'

MI5

His Fellowship at an end, Blunt left Cambridge in June 1937. An application for a Fellowship at King's had been rejected and he had failed to land the directorship of the Fitzwilliam Museum in Cambridge. In fact, as he readily admitted, he did not do a great deal between leaving Cambridge and the start of the war. But he did recruit three students to the cause – Michael Straight, John Cairncross and Leo Long. Straight was an American, the glamorous scion of the very wealthy Whitney family. He joined the Communist Party at Cambridge and became part of the Cambridge cell, mainly because, like everyone else, he was so impressed by John Cornford. He described himself as an 'amateur communist', but, on Cornford's instructions, he infiltrated the Cambridge Union on behalf of the Communist Party. After Cambridge, he went home to America and later insisted that he never passed anything secret to the Soviets. Regarding Cairncross, who did not like Blunt, the only part Bunt played in his recruitment was introducing him to Guy Burgess. Leo Long, like Cairncross, came from humble beginnings and, like Blunt he was galvanised by the Spanish Civil War. He became a committed communist and joined the Apostles.

The Russian *rezidentura* in London fell silent in the midst of Stalin's purges and Blunt's work for them also dried up. He had distanced himself from communism, on the advice of Moscow, although he failed to hide his admiration for it in articles he wrote at the time. In September 1937, he started work at the Warburg Institute as general editor of the institution's publications. He enjoyed it greatly. He also worked at the Courtauld Institute.

Meanwhile, he spent a great deal of time with Guy Burgess who continued to live outrageously.

In March 1939, as the world headed inexorably towards war, Blunt was appointed deputy director of the Courtauld. In August he published the first volume of *The Drawings of Poussin* and *Artistic Theory in Italy* was being prepared for publication. The German-Soviet Pact of August did not bother him. He later argued that it was 'a tactical necessity for Russia to gain time… it gave them time to rearm and to get stronger to resist what was clearly going to happen'. On 1 September, Germany invaded Poland and war was declared. Blunt had been on holiday in Cannes with Burgess and the two rushed back to London.

Advised by Moscow that it would be best for him to do his wartime service in Military Intelligence, he reported to barracks at Minley in Hampshire on 16 September to undergo training. Ten days later, however, he was called back to London for an interview with Brigadier Kevin Martin, deputy director of Military Intelligence. A very nervous Blunt was informed by Brigadier Martin that his communist past had been discovered as well as the fact that he had visited Moscow in 1935. He passed off his interest in Marxism as purely intellectual and got away with it, returning to Minley.

By the middle of December, Captain Blunt was in Boulogne, serving with the Army Intelligence Corps at the head of a unit, Field Security 18, charged with overseeing port security for the British Expeditionary Force. Blunt was viewed by his men as 'rather aloof', but pleasant enough, although he was very obviously not really cut out to be a soldier. His section uncovered no instances of espionage but Blunt was happy to occupy himself 'driving around the countryside looking at minor Gothic churches and good eighteenth-century panelling,' as he wrote in a letter to a friend. He kept his homosexuality very much under wraps.

As the Germans advanced closer to Boulogne, Blunt's section

was ordered to evacuate and soon he was back in London. In June 1940, he started work with MI5. He was just what the Secret Service was looking for. Guy Liddell and Dick White wanted to replace the former staff of aristocrats and members of the upper class with brilliant men and women. The fact that Blunt had left-wing views and was gay did not stand in his way. Liddell and White knew perfectly well that their new approach to recruitment would run the risk of such people coming into the organisation.

He moved into a flat at 5 Bentinck Street owned by Victor Rothschild in 1941, along with Tess Mayor and her friend Patricia Rawdon-Smith who, somewhat incongruously, had slept with Blunt several years previously, the only woman known to have done so. In 1941, Guy Burgess also moved in and it became a chaotic party house often filled with spies.

A Fully-fledged Spy

After the hiatus provided by Stalin's purges, the London *rezidentura* finally opened for business again in the autumn of 1940, headed by Anatoly Gorsky, nominally second secretary at the Soviet Embassy, who was running eighteen agents, including the Cambridge spies. He was both astonished and delighted to learn that Philby and Blunt were now employed by British intelligence and that John Cairncross was working as private secretary to Lord Hankey, Chancellor of the Duchy of Lancaster. As previously, some in Moscow wondered if this might be a double cross by the British but they persevered. Blunt was soon delivering military intelligence documents to Gorsky. In fact, between 1941 and 1945, he passed 1,771 documents to the Soviets. No longer merely a recruiter for Soviet Intelligence, he was now a fully-fledged spy. Why did he make the journey from recruiter to document-passing traitor? He never really explained it, even after he had been exposed as a spy. He sometimes shrugged his shoulders, saying 'Cops and robbers', or 'Cowboys and Indians', as if it was all a game to him. But, this was a man with high moral standards and he must have seen it as simply the right thing to do. It is worth pointing out, however, that, like most of the others, he did accept small financial rewards of £100 on several occasions. Some have suggested that his commitment to communist ideology was not that strong and even his handlers noticed his lack of political enthusiasm. But he liked the danger of spying and luxuriated in the knowledge that he was good at it, able to live his double life.

In February 1941, Blunt became Guy Liddell's personal assistant and he also worked for Dick White in German counter-espionage. His principal work was the monitoring of foreign embassies. He was pleased by the German invasion of Russia because it made the Soviets allies again and, this being the case, he felt his espionage had some justification. He also falsely claimed that, after the Soviet-German pact, the material he passed was 'almost entirely about the German Intelligence Services'.

Gorsky, for whom the Cambridge spies did not have a lot of time, was replaced by the charming and efficient Boris Kreshin – codename 'Bob' and later 'Max'. Blunt liked him and Kreshin certainly approved of Blunt, describing him as a 'thorough, conscientious and efficient agent'. Blunt responded in kind, delivering more material than ever. At MI5, he was regarded by colleagues as charming, although one of those with whom he did not work closely described him as 'an ice-cold bastard… anyone who was not important to him did not exist'.

In 1941, he bumped into an old Cambridge friend, the ardent communist and former Apostle, Leo Long, who was working for MI14 which specialised in intelligence about Germany. Blunt simply asked him for 'every piece of information that could be useful to the Russians'. Thereafter, they would meet in a pub in Portman Square or at a snack bar, Rainer's, on the corner of Jermyn Street. Long would pass handwritten notes of his department's work for the week under the table to Blunt.

In 1943, he was promoted to major, but, around this time it was all getting too much for him. He fell ill and was sent to a nursing home in Wales to recuperate. On his return he became involved in the planning for the invasion of Europe, working on the scheme to deceive the Germans about plans for the D-Day landings, persuading the Nazis that the main assault would take place in the Pas-de-Calais area, thus forcing them to concentrate their forces there. He was also involved in the Double-Cross System in which Nazi agents in Britain were captured or surrendered, and were then used by MI5 to broadcast fake information back to their controllers in Germany.

Critical to the Allied war effort was the decryption of enemy communications that was carried out at Bletchley Park in Buckinghamshire using Enigma machines. This was designated as 'Ultra', standing for 'ultra-secret' and Blunt began passing to the Russians the results of the decryption of Wehrmacht intercepts. It was a risky business sharing such secrets, because if the Germans discovered that their codes had been broken, they would simply change the wheels on the Enigma machines and thus prevent Allied codebreakers from decrypting the messages. Former Cambridge man, and fellow Soviet spy, John Cairncross, was working at Bletchley and it is possible that Blunt may have been what is termed his 'cut-out', the conduit through which his material was passed to the Russians.

However, although it was suggested when he was exposed as a spy that his spying was responsible for many deaths, there is no evidence to support this and the Soviets in the NKVD were concerned that the material he gave them was not especially damaging to Britain. Even so it was undoubtedly harmful, relating as it did to the Double-Cross System, the fact that the Enigma code had been broken and the dates of the D-Day landings.

A Secret Royal Mission

Like everyone in Britain after the war, Anthony Blunt was exhausted but he was still working hard, a couple of days a week at MI5 from April 1945 and readying the Courtauld for re-opening to students in October. That April, he accepted another position – Surveyor of the King's Pictures. Many were surprised that a man with the convictions of Blunt could accept such a position, especially as it was unpaid. Perhaps there was an element of desperation about it. Surely, he might have thought, no one in such a role could be suspected of being a Soviet spy? It was undoubtedly good for his career. Soon after his appointment, he was invited onto the executive committee of the influential National Art Collections Fund. He did not really enjoy the life of the courtier, however, bemoaning 'excruciating weekends' at Windsor, although the Royal Family appreciated his politeness and discretion.

It was this discretion that took him on a secret mission for George VI in August 1945 when he was asked to accompany Owen Morshead, the Royal Librarian, to Friedrichshof Castle, near Frankfurt in Germany. At the castle, residence of the Landgraves of Hesse, were reputed to be 4,000 letters written by Queen Victoria to her daughter, the Empress Frederick of Germany, mother of Kaiser Wilhelm II, as well as other important letters and documents. It was said that they needed to be rescued because they were 'exposed to risks owing to unsettled conditions after the war'. The truth was, it was feared that the contents of some of these letters would appear in American newspapers, especially since letters from the Duke of Windsor – the former Edward VIII – to his cousin, Philip, Landgrave of Hesse were said to be amongst them. It has been suggested that, in the letters, the Duke made clear his sympathy with the Nazi cause.

The two men flew to Germany on 3 August, Morshead

particularly pleased to be accompanied by Blunt whose German was impeccable. Their task was not just to find the relevant papers, but also to persuade 73-year-old Princess Margaret of Hesse to allow them to take them back to England. Having lost three sons in the war, Princess Margaret did not feel particularly well-disposed towards Britain, but she was finally persuaded and they were safely returned to the castle in 1951.

Blunt made three more trips on behalf of the Royal Family in the next eighteen months in order to recover royal treasures. Of course, the British Crown had no ownership of or right to these articles but claimed to be putting them into safekeeping to prevent them being looted by occupying forces, something that was sadly prevalent at the time.

Detection

Blunt left MI5 when the Courtauld reopened in October 1945 but, after a gap of a year, continued to meet Boris Kreshin occasionally for the next five years. Admittedly, he did not have a great deal to pass on. He mainly seems to have passed documents given to him by Burgess. Once again he seemed to be under intolerable stress and he became even paler and thinner than normal. In 1947, he became Director of the Courtauld and moved into a spacious apartment on the top floor of the institute, his home for the next 25 years.

In February 1950, the spying community was horrified by the arrest of the atomic scientist, Klaus Fuchs, charged with passing atomic secrets to the Soviets while working at Los Alamos during the war. He had been uncovered by the decryption project, Venona. This led Guy Burgess to speak to his handler about asylum for him and Kim Philby, but that was not at all what Blunt wished. In fact, his handler reported to Moscow that Blunt would rather commit suicide if danger of exposure was threatened. Venona, however, failed to expose Philby, Burgess or Blunt, although it did uncover Donald Maclean. As we have seen, he and Guy Burgess famously defected in May 1951. When Burgess had returned to Southampton from Washington on the Queen Mary, after being suspended by MI5, Blunt had met him at the docks and taken him back to his flat. He insisted later, however, that he had given Burgess and Maclean no warning of Maclean's imminent arrest. Blunt is rumoured to have searched Burgess's flat before MI5 got to it, trying to remove anything incriminating, but failed to do so and a treasure trove of material was found, some of it implicating John Cairncross. Naturally, the case of the 'Missing Diplomats', as they were described, became a huge news story and, as a close friend of Burgess, Anthony Blunt's name was dragged into it. For a few days, he was a prisoner in his own flat, reporters swarming around the entrance to the Courtauld downstairs.

Suspicion had already begun to fall on Blunt by this time. He was interviewed a number of times, once by Jim Skardon, but not even the great interrogator could get him to admit he was a spy. The suspicions would not go away, however, even as Blunt became an extremely powerful figure in the world of art history in the next ten years. His expertise in seventeenth century French and Italian art meant that his advice was sought everywhere on purchases for collections around the world and on attributions of paintings. He lectured in Britain and abroad and he edited the catalogues of the Royal Collection as well as the series of books, 'Studies in Architecture', published by Zwemmer.

Between 1951 and 1964, he was interviewed by MI5 no fewer than 11 times, but at no point did he break. The pressure was huge, particularly in September 1955, when *The People* published a story claiming that a third man had been involved in helping Burgess and Maclean make their escape. As ever, it was a defector who had thrown the stone into the pond and one of the ripples was the third man angle. A month later, following a leak by J Edgar Hoover, the British press named Kim Philby as the third man. As we have seen, Philby wriggled his way out of this accusation, but the Burgess and Maclean story reared its ugly head once more in February 1956 when the two men rematerialised at the National Hotel in Moscow. Blunt had a new worry to add to the many that he already had – Burgess's return to England. If that happened, he would be called as a witness at his trial. His health deteriorated, forcing him to take time off work and remove himself from various committees.

Finally, in January 1964, MI5 found evidence that Anthony Blunt was, indeed, a spy. In Washington, the Cambridge alumnus, Michael Straight, under consideration for the chair of the National Endowment for the Arts, was worried that his left-wing Cambridge past might be revealed. He confessed, therefore, to his recruitment by Anthony Blunt as a spy in the 1930s while he was an undergraduate at Trinity College. He told all to MI5 officer, Arthur Martin, in America to interview another suspected spy, John Cairncross. It was now widely recognised at MI5 that Blunt was a spy, and that he had been part of Burgess's ring. There just was not enough evidence to do anything about it. And anyway, after a series of embarrassing spy cases, the service was reluctant to go public with another. It was decided that, in return for full cooperation and a confession, Blunt would be offered immunity from prosecution and confidentiality. He would even get to keep his job at the Palace. This was justified by Margaret Thatcher in her 1979 speech to Parliament: 'Any action could, of course, have alerted Blunt's former Russian controllers, and others who were already under suspicion, that he had confessed.' It is hard, however, in the light of George Blake's 42-year sentence and John Vassall's 18 years, not to view it as the establishment simply looking after one of its own. He was even given an honorary advisory position after his retirement as Surveyor of the Queen's Pictures.

Anthony Blunt was interviewed once or twice a month for the next eight years, but had already divulged a huge amount by the end of 1964. He told his inquisitors, Arthur Martin and Peter Wright, the names of his Soviet handlers, confirmed that he had supplied details of the internal structure of MI5 to them, as well as details of operations. He told them he had handed over German intercepts, had informed Moscow that the offices of the British Communist Party were being bugged and confirmed that he was aware that Burgess and Maclean had been recruited as Soviet spies. He admitted to recruiting Leo Long and that he knew John Cairncross was also working for the Soviets. Wright and Martin wanted him to name names in MI5 but they were to be disappointed on that front. Wright later wrote: '… although Blunt under pressure expanded his information, it always pointed at those who were either dead, long since retired, or else comfortably out of secret access and danger'.

They brought Michael Straight over to jog his memory but all Blunt did was thank him for coming clean, thereby allowing him to unburden himself.

Exposure

Blunt's health continued to give cause for concern and, in 1972, it became serious when he was diagnosed with bowel cancer. As he was not expected to survive, plans were made at MI5 to make public his extraordinary story. He survived, but by 1975, the tools of his trade, his eyes, began to deteriorate with cataracts. He tried to conceal his debility, but he was unable to distinguish colours and could only see things at very close range.

It was his old acquaintance, Goronwy Rees, who finally exposed him to the world. Rees had come close before, in newspaper articles, but after his diagnosis with terminal cancer, he resolved to expunge his hatred of Blunt by revealing his secrets. He had always disliked him, but had become obsessed with him, blaming him for all his ills while watching him become ever more successful. Now was his moment and he poured out what he knew to the writer Andrew Boyle who was writing a book – *Climate of Treason* – about the Cambridge spy ring. As Blunt agitated in September 1979 to see a copy of the book, due for publication in November, he learned that Boyle had decided not to name Blunt, but instead to use the pseudonym 'Maurice' for him in order to avoid any lawsuits for defamation. The request for sight of the book made its way into the satirical magazine *Private Eye* and Blunt's name was mentioned in connection with it. On 8 November, four days after extracts from *Climate of Treason* had appeared in *The Observer*, *Private Eye* revealed that 'Maurice' – the fourth man in the Cambridge spy ring – was, in fact, Sir Anthony Blunt. Boyle, meanwhile, refused to confirm or deny it, insisting that it was the responsibility of the government to reveal the truth of the matter.

Prime Minister Margaret Thatcher was, according to Cabinet Secretary Robert Armstrong, 'personally affronted by Blunt's immunity'. Thatcher viewed the whole matter as the establishment circling its wagons to protect itself and one of its own. Therefore, Downing Street had Labour MP, Ted Leadbitter, ask a question about Blunt at Prime Minister's Questions on 15 November. In answer, Thatcher read out a statement, saying:

'It was considered important to gain Blunt's cooperation in the continuing investigations by the security authorities, following the defections of Burgess, Maclean and Philby, into Soviet penetration of the security and intelligence services and other public services during and after the war. Accordingly, the Attorney-General authorised the offer of immunity to Blunt, if he confessed. The Queen's Private Secretary was informed both of Blunt's confession and of the immunity from prosecution, on the basis of which it had been made. Blunt was not required to resign his appointment in the Royal Household, which was unpaid. It carried with it no access to classified information and no risk to security and the security authorities thought it desirable not to put at risk his cooperation.' She added: 'There is no doubt that British interests were seriously damaged by his activities,' she said. 'It is unlikely that he put either British military operations or British lives at risk.'

Naturally, there was a media frenzy and Blunt was hounded by the press wherever he went. According to his former pupil, the art critic, Brian Sewell, who helped to protect Blunt at this time from the media, he remained calm, even 'business-like'. He was stripped of his knighthood and Trinity College removed his Honorary Fellowship. He resigned from the Royal Academy after they had made an unsuccessful attempt to expel him. The media response to his exposure was savage and in his working life people strove to expunge his name from everything. Life did calm down to some extent, but by 1981, he had visibly aged and was complaining to his doctor about chest pains, palpitations and shortness of breath.

On the morning of 26 March 1983, seated at his desk at home in Highgate, Anthony Blunt had a heart attack and died. He was 75 years old. In his unpublished memoirs, Blunt admitted that spying for the Soviet Union had been a mistake:

'What I did not realise is that I was so naïve politically that I was not justified in committing myself to any political action of this kind. The atmosphere in Cambridge was so intense, the enthusiasm for any anti-fascist activity was so great, that I made the biggest mistake of my life.'

John Cairncross: The Fifth Man

Lesmahagow

The large South Lanarkshire village of Lesmahagow is situated about 20 miles south-east of Glasgow. Once the main road south ran through the village but, by 1986, it was bypassed by the M74 motorway. Its economy too, was bypassed – by the decline of coal mining on which it had thrived since the middle of the nineteenth century. However, coal extraction was at its peak in the area when John Cairncross was born there in 1913. He has often been described as working class, in contrast to the other members of the Cambridge spy ring, but that is not quite the case. His father was the owner of an ironmongery shop and he also owned his own house, as opposed to renting it. That would make John Cairncross lower middle class. So, although not by any means wealthy, the Cairncross family was not doing badly.

By the time John was 13, the effects of the global slump were making themselves felt in the area but mine owners were reluctant to see their profits decline even as coal production fell. Miners' weekly pay had, therefore, been reduced from £6 to £3 18s over a period of seven years. This led to a strike which grew into a general strike in May 1926. Most miners were back at work by November, but British coal-mining areas were decimated, Lesmahagow included. Cairncross will have seen the devastating effects of this as a teenager. Poverty was rife, with many having to rely on handouts from the parish and the local council.

During these tumultuous years, John and one of his brothers, Alec, went to school in their home village and then to Hamilton Academy, a prestigious Lanarkshire school. (Cairncross's three brothers would all go on to become professors, Alec gaining a reputation as a noted economist.) In 1930, John moved to Glasgow to attend Glasgow University, at a time when both city and university were mired in economic problems. His intellectual performance was impressive from the off. At the age of just 17, he scored the fifth highest marks in the bursary exams, receiving both a bursary from the university and a Carnegie Trust Grant, like his brother Alec before him. He won the prize for highest achieving student in his year group in both French and German for the two years he attended the university. His third year was to be spent studying abroad and he opted for the Sorbonne in Paris where he enjoyed the work of Molière, Racine, Corneille and La Fontaine, men whose writing would become a huge part of his life in years to come. In fact, he decided to remain at the Sorbonne for a further year.

He claimed later that he had largely ignored politics in his first year in Paris, describing himself as 'wrapped in a kind of academic cocoon'. But things were changing in Europe and, returning in 1933, he came into contact with members of Action Française, a nationalistic, anti-communist and anti-Semitic movement. He also met Jewish refugees who had fled Germany where, in January of that year, Adolf Hitler had come to power. In fact, having earned his degree, Cairncross cycled to Germany in order to ascertain for himself just what was going on there. As might be expected, he came up against anti-Semitism and a growing militarism. He recognised the part played in the growth of National Socialism by Germany's dire economic situation and the shame of defeat in the First World War. This experience confirmed him in his opposition to Nazism and the belief that only the Soviet Union could offer any opposition to its expansionist plans.

Cambridge

Cairncross's brother Alec persuaded him to complete his studies at Cambridge. As before, he impressed in his entrance exam and was admitted to Trinity College, starting in the autumn term of 1934. He was, like Alec, surprised by the environment into which he entered, one of, as he put it, 'prevailing authoritarianism', with strict rules and curfews to be adhered to. He was dismayed by the lack of women and the 'sexual repression [that] thickened the air.' Needless to say, he performed impressively, emerging with a First Class Honours degree in modern languages.

He mixed socially with several communists in the hotbed of communism that was Cambridge in the 1930s. The most important of these was Anthony Blunt who actually had the rooms beneath his. Blunt was not a favourite of the Scotsman, though, as he later told his MI5 interrogators: 'Blunt was always something of a patrician, very stand-offish and not very accessible to undergraduates outside his immediate circles.' Cairncross had little choice but to socialise with him, however, as Blunt ran the Modern Languages Club. For his part, Blunt, the KGB recruiter, believed that Cairncross, with his hatred of Nazism and support of communism, was probably ideal recruitment material. Cairncross attended several meetings of the Cambridge Communist Party but claimed to have been put off by its lack of realism and its conspiratorial nature: 'I was attracted to Communism in the first place by its clear desire to secure a line-up against Germany and also by its approach to the study of literature and philosophy whereby social developments were linked with the evolution of thought and art.' He claimed never to have become a member of the party.

Blunt told Guy Burgess about Cairncross and Burgess made a point of meeting him in 1937 at a party thrown by Blunt. Telling Moscow about him, Burgess was less than complimentary, describing him as 'lower middle class... speaks with a strong Scottish accent and one cannot call him a gentleman'. He let them know that Cairncross had never really been a member of the party, but that they should work with him. He was given the codename 'Molière'.

A Soviet Spy

Having graduated with a First Class degree from Cambridge, Cairncross failed in his first ambition, to find work as an academic. He believed that he had not made the necessary contacts in his time at Cambridge and this had closed that avenue to him. The Civil Service seemed like the only option to him and, after cramming throughout the summer of 1936, he, naturally, came top in the Foreign Office and Home Civil Service exams. After also topping the oral exam, he was in, as a Third Secretary at the Foreign Office.

Starting out in the American Department, working on what he considered trivial issues, he was transferred in February 1937 to the Spanish section of the Western Department. Another move followed that year, to the Central Department. He had travelled in Spain in 1936 and, of course, the civil war had made the country something of a test tube for the global conflict to come. Cairncross was responsible for scrutinising the news from Spain and handling the exchanges of British prisoners captured by Franco's Nationalists.

There are several reasons why Cairncross agreed to become a spy. The principal one was that the war that was inevitably coming would, in the mind of Cairncross and many others, be calamitous for Britain without the help of the Soviet Union. And, if the British government continued to pursue a policy of appeasement, disaster was inevitable. Cairncross, therefore, believed he had to take action of some kind to help Britain survive. There was also his fear that, if he did not agree to work with the Soviets, he could be subject to blackmail about his communist connections at Cambridge, placing his current job at the Foreign Office in jeopardy.

Unfortunately, he did not get on with his colleagues or his bosses. Not long after he arrived in the American Department, even though his position was fairly junior, he was in trouble for opposing the views of a senior official, Sir Robert Craigie, who gave support to German colonial claims. He was thought of as dull by his fellow workers and lunch with him was a tedious experience, even though he was evidently a very clever man.

This was not helped by his own conviction that he was better and more intelligent than anyone else.

During his two years at the Foreign Office, Cairncross supplied his handlers with material that dealt with Germany and the Spanish Civil War – 'whatever he could lay his hands on', according to Modin. Later, he said that he did not pass on very much and that none of it was very secret, claiming he only really duplicated what Maclean was already giving them. It is difficult to estimate the seriousness of his espionage, a fact confirmed by writer Christopher Andrew, who has enjoyed access to the KGB archives, and the KGB's chief archivist, Vasili Mitrokhin.

As we have seen, Stalin's purges between 1936 and 1938 devastated the London *rezidentura*. Deutsch was summoned back to Moscow and Cairncross was passed to Anatoly Gorsky who was almost immediately also ordered back to the Russian capital for training. For nine months, Cairncross, like the other spies in London, was out of touch with Moscow Central. He claimed that he passed on no material until the German invasion of Russia in June 1941, but this seems unlikely to be true, as he was providing Moscow Central with information from the Treasury.

The Treasury

In 1938, Cairncross was transferred from the Foreign Office to the Treasury, escaping what he perceived as the snobbery that had blighted his time there. There is evidence, however, that his performance was regarded as poor and they were glad to move him on. He was happier at the Treasury, but it presented the Soviets with a problem. John Herbert King, another Soviet spy at work in the Foreign Office, was arrested and sent to prison. This left Donald Maclean as their chief source of information there but it was expected that he would soon be sent abroad. Cairncross had been lined up as his replacement in the Foreign

Office. To make matters worse, his work in the Treasury did not involve classified material and his value to them plummeted. Nonetheless, the Treasury was a conduit for material from every corner of government and Cairncross was still able to pass some useful information,

Although long gone from the Foreign Office, he remained in touch with a number of his former colleagues, allowing him to provide information about the British appeasement policy towards Nazi Germany. In 1952, while being questioned by MI5, he told them:

'In October 1938 I moved to the Treasury but continued in the normal course of social relations to see something of my Foreign Office friends. I also carried on the habit of making occasional entries on European events in my diary on the basis of my discussions with these friends. Round about Easter 1939, after the invasion of Czechoslovakia by Hitler, Burgess and I had lunch together and the previous argument about Chamberlain's intentions came up. He asked me to substantiate my views and I made notes, both of recent conversations and some held immediately after seeing Burgess, and let him have access to them.'

These notes were never returned to Cairncross, nor did Burgess destroy them. A number of years later, when they fell into the hands of MI5 after Burgess's defection, they helped to expose him as the 'fifth man'.

We have already seen the seeds of discontent that were sown amongst British communists and intellectuals by the pact signed by Germany and the Soviet Union on 23 August 1939. Some, such as Goronwy Rees, simply abandoned communism for good. In common with the other Cambridge spies, Cairncross believed Stalin had little option but to align with Hitler, given that the British government had failed to engage with the

Russians in the struggle against German expansionism.

At the start of the war, Cairncross tried to get back to the Foreign Office but his request was rejected. Next, he suggested a posting to the Government Code and Cypher School at Bletchley Park. No doubt these requests were made in accordance with Moscow's wishes. However, after a further year at the Treasury, he was given the position of Private Secretary to Lord Maurice Hankey, Chancellor of the Duchy of Lancaster, a man with a bewildering range of responsibilities that took in wartime scientific research, intelligence affairs and running the Post Office. Hankey was privy to all matters discussed in Winston Churchill's Cabinet and, therefore, so was John Cairncross. He was happy in this job and admired his boss. He mixed with important people and was paid a great deal more than previously which permitted him to move into a flat in the exclusive Dolphin Square in Pimlico. This soon became a mixed blessing as he was fortunate to escape with his life when Dolphin Square was hit by a German bomb, forcing him to move in with his brother Alec.

His time in Lord Hankey's office provided Moscow with rich pickings amongst which were the minutes of Cabinet meetings. Cairncross – now codenamed 'Liszt' – developed the habit of working late and simply removing the documents to be copied overnight, returning them early the following morning. He was prodigious, handing over to Gorsky some 3,449 documents, covering a variety of subjects, from bacteriological warfare to counter-intelligence investigations. It has been claimed that he was the first spy to alert the Soviets to Anglo-American efforts to build an atomic bomb, but, despite having been in a position to leak atomic secrets as secretary at meetings of the British Scientific Advisory Committee, Cairncross always denied this. In 1994, however, Yuri Modin contradicted him: 'Lord Hankey's private secretary became the first agent to inform the NKVD that the Americans and British had been working since late 1940 on the joint manufacture of an atomic bomb.' Other evidence would suggest that Cairncross was, indeed, letting the Russians in on the development of the atomic bomb at an early stage. This, of course, jeopardises his claim that his sole reason for spying was to ensure the survival of Britain. Had Hitler's invasion of the Soviet Union been successful, the atomic secrets imparted by him and others to the Russians would have fallen into the hands of the Nazis.

Bletchley Park

Bletchley Park, known in the Domesday Book in 1086 as part of the Manor of Eaton, was by 1938 destined to be a housing estate. In May of that year, however, Admiral Sir Hugh Sinclair, head of MI6, bought the mansion and 58 acres of land for £6,000, using his own money for the purchase because the government could not afford it. He intended it for use by the Government Code and Cypher School (GC&CS) and MI6 in the event of war. The beauty of its location was that it was very close to Bletchley railway station which stood at the intersection of the Varsity Line that ran between Oxford and Cambridge from which institutions it was expected most of the codebreakers would come, and the West Coast railway line that connected all of the main cities of Britain. The main road to London was also close by.

GC&CS had actually been in operation since 1919, its objectives to ensure the security of codes and ciphers used by government departments, and to study the communications of foreign powers, breaking the codes and ciphers used in these where necessary. Initially, the Soviet Union had been the focus of its activities, but the threat of Nazi Germany had persuaded GC&CS to focus on it. The organisation's task had been rendered more difficult by Germany's introduction in 1926 of a new family of cipher systems named Enigma. An Enigma machine looks somewhat like a typewriter, only it is much more complicated. Enclosed in a wooden case, it has a keyboard and a lamp board, each bulb on the board representing a different letter of the alphabet and it works on the basis of an electromechanical rotor mechanism that scrambles the letters of the alphabet. When a key is pressed, an electrical signal is created that illuminates a different letter on the board. When the operator types a message, he or she writes down the illuminated letters. This outwardly simple machine was capable of generating a cipher with billions of permutations. The Germans were convinced it was impossible to crack and, before the war, the British were of the same opinion.

The cipher team at Bletchley was led by Commander Alastair Denniston who was tasked with the recruitment of people – men, mostly – from Britain's elite seats of learning. Amongst them were mathematicians such as Alan Turing and Gordon Welchman. Before the war cryptography had been all about language; now, it was all about machine-based solutions and mathematics. Turing designed a machine named 'Ultra' that broke Enigma's codes. Soon about 20,000 messages were being deciphered each month by teams at Bletchley working in shifts round the clock to sort through and prioritise the material. Incredibly, by 1944, there were around 10,000 people working for GC&CS.

The Russians were being kept in touch with the codebreaking activity by a number of different sources, one of whom was John Cairncross. He was posted to Bletchley Park in May 1942, arriving there in August after training. He would have found an installation that was heavily guarded; there was a password system for entry, the password changing daily. Staff were left in no doubt that failure to comply with the rules would result in the direst consequences, up to and including being shot by a guard. Internally, information was compartmentalised to prevent too many people knowing what was going on. Cairncross was told that the Russians had not been informed about Ultra because the British could not trust them, information that made him furious. He claimed that he had wanted to stop spying when he got to Bletchley Park, but knowing that such information was being withheld from an ally made him resolve to carry on.

He was put in Hut 3, a section with the task of translating deciphered German Army and Air Force material received from Hut 6, one of the cryptoanalysis sections, interpreting it and transmitting it to the appropriate people. It was challenging work. Cairncross described it as 'the correction and restoration of words blurred, distorted or omitted' and it required, in his words, 'a generous dose of imagination, and a corkscrew mind'. But, he was good at it, enjoyed the work and liked the people. It was a difficult working environment, however, poorly ventilated, boiling hot in summer and freezing in winter. He spent his days off in London, but described it generally as a 'semi-monastic life'.

Of course, on his days off, he was also passing material to Gorsky – two volumes of a training manual, for instance, and information about how to read Tunny traffic, the product of another family of cipher machines. The Russians would have learned that the British had, indeed, broken the Enigma codes as well as the codes of other systems. He would walk out of Bletchley Park unchallenged with decrypts stuffed down his trousers, head for London and hand them over. Crucially, his material helped the Russians destroy 600 planes of the Luftwaffe in strikes that preceded the Battle of Kursk in July and August 1943. The Soviet Union would go on to win the battle, helped in no small way by Cairncross's provision of information regarding German forces and technical details about the Tiger tank being used by the Germans. In late 1944, Moscow awarded him the Order of the Red Banner for his work on Kursk.

MI6

The work at Bletchley was stressful and physically demanding. Shiftwork was exhausting and Cairncross felt his eyesight was suffering from his constant straining at decrypts. Coinciding with this was the desire expressed by Moscow for him to engineer a move into the Secret Intelligence Service. He networked and cajoled to obtain the transfer, but was initially turned down; he was too valuable in the military section. Eventually, Professor Frederick Green, whom Cairncross knew from Cambridge, now acting as the liaison officer between GC&CS and Section V of MI6, pulled some strings and Cairncross was moved.

His MI6 career began in June 1943, working under David Footman, head of the German section of Section V based at Glenalmond, an Edwardian mansion in St Albans. The closeness to London allowed him to commute from his flat there which suited him after the rigours of life at Bletchley. The work was not dissimilar to what he had been doing there, the focus being on communications made by the counter-intelligence section of the Sicherheitsdienst (SD), the intelligence agency of the Nazi Party, and the SS. As before, his job was to analyse information provided by the decrypts that had been broken at Bletchley Park.

In November 1944, Cairncross came under the control of a new handler – Boris Mikhailovich Krötenschield, codenamed 'Kretchin'. Krötenschield gave him £250 in late 1944 as a symbol of how impressed the Soviets were by his work. One of his tasks was the destruction of old intercepts but he was able, instead, to pass around 1,500 of them to Krötenschield. What was particularly useful to the Soviets was the fact that some of these came from German counter-intelligence units that were actually at work inside the Soviet Union. Soon, however, a move to the department dealing with the Balkans changed this and he no longer had access to much material concerning the Soviet Union.

Cairncross was a valuable asset, even if in 1943 he was only able to supply Moscow with 94 documents, as opposed to 1,454 in 1942. In 1944, however, his tally rose again to 794. By 1945, he was undoubtedly losing interest in his work. He was by then in the political department of SIS but its work was being wound down as the war drew to a conclusion. What was next for him? He had been asked to stay on, but he became concerned that he would be sent abroad and might end up running agents. Instead, he opted for a return to the Treasury with the rank of Principal, starting there in June 1945. By this time, he later claimed, he had lost interest in helping the Soviet Union, possibly influenced in this by Stalin's harsh regime. It might also have had something to do with his new handler, Ivan Milovzorov, who seems to have been fairly inept. Milovzorov was disliked not just by Cairncross, but also by the other Cambridge spies. Cairncross's output fell away as a consequence, although he also claimed that he had very limited access in his new role to classified material. In fact, his espionage stopped altogether for a few months in September 1945 when Igor Gouzenkho, an officer in the intelligence staff in the Russian Embassy in Ottawa, Canada, defected along with hundreds of top-secret documents. Cairncross was out of action until June 1948.

The Soviets were at this time really after nuclear secrets and were pleased when, in January 1950, he was transferred to the department of the Treasury that dealt with the financing of defence research. He shared an office with a Treasury official, George Oram, who did have access to classified material which he very conveniently kept in a drawer he shared with Cairncross. This allowed Cairncross to get some British atomic secrets to the Soviets. He also had access to information about high-grade weapons research as well as signals intelligence, communications technology, and a good deal more. Moscow was delighted.

In 1951, Cairncross married 35-year-old Gabrielle 'Gabi' Oppenheim who came from a family of German commodity traders. By now, he was working in the Ministry of Supply but the work was insufferably dull. Nonetheless, he had access to a wide range of documents from various government departments including the War Office, many of which, of course, he passed to his handler. In June and July of 1951, he passed on 1,339 documents.

Exposure

The vanishing act perpetrated by Guy Burgess and Donald Maclean in May 1951 was devastating for John Cairncross. When his name was discovered in Maclean's diary, it also brought suspicion down on him. Adding to his problems was the discovery in Burgess's flat of the notes on the Foreign Office he had given Burgess in 1939, the handwriting proof that they were written by Cairncross. From out of nowhere – his name had never previously come up – he was a suspect and was called in for questioning. Jim Skardon, who had cracked Klaus Fuchs, was brought in to interrogate him. After Cairncross denied everything, Skardon produced the handwritten notes found in Burgess's flat, noting that Cairncross was struck 'practically speechless' by them. As Cairncross described the moment: 'I froze as soon as I recognised my own handwriting... I was thunderstruck and muttered that I was out of my depth. Skardon simply smiled at my confusion and commented that he was swimming nicely.' Cairncross had tried to get the notes back from Burgess but Burgess had merely told him that he had lost or destroyed them. He told Skardon that the notes had been written simply to clarify his own thoughts and, he claimed, he had no idea that Burgess would hand them over to the Russians but he was cautioned.

Obviously, his career in the civil service was over. While

it was decided whether his case would be taken forward, he was suspended from his job, and airports and ports were informed so that he would not be tempted to defect or escape the country.

At a second interview, he provided a signed, formal statement in which he acknowledged having been interested in communism at Cambridge but also asserted that he had been completely unaware that Guy Burgess was a Russian spy. He claimed to have naively believed that Burgess would be a useful contact to have. At the same time, he noted that he had been concerned that Burgess might use the notes to blackmail him into revealing secrets. That, of course, suggested that Cairncross was indeed aware that Burgess had sinister motives. In a third interview, Skardon pursued this avenue of enquiry and went over the other issues that had come up. He emerged from the interview believing that Cairncross was 'coming clean' about everything. It seemed that, by sticking to his story that, at the time, he regarded the notes to Burgess as simply 'an interdepartmental exchange of information', he had escaped the clutches of MI5.

Penniless and Unemployed

Cairncross was in a perilous position. He had lost everything and needed to quickly find employment of some sort. Of course, he had his academic capabilities and learning to fall back upon. He was, after all, an expert on French seventeenth-century poets and playwrights such as Racine, La Fontaine, Molière and Corneille. But his efforts to land a position in academia failed. He and Gabi moved to Rome where she was employed as a secretary for the United Nations Food and Agriculture Organisation (UNFAO) and he worked as a translator and journalist, writing for *The Economist*, *The Glasgow Herald* and *The Observer*. He also published a book, *New Light on Molière* in 1956, the first of three he would write about the great French playwright. By that time, he and his wife had relocated to Geneva. A year later he was appointed chief editor for The Economic Council for Asia and the Far East, based in Bangkok. He published a translation of Racine's play, *Phaedra*, in 1958 and was approached by Penguin Books to translate another two plays. In 1963, *Phaedra*, *Iphigenia* and *Athaliah* appeared in a single volume. In 1959, he published a collection of his poetry, *By the Lonely Sea*.

In 1963, he and Gabi separated, and Cairncross moved to Karachi to work on Pakistan's Planning Committee. Soon his academic ambitions were realised when he landed a job as a lecturer in Romance Languages at Case Western Reserve University in Cleveland, Ohio. It was not long, however, before MI5 came calling, alerted by his application for a visa to work in America. Many in the Secret Service were still not persuaded of his innocence and they wondered if he might give them more if he was outside the jurisdiction of MI5. Arthur Martin, a veteran of the Fuchs and Maclean investigations, and already in the United States, was delegated to go and visit him in Cleveland. Martin was an impressive individual, later described by Cairncross as 'one of the most effective intelligence officers I have ever met'. When he met him in 1964, the MI5 man made it clear that he did not believe Cairncross had divulged everything in 1952. It was the moment that Cairncross realised that there was no point in continuing to lie and he gave Martin a more complete confession than in his previous statement. The text of this is still secret but it is clear he confessed that he had been recruited by Russian intelligence in 1936 and had continued working for them until 1951.

Of course, this confession was inadmissible in a British court – it was outside MI5's jurisdiction, as previously noted, and it was not made under caution. Indeed, John Cairncross was never prosecuted by the British authorities, thus escaping the long custodial sentence that was the fate of his fellow spies, George Blake and John Vassall. Of course, his university career was over and in 1967, he returned to Italy and worked for the UNFAO as a translator. His job took him, on occasion, to Britain where he was subjected to further interviews. In 1970, he moved to Provence in France.

John Cairncross's espionage was made public in 1979, in the furore surrounding the exposure of Anthony Blunt as a Soviet spy. The former Assistant Private Secretary to three Prime ministers, Jock Colville, informed the *Sunday Times* journalist, Barrie Penrose, that Donald Maclean had not been the only spy in the Foreign Office. Penrose concluded that it could only be John Cairncross. He approached Cairncross and the former spy's confession was splashed across the front page of the newspaper. In 1981, Prime Minister Margaret Thatcher confirmed that Cairncross had spied for the Soviets and further confirmation was provided by the KGB defector, Oleg Gordievsky, in 1990.

By 1995, Cairncross was living once again in the South of France, married to opera singer, Gayle Brinkerhoff. He died in October that year, aged 82.

Cold War Traitors

Introduction

The Cold War. It evokes strong imagery – trenchcoated men hugging shadows, dark, smoke-filled basement rooms with swinging electric lights illuminating an interrogation, prisoner exchanges at mist-shrouded checkpoints and spies meeting their handlers in the corners of seedy bars. These images come from the many films that have been made about this period, but what was the Cold War really like? What happened during an era that was named for something that did not actually happen – that is, war?

The term 'Cold War' was coined by the British writer, George Orwell, in his 1945 essay 'You and the Atomic Bomb'. Orwell was writing about the fact that the world was living under the constant threat of nuclear warfare and in his piece refers to the notion dreamt up by American philosopher, James Burnham, that the world was polarised:

> 'Looking at the world as a whole, the drift for many decades has been not towards anarchy but towards the re-imposition of slavery… James Burnham's theory has been much discussed, but few people have yet considered its ideological implications – that is, the kind of world-view, the kind of beliefs, and the social structure that would probably prevail in a state which was at once unconquerable and in a permanent state of 'cold war' with its neighbours.'

The first time it was aired in reference to the contemporary tension between the United States and Russia was in a speech by Bernard Baruch, an influential businessman and adviser to US presidents, who said in a 1947 speech: 'Let us not be deceived;

we are in a cold war.' And the Cold War had to remain just that – cold – because the alternative was too horrific to contemplate – nuclear catastrophe, the tit-for-tat of nuclear warfare that would have left the world uninhabitable, if indeed anyone was left alive to inhabit it.

The Cold War is generally accepted to have lasted from 1947 until the 1991 dissolution of the Soviet Union, but it could well be said that it began before 1947, as the two great powers, the Soviet Union and the United States, jockeyed for position in the early 1940s with an eye on post-war mastery of the world. The Soviets exploited the political sensibilities of scientists with communist sympathies, such as Klaus Fuchs and Alan Nunn May, who were working on the development of the atomic bomb. For these scientists, it was quite simple – they believed that if both sides had the secrets of the bomb, it would not be used. Mutually assured destruction ensured that, in order to avoid annihilation, neither side would dare to deploy nuclear weapons.

The Cold War also created other types of spies. George Blake was a committed communist who never considered himself British and, therefore, felt at ease with his decision to be a double agent; John Vassall, Geoffrey Prime and Michael Bettaney also betrayed their country out of sympathy for the communist cause, but there were other elements to their treachery – homosexuality in the case of Vassall, inadequacy and sexual deviancy in the case of Prime, and alcoholism and attention-seeking in the case of Bettaney.

No matter their motivation, several of the traitors in this chapter lived in the shadowy, edgy double world of the spy for lengthy periods; and each of them did untold damage to their country.

Alan Nunn May:
The Nondescript Traitor

'Like a suburban bank clerk'

He was a pretty unexceptional sort of man, 'shy with a dry sense of humour', as someone described him. Other descriptions rendered him as 'colourless', and 'like a suburban bank clerk'. And yet, this unremarkable little man with his bald head, wire-rimmed glasses and toothbrush moustache caused untold damage to the interests of the West between 1940 and 1946 by passing secrets of British and American atomic research to the Soviet Union.

Born into a fairly well-off family in 1911 at Moseley in Birmingham, Nunn May was educated at the public school, King Edward's, and won a scholarship to Trinity Hall, Cambridge where he proved to be a brilliant scholar, gaining a First Class degree in the Mathematics Tripos in 1931 and graduating as a Bachelor of Arts in 1933 while also obtaining a First Class degree in the Natural Sciences Tripos. In 1936, he earned a PhD and, in that year, fulfilled an ambition by visiting Leningrad. He had already joined the Communist Party of Great Britain.

It was the 1930s, and, as we have seen, left-wing sympathies were all the rage at Britain's universities, these attitudes partly driven by a fear of fascism. It must be remembered, too, that the political and social experiment of the Soviet Union was still new and fresh, leading many to imagine a more hopeful future, especially after the tragedy of the First World War. Students welcomed the hunger marchers and were hell-bent on disrupting meetings of Oswald Mosley's blackshirted fascists. In 1936, as we have seen, many of the idealists who had espoused these left-wing sympathies travelled to Spain to fight against Franco's version of fascism in the Spanish Civil War.

As all this went on around him, however, Alan Nunn May merely looked on. He was not a man of action. Rather, he studied and took on board the philosophy but he did not apply it in any particular way. The most radical thing he did was to join the board of the *Scientific Worker*, the organ of the National Association of Science Workers which provided a home for many communists. The class struggle was sidelined, however, when war broke out in September 1939.

The 'Tube Alloys' Project and Canada

As a scientist, 29-year-old Nunn May was in a reserved occupation and was, consequently, not subject to call-up. His burgeoning reputation in the field of experimental physics led to him associating with some highly respected scientists and, in spring 1942, he was invited to join the 'Tube Alloys' project – codename for the British and Canadian nuclear weapons development programme, based at the Cavendish laboratory in Cambridge. As the work was highly classified, Nunn May had to sign the Official Secrets Act. His pro-Russia views were not considered unusual. Pro-Russia meant he was anti-fascism and that was, of course, desirable. In fact, there were a good many scientists with leftist views. Russia was, after all, an ally at the time.

For eight months, he worked in Cambridge and, during that time, there is no evidence that he was in touch with Russian intelligence, although it is now known that the Director of Intelligence at Moscow Central was aware of him. It is, of course, possible that he was, in fact, already working for the Russians at Cambridge.

The Canadian assignment was an indication of how highly regarded he was as a scientist. He went as the senior member of a

British team of scientists, sent to work with Canadian scientists in Montreal where they would be safer, away from the war, working on their heavy water project. The members of the team and their wives left for Canada in January 1943 and, as ever, on the voyage across the Atlantic, Nunn May remained his aloof and distant self.

The Montreal site was at Chalk River, west of Ottawa. Nunn May did not work directly on the atomic bomb, but he knew a lot about it, about the graphite piles at Hanford in Washington State and about plutonium production. He visited the American atomic research operation in Chicago three times and probably got to know more about the development of the bomb than any other British scientist. But General Leslie R Groves, the director of the Manhattan Project, disapproved of his visits and prevented Nunn May from making a fourth one in the spring of 1945. His misgivings later proved to be entirely justified, of course. The General explained it:

'By that time May had spent more time and acquired more knowledge at the Argonne [the National Laboratory near Chicago] than any other British physicist. Although I had absolutely no reason to suspect him, I did not like him to acquire such a wide knowledge of later developments. It is for that reason that in the spring of 1945 I declined to approve a proposed fourth visit of one month's duration. May never returned to the Chicago laboratory and never visited any other Manhattan District installation.'

The Americans were reluctant to share their secrets and Nunn May was very frustrated by this. He was already irritated that the Russians were not being taken into British and American confidence, conveniently ignoring the fact that the Russians could hardly be said to be open and honest about what they were up to. For him, though, the world's hope for the future lay with the Soviet Union. In his eyes, therefore, they could do no wrong.

Contact

The Soviet agent chosen to make contact with Nunn May in Canada was Lieutenant Pavel N Angelov, of the Russian Intelligence Service. He was codenamed 'Baxter', while Nunn May was given the name 'Alek'. By some unknown means, Nunn May was told he would be contacted by Baxter who would approach him and utter the phrase 'Best regards from Mikel'. Initially, the Soviets were not directly seeking information about the atomic bomb. Rather, they told him, they wanted to know about uranium and atomic energy. That spring and summer of 1945, they met on several occasions, Nunn May providing information that was then sent by cable to Moscow Central. If there were handwritten notes, these were conveyed by diplomatic bag. In April 1945, he was paid $200, the banknotes pushed into a whisky bottle for the sake of secrecy, together with a second full bottle which was also handed over.

Shortly after the first atomic bombs were dropped on Hiroshima and Nagasaki on August 6 and 9 respectively, Nunn May provided the Russians with perhaps the most valuable items possible – minute samples of separated uranium isotopes along with details of the Hiroshima and Nagasaki bombs. The isotopes were personally carried to Moscow by the assistant military attaché from the Russian Embassy in Ottawa.

Details of electronically controlled anti-aircraft shells being developed by the Americans were also sent. Around this time, Nunn May warned Baxter that he would be returning to England at the beginning of September to take up a post at King's College, London and he was anxious that the Russians should be able to make contact with him once he was there. Arrangements were made by KGB Colonel Nikolai Zabotin for a meeting on either 7, 17 or 27 October at 11pm on the street in front of the British Museum. The identifying phrase would again be 'Best regards from Mikel'. In the meantime, Nunn May paid a visit to a uranium plant at Petawawa in southern Ontario and, at his last meeting in Canada, he passed on information about that. He told them he would be returning to Canada for a month in the following year. The Russians paid him $500 for his work so far.

Russian agents in London suggested that it would be too dark to meet at 11 at night. Eight in the evening was agreed to be a better time and the passwords were changed. The contact would say 'What is the shortest way to the Strand?' and Nunn May would reply 'Well, come along. I am going that way'. Nunn May would launch their conversation with the familiar phrase 'Best regards from Mikel'.

Confession

Nunn May started at King's towards the end of September 1945 but the work in which he was involved was no longer top secret. On 5 September 1945, however, GRU cipher clerk Igor Gouzenko, defected to the West in Ottawa, a defection that, as we have seen, gravely worried Kim Philby. Gouzenko, worried that he and his family were about to be sent back to Russia, had walked out of the Soviet Embassy carrying a suitcase filled with documents, code books and deciphering materials. As a result, numerous Canadians were exposed as Soviet spies and a spy ring of about 20 people, led by the Polish-Canadian politician, Fred Rose, was also revealed.

Amongst the documents Gouzenko handed over was one that named Nunn May as a Soviet spy and there were also details of his proposed October meeting outside the British Museum. Instead of immediately arresting him, however, Special Branch decided to exercise patience, choosing to wait and see if he would keep his appointment, given that the Russians had probably worked out that Nunn May's name was in the stolen material. Of course, he failed to turn up on the agreed dates and, when they waited again the following month, once again he was a no-show. He would have known nothing of Gouzenko's defection as it was not made known to the press until February 1946, but there can be little doubt that he would have been warned by his Soviet masters.

Finally, as arrests continued in Canada, Nunn May was brought in for interrogation by Commander Leonard Burt of Special Branch in the middle of February. The venue was Shell-Mex House on the Strand in London. By all accounts, the scientist was composed, showed no signs of fear or concern. When informed that there had been a leak of information relating to atomic energy in Canada, he replied that this was the first he had heard of it. He denied any knowledge of Zabotin, Angelov or Baxter or that he had been approached to give classified information while in Canada. Towards the end of the questioning, he insisted that he was not prepared to divulge information that would implicate his friends. This suggested that he was, indeed, holding something back.

On 20 February, Burt returned to the fray with evidence from Canada that Nunn May had associated with the Russians there and that an appointment had been made for his return to England. Realising at last that it was the end of the road, Nunn May broke down in tears, insisting: 'No, I did not keep that appointment as when I returned I decided to wash my hands of the whole business.' Still, however, he refused to reveal his contacts' names or accept that what he had done was wrong. He dictated a written confession, ending by saying: 'The whole affair was extremely painful to me and I only embarked upon it because I felt this was a contribution I could make to the safety of mankind. I certainly did not do it for gain.'

Arrest and Trial

Alan Nunn May was arrested on the afternoon of 4 March 1946, at King's College by Detective-Inspector William Whitehead of Special Branch and charged under the Official Secrets Act at Bow Street police station. He chose to make no comment.

Meanwhile, in Canada, the Soviet Embassy issued a statement claiming that any information received from Canadian and British nationals was of little consequence 'in view of the far more advanced technical attainment in the USSR'. It went on to say that those Soviets involved had been recalled to Moscow and ended with an accusation that the Canadian media were simply trying to create bad blood between the two countries. Of course, this disingenuous statement was designed to downplay the magnitude of what Nunn May had revealed, information they claimed was generally available in published pamphlets and documents. This was patently untrue.

Nunn May's trial and conviction passed relatively quietly. Even though his case was the first to confirm that the Soviet Union had gained atomic secrets by espionage, the public was at that time more preoccupied by World War Two traitors such as William Joyce and John Amery. And, of course, many, including a number of scientists who had worked on the development of the bomb, believed that we should share our nuclear information with the Russians in order to prevent another war, one with even more catastrophic consequences.

The trial began on 1 May 1946, before Mr Justice Oliver and with the Attorney-General prosecuting as he had done at several other such trials. Gerald Gardiner KC appeared on behalf of the accused. As expected, Alan Nunn May was found guilty. Sentencing him, the judge said: 'I think you acted not as an honourable man but as a dishonourable man. I think you acted with degradation. Whether money was the object of what you did, in fact you did get money for what you did. It is a very bad case indeed.' He was sentenced to ten years' hard labour.

Nunn May was sent to Wakefield Prison in Yorkshire to start his sentence without having identified the people to whom he had given the information and without, in fact, helping the investigators in any way. There were moves to have his sentence reduced. The Association of Science Workers of Great Britain (AScW) was of the opinion that it was particularly harsh when the maximum sentence under the Atomic Energy Bill was five years. They also noted that his scientific contribution to the war effort was not taken into account in the sentencing. Questions were also asked in Parliament about the severity of the sentence, one MP calling into question the ethics of atomic bomb secrecy. The Home Secretary, James Chuter Ede, wholeheartedly disagreed and was supported in his assertion by loud cheering in the Commons chamber.

Nunn May was released in late 1952, having served six and a half years but was, naturally, unable to find employment with any British university. Instead, he went to work for a scientific instruments company. In 1953, he married Hilde Broda, former wife of the Austrian scientist, Engelbert Broda, a man also suspected of passing nuclear secrets to the Russians. In 1961 Nunn May went to work at the University of Ghana, researching into solid-state physics. He returned to Cambridge in 1978 and it was there that he died 25 years later of pneumonia. He was 91.

But this quiet man did not ultimately go quietly. A month before he died, he dictated a confession to a family friend which was published by *The Guardian*. It began 'This is a disclosure of how I became a Russian spy'. He said that he believed a report received in America around 1942 that the Germans were developing radioactive 'dirty bombs' and that he feared these would be used in the Soviet Union which Hitler had invaded in 1941. He had warned the Russians through his Communist Party contacts, but, although his warning was not taken seriously, he had put himself firmly on their radar. When he travelled to Canada to work, the Soviets wanted him to set up a radio communication centre to transmit information to them. He refused to do so, believing it to be inherently dangerous but he still became an informant for them, believing that they should be kept informed of developments in the West. To the end, he maintained that his betrayal was worthwhile in order to save the world from nuclear disaster.

Klaus Fuchs: The Traitor Who Gave the Russians the Bomb

The Red Foxes

The Fuchs family were known in their home town of Rüsselsheim as the 'red foxes' – Fuchs being German for fox – because of their socialist views. Those leftist views would heavily influence the life of the atom spy, Klaus Emil Julius Fuchs, whose betrayal of America's Manhattan Project to the Soviet Union would imperil the peace of the post-war world.

He was born in 1911, the son of a Lutheran pastor and enrolled at the University of Leipzig, where his father was professor of theology, in 1930, to study mathematics and physics, later continuing his studies at Kiel University. Around this time, he began to develop his interest in politics, joining the student section of the Social Democratic Party of Germany (SPD) and its paramilitary wing, the Reichsbanner Schwarz-Rot-Gold. The SDP was the oldest political party in Germany and was chiefly responsible for the creation of the Weimar Republic after the First World War. A year after starting at university, the 20-year-old Fuchs was devastated by the death by suicide of his mother and then, in 1932, he was expelled from the SDP for supporting the Communist Party candidate in the presidential elections of March 1932. The SDP, along with the Centre Party and the Deutsche Volkspartei, had put its weight behind the incumbent Paul von Hindenburg in an effort to stop Adolf Hitler claiming victory. The Communist Party had broken ranks, however, by choosing to put forward its own presidential candidate, Ernst Thälmann. Fuchs and his three siblings joined the German Communist Party, the KPD and, by this time, he was speaking at public meetings and taking part in activity aimed at disrupting Nazi gatherings. During one such attempt, he was severely beaten and thrown into a nearby river.

A Refugee in England

In 1933 after Hitler was elected Chancellor, Fuchs left Kiel, where the National Socialist German Workers' Party (NSDAP) was particularly powerful, for the Kaiser Wilhelm Institute for Physics in Berlin. In February 1933, the Reichstag was destroyed by fire and, with opposition parties being blamed for the outrage, Fuchs was forced into hiding in the apartment of a fellow Communist Party member. Expulsion from the Kaiser Wilhelm Institute followed in October 1933 but by then he had already gone to live in Somerset in England with Ronald and Jessie Gunn, whom he had met at a conference in Paris.

He found work as a research assistant to Neville Mott, professor of physics at Bristol University, gaining his Ph.D. in physics there in 1937. Moving to Edinburgh University, he worked under another German refugee, Max Born, who was instrumental in the development of quantum mechanics and would go on to win the 1954 Nobel Prize in Physics. Fuchs gained a Doctorate in Science degree from Edinburgh and applied for British citizenship in 1939. By June 1940, his application had still not been approved and he was interned as an enemy alien, despite his previous, well-documented opposition to the Nazis in Germany. Initially held on the Isle of Man, he was then sent to Sherbrooke in Quebec in Canada but even while interned, he continued to publish scientific papers in partnership with Max Born. On Christmas Day 1940, his captivity ended and he returned to Edinburgh to continue his work with Born who had lobbied for his release.

Fuchs's life changed in May the following year when he was invited by the German-born physicist, Rudolf Peierls, chair in applied mathematics at the University of Birmingham, to work on the 'Tube Alloys' project – as we have seen, the programme to develop nuclear weapons in partnership with Canada. In August 1942, Fuchs was finally granted British citizenship and signed the Official Secrets Act. His signature to the act was rendered pointless, however, when, in late 1942, he made contact with an old communist friend from his internment in Quebec – a Jewish German economist named Jürgen Kuczynski who had participated in the anti-fascist resistance in Germany and had fled Nazi persecution to Britain in 1936. Now teaching at the London School of Economics, Kuczynski put Fuchs in touch with Simon Davidovitch Kremer, the secretary to the military attaché at the Russian Embassy. Kremer was also an agent of the Soviet military intelligence directorate, the GRU. A courier – Kuczynski's sister Ruth, a major in Soviet intelligence – was found for Fuchs as he would be unable to justify numerous trips to London. Fuchs was given the codename 'Charles'.

In late 1943, Fuchs and Peierls moved to Columbia University in New York City to continue their work. They were engaged on behalf of the Manhattan Project, on research into gaseous diffusion as a means of enriching uranium. Fuchs now fell under the control of another Soviet intelligence organisation, the NKGB.

In early 1944, Fuchs was told to meet a man named 'Raymond'. Following instructions, he left his hotel, the Brabazon Plaza, and made his way to the subway in the Lower East Side of New York. It was Saturday afternoon and the subway was much quieter than it would have been during the working week. Before he stepped out of the train, Fuchs produced a tennis ball from his coat pocket. This was his signal to Raymond who would be waiting on the platform for him. Raymond was actually Harry Gold – born Henrich Golodnitsky – a 34 year-old Swiss-born American laboratory chemist who had immigrated to the United States at the age of four. Raymond made himself known by carrying a pair of gloves in his right hand and a book with green binding in the other. The two approached each other and shook hands before heading for a café. Gold reported back to Moscow on his new charge:

'He (Fuchs) obviously worked with our people before and he is fully aware of what he is doing... He is a mathematical physicist... most likely a very brilliant man to have such a position at his age (he looks about 30). We took a long walk after dinner... He is a member of a British mission to the U.S. working under the direct control of the U.S. Army... The work involves mainly separating the isotopes... and is being done thusly: The electronic method has been developed at Berkeley, California, and is being carried out at a place known only as Camp Y... Simultaneously, the diffusion method is being tried here in the East... Should the diffusion method prove successful, it will be used as a preliminary step in the separation, with the final work being done by the electronic method. They hope to have the electronic method ready early in 1945 and the diffusion method in July 1945, but (Fuchs) says the latter estimate is optimistic. (Fuchs) says there is much being withheld from the British. Even Niels Bohr, who is now in the country incognito as Nicholas Baker, has not been told everything.'

Within a few weeks of this meeting, Fuchs was passing information about the US nuclear weapons programme to Gold who passed it to Anatoli Yakovlev, a Soviet consul in New York who was also a Soviet intelligence officer controlling a number of agents in the United States. The information was then smuggled back to Moscow in diplomatic bags. At one of their meetings, Fuchs was offered $1500 but he refused to accept it. He was instructed to get himself a job at the atomic bomb laboratory at Los Alamos in New Mexico which he duly did in August 1944, working in the Theoretical Physics Division, under the German scientist, Hans Bethe. He was now involved in the actual construction of the bomb.

This may have actually been the happiest time of Klaus Fuchs's life. In his time off, he went mountain climbing and in winter he skied. There was a great deal of enjoyable socialising with the other scientists and their families. He was being well-paid and he bought a car, a second-hand Buick. He was relaxed and fit and healthy. Security was not too bad at Los Alamos; there was a barbed wire fence and passes were needed to move to the different sections of the facility. The local people were completely unaware of what they were up to but the scientists and their families were free to go into Santa Fe as and when they wished.

The Russians had lost track of their precious spy around this time. He had missed a few meetings in New York and they became worried that he had been compromised or even arrested. Harry Gold travelled to Cambridge, near Boston, to make enquiries at the home of Fuchs's sister Kristel Heineman. All she could tell him was that he was somewhere in the south-west but was due to holiday with them in early 1945. When Gold met Fuchs again, he was excited to discover what the scientist was involved with, asking him to write down everything he knew about the Manhattan Project. Fuchs provided details of the design and construction of the bomb and the location where the plutonium was produced. Of crucial interest to the Soviets was information he provided about the implosion lens, a device designed to explode inwards that was used to actually detonate the bomb.

On 2 June 1945, in a quiet suburb of Santa Fe, Fuchs passed to Gold a wad of papers that contained all the details of the final stages in the development of the atom bomb. He also provided the date of the first explosive test of the device – 16 July – telling him it would be in the Alamogordo Desert. Fuchs was indeed present at what was codenamed the Trinity test, and like other witnesses, was humbled and amazed by its power.

When President Truman met Stalin in August at Potsdam, he told him that America had developed a powerful new bomb that was going to be dropped on Japan in order to end the war but apparently Stalin did not show a great deal of interest. The reason was, of course, that, thanks to Fuchs and a couple of other Soviet spies at Los Alamos, he already knew just about everything there was to know about the new weapon.

Return to England

Fuchs returned to England in July 1946, to a job as head of the Theoretical Physics Division at the Atomic Energy Research Establishment at Harwell but, as soon as he got back, he contacted members of the British Communist Party in order to resume contact with the NKVD. Eventually, he was put in touch with Aleksandr Feklissov, the Soviet Secret Service's London deputy station chief, responsible for scientific and technical intelligence. Fuchs provided Feklissov with all the Russians needed to build a hydrogen bomb, from a project being worked on at the University of Chicago by Edward Teller and Enrico Fermi. He also gave them the results of the third series of American tests at the Pacific Proving Grounds at Eniwetok Atoll. Around this time, Fuchs began accepting payment from the Soviets. He had money troubles; his father was now dependent upon him and one of his brothers was ill with tuberculosis. They paid him £200 but he immediately returned half of it, reasoning that people would wonder where all that money had come from.

It all began to unravel in March 1948 when the British newspaper, the *Daily Express*, revealed that MI5 was investigating three scientists who were thought to have once been members of the Communist Party of Great Britain. Moscow immediately ordered Feklissov to distance himself from Fuchs and, to make matters worse, one of Fuchs's former contacts in the United States – Ursula Beurton (aka Ruth Kuczynski) – had been brought in for questioning by the FBI. The Russians reasoned that, even if Fuchs was not arrested, it was unlikely that he would be allowed to work again in the field of atomic research. Nonetheless, Feklissov continued to meet him.

By 1948, Fuchs was having second thoughts as he liked the people with whom he worked at Harwell and felt bad about his betrayal of them and their work. He resolved to give the Soviets less material until he had worked out how to proceed. Then, to his horror, in the spring of 1949, he discovered he had a spot on his lung. A terrible period ensued and, even after his illness had gone, he remained in bed staring at the wall, undoubtedly struggling with his complex loyalties. He may even have resolved to give up his double life and devote everything to Harwell, but by this time it was too late.

As with Donald Maclean, it was the Venona project that uncovered the treachery of Klaus Fuchs and, as before, the British were compromised by this knowledge, unwilling to arrest Fuchs because this would let Moscow know that their codes had been broken. Some of the first messages that were decrypted spoke of a scientist at the Manhattan Project who went by the codenames 'Charles' and 'Rest'. He had provided information that was 'of great value' according to one message sent from Moscow to New York on 10 April 1945. The message went on to say that the information he passed included 'data on the atomic mass of the nuclear explosive' and details about how the atomic bomb was exploded. By September 1949, they were convinced of Fuchs's guilt. His telephones were tapped and his mail was intercepted. They even installed microphones in his home at Harwell. Surveillance was initiated but all that was revealed was that he was having an affair with the wife of his line manager at Harwell.

Arrest and Trial

It was finally decided to question Fuchs and the man chosen to do it was Jim Skardon, MI5's chief investigator, who had interrogated Kim Philby. Skardon, a man of infinite patience, tact and tenacity, met Fuchs at Harwell on 21 December, questioning him for four hours. Naturally, Fuchs denied involvement in any espionage and insisted that there was no evidence of him spying. At the end of that first meeting, there was, of course, the question of what Fuchs would do. He might try, if he was guilty, to flee or he might even take his own life. Some thought he should be taken into custody to forestall either of these events but Skardon remained unconvinced that Fuchs was, in fact, a spy, and did not believe he would run away or kill himself. He let him stew for a few days and then returned to Harwell on 30 December. At the first meeting, they had discussed Fuchs's life in Germany and his work in Edinburgh. Now they turned to the time he had spent in the United States. Still, Fuchs insisted that he was not guilty of anything.

At this point, Percy Sillitoe, head of MI5, contacted Sir John Cockroft, director of the Atomic Energy Research Establishment, to say: 'We have had Fuchs' activities under intensive investigation for more than four months. Since it has been generally agreed that Fuchs' continued employment is a constant threat to security and since our elaborate investigation has produced no dividends, I should be grateful if you would be kind enough to arrange for Fuchs' departure from Harwell as soon as is decently possible.' Sir John intimated to Fuchs that it would be in everyone's interest if he resigned at once and perhaps found a university post.

Three days later, Skardon was back, informing Fuchs that his time in New York was now under the microscope. Again, Fuchs denied everything but admitted to Skardon that he was leaving Harwell, and suggested that he was thinking of taking a holiday. At the end of this third meeting, Skardon at least felt there was a kind of mutual trust between him and his quarry.

Fuchs appears to have had something of an epiphany a few days later and asked to see Skardon again. For two hours they talked but Fuchs remained intransigent. Skardon suggested lunch and Fuchs drove them into nearby Abingdon where they stopped at a pub. Afterwards, they returned to Harwell. As soon as they entered Fuchs's house in which they had been meeting earlier, Fuchs announced that he had decided to confess. As Skardon later wrote:

'During the meal he seemed to be resolving the matter and to be considerably abstracted… He suggested that we should hurry back to his house. On arrival he said that he had decided it would be in his best interests to answer my questions. I then put certain questions to him and in reply he told me that he was engaged in espionage from mid-1942 until about a year ago. He said there was a continuous passing of information relating to atomic energy at irregular but frequent meetings… "Since that time I have had continuous contact with the persons who were completely unknown to me, except that I knew they would hand whatever information I gave them to the Russian authorities. At that time, I had complete confidence in Russian policy and I believed that the Western Allies deliberately allowed Russia and Germany to fight each other to the death. I had therefore, no hesitation in giving all the information I had, even though occasionally I tried to concentrate mainly on giving information about the results of my own work. There is nobody I know by name who is concerned with collecting information for the Russian authorities. There are people whom I know by sight whom I trusted with my life.'"

The irony was, of course, that until his confession, there was little chance of Fuchs being prosecuted as the only evidence against him was derived from Venona and that could not be used in court.

Needless to say, the case broke sensationally in the media but the trial at the Old Bailey held little drama, lasting less than 90 minutes. Fuchs was found guilty of four charges of breaking the Official Secrets Act by 'communicating information to a potential enemy' and the judge, Lord Rayner Goddard, sentenced him to the maximum allowable for espionage at the time – 14 years. Fuchs had been labouring under a misapprehension, however. On the way into court, his senior counsel, Derek Curtis-Bennett had said to him: 'You know what the maximum penalty is?' Fuchs had replied: 'Yes, I know. It's death.' 'No' replied Curtis-Bennett, 'It is 14 years.' During the time he had been held on remand in Brixton Prison, it seems that he had been under the misapprehension that he would be hanged.

He served nine years and four months of his sentence, and was released from Wakefield Prison on 23 June 1959. He immediately flew to East Germany where he was appointed deputy director of the Institute for Nuclear Research near Dresden. He married an old friend from his university days, Margaret Keilson, and died on 28 January 1988.

Meanwhile, enquiries in the United States led to the

uncovering of Harry Gold, Fuchs's contact. The FBI had questioned hundreds of suspects and had even spoken to Fuchs's sister, Kristel, but Gold was undone by the discovery at his apartment of a map he had bought in Santa Fe when he had gone there to meet Fuchs. On 22 May he confessed and Fuchs confirmed his identity when shown a photograph of him. In 1951, he was sentenced to 30 years' imprisonment but was paroled in 1965 after serving less than half that time.

J. Edgar Hoover, long-time head of the FBI, noted that, 'Fuchs said he would estimate that the information furnished by him speeded up by several years the production of an atom bomb by Russia.'

Harry Houghton and Ethel Gee: When Harry Met Ethel

A Weak Englishman

It is a story of five people – three highly skilled Soviet spies, an inadequate Englishman with a bloated sense of himself and the woman who made the mistake of falling in love with him. It began at Portland, a rugged, grey peninsula on Dorset's Jurassic Coast and ended near the Old Vic Theatre on the corner of The Cut and Waterloo Road in London.

The weak Englishman at the heart of the tale was Harry Frederick Houghton, born in Lincoln in 1905 and done with school at the age of 14. He joined the Royal Navy and ended the Second World War as a master-at-arms, the equivalent to a chief petty officer. He next joined the civil service and in 1951 was appointed to the staff of the British Embassy in Warsaw as a wages clerk in the department of the naval attaché. His wife Peggy accompanied him to Warsaw but this did not prevent

Houghton from beginning an affair with a Polish woman called Katrina who happened to be 20 years younger than him. Harry was having a ball, enjoying an exciting social life with his new love and her friends but, of course, it was expensive keeping a young lover entertained. Oblivious to the reason her husband constantly had no money, Peggy suggested he could boost their income by selling coffee on Warsaw's lucrative black market. When that began to bring in some much-needed cash, he broadened his portfolio of illicit goods to include, amongst other things, pharmaceuticals, at that time, like coffee, in short supply in the Polish capital.

However, stories of his black marketeering and heavy drinking and rumours of domestic abuse came to the ears of his superiors and he was ordered home in 1952. Prior to his departure, Katrina passed to him the names of some Poles in London that she suggested he should contact. What Houghton did not know, however, was that the names were actually provided to her by Urząd Bezpieczeństwa (UB), the Polish Secret Police who had started taking a keen interest in him. Houghton returned to London and a few months later contacted one of the names on the list – a man named Tadeusz. The two men met at a pub in Earl's Court in London and hit it off immediately.

Houghton was appointed to a new post at Portland in Dorset, working for the Admiralty in the records department of the Underwater Detection Establishment (UDE), a research department, that dealt with underwater detection systems and weapons. In 1953, he and his wife moved to Meadow View in Broadwey, near Weymouth, just across the isthmus that joined Portland to the mainland. He still visited London to meet with Tadeusz but his main focus was to get his hands on extra cash to entertain his new girlfriend, Ethel Gee, known as 'Bunty'.

Bunty lived on Hambro Road, in Portland, a street of redbrick, terraced houses, with her mother, her bedridden aunt and uncle, all of whom were in their eighties. Caring for them had severely curtailed her social life and she remained unmarried at 41. She worked as a filing clerk at the UDE and handled documents of the utmost secrecy dealing with Britain's underwater warfare plans and the Royal Navy's first nuclear submarine, HMS *Dreadnought*. Bunty Gee fell for Harry Houghton and the two of them would jump in his car and go for drinks in the pubs in the surrounding area.

On one of his visits to London, he complained to Tadeusz about his lack of cash to entertain his mistress and about his increasingly difficult marriage, information that was channelled back to the Russians who decided the time was right to engage Houghton in the role they had long envisaged for him – that of spy.

A Spy Is Born

In late 1953, again drinking in London with Tadeusz, who was accompanied by a Polish friend, he was told that help was at hand. He could earn a lot of money by supplying information about the work that was going on at the base. To start with, they asked him to supply details of the equipment that was being used as well as the name of every scientist working there. Houghton jumped at the chance and was told to await instructions. An anxious wait followed with his financial situation worsening all the time. Eventually, he received a phone call at the base, the voice on the other end of the line introducing himself as a friend of Katrina. They arranged to meet the next day outside Dulwich Picture Gallery in southeast London. Houghton was instructed to carry a pair of brown kid gloves and a copy of *The Times* to meet a man named 'Nikki' at the gallery. Nikki explained to him that he would be sent a brochure for a vacuum cleaner when they needed to see him and the following Saturday, after receipt of this brochure, he was to bring films of secret naval documents to the Toby Jug pub on the Kingston by-pass in Surrey. He was given a Minox camera, a miniature photographic device made in Germany that was *de rigueur* for spies. Houghton was shown how to use it and sent on his way.

Houghton successfully carried out his first assignment and followed up with more photographed documents. He almost came a cropper, however, when his wife found a package containing what appeared to be secret Admiralty documents. She spoke to a few friends about it and the information soon reached the ears of the UDE's security personnel. Luckily for Houghton, however, it was no secret that the Houghton marriage was in a parlous state and the security officers involved suggested that her claim was little more than the ranting of an over-emotional wife. No action was taken apart from the precaution of moving Houghton to the repair unit office, thus ending his access to classified documents. This, of course, meant the end to his income from espionage.

In 1956, Houghton and Peggy finally separated and he moved to a caravan at Warmwell, about 13 miles from the base, using a loan from Bunty Gee for its purchase. He would later move onto Portland itself. His relationship with Bunty was flourishing and she often spent the night in the caravan. They would also travel up to London to go to the theatre or cinema, staying overnight as 'Mr and Mrs Houghton'. Eventually, in 1958, Peggy divorced him and he was able to move back to the Broadwey cottage.

Nikki still pressed him for information, particularly anything relating to Britain's anti-submarine defences. He left Houghton in no doubt that he had somehow to get his hands on this material. A few days after this particularly difficult meeting, a man turned up on Houghton's doorstep, introducing himself as Gordon Arnold Lonsdale, a friend of Nikki. Stocky, with a winning smile and dark hair, Lonsdale spoke with a North American accent but told Houghton he was a Soviet agent. He needed, he said, pamphlets on submarine detection. Houghton's protests that he was no longer in a position to access such material fell on deaf ears, Lonsdale merely telling him, as Nikki had, that it was 'an order'. Aware of Houghton's relationship with Bunty Gee, Lonsdale suggested that she might be the means by which they could obtain the relevant documents. After all, Lonsdale pointed out, she worked in the UDE records office and such documents crossed her desk every day.

When Houghton met up with Bunty that evening, he explained that he had been visited by an old friend, a US Embassy naval attaché named Alex Johnson. He wanted her to meet him and had bought three tickets to the Bolshoi Ballet, performing at that time in London. Lonsdale charmed Bunty but Houghton later told her that Johnson was blackmailing him over his black-market activities in Warsaw. The price of his silence was information about the UDE. Lonsdale wanted this information, claimed Houghton, to ensure that Britain was adhering to NATO agreements that guaranteed it would share details of its work in the area of underwater defence with the United States. Did Bunty believe this story? It is impossible to say, but she agreed, without hesitation, to comply with Harry's request. She got into the habit of stuffing a wad of documents into her bag at night and walking out with them. They were photographed and returned next morning. The pair were well remunerated for the work. The cottage was refurbished and they began to live the high life, Harry flashing the cash in the local hostelries.

Naturally, people's suspicions were immediately aroused and a couple of locals reported their concerns – Fred Hosking, a dockyard police officer, told his senior officers, and a neighbour passed on her suspicions to the local police. Peggy Houghton's story was recalled by security officers at the base but this time the misgivings about Harry Houghton were not brushed aside. MI5 became involved and several of the organisation's officers met with Admiralty intelligence officers at the base. Bert Smith, head of Dorset CID, was also present. Houghton was put under surveillance, and the job was handed to the young detective sergeant Leonard Burt who had been involved in other notable cases including those of the atomic spies, Klaus Fuchs and Alan Nunn May. Burt was to liaise with Jim Skardon of MI5 who, as we have seen, had interrogated Klaus Fuchs and would be closely involved in the investigation of the Cambridge Five.

In spring 1960, Harry Houghton was followed to a rendezvous in London with Gordon Lonsdale. The Canadian Lonsdale was posing as a salesman of a variety of goods including jukeboxes, burglar alarms, and bubble gum dispensing machines, and the agents following Houghton wondered if they were perhaps involved in a business together, something that could explain Houghton's new-found wealth. When it became clear that he was involved with Bunty Gee of the records office at the base, however, alarm bells began to go off.

One Saturday in early July 1960, as Houghton and Gee drove away from Portland in his car, a brand-new Renault Dauphine, they failed to spot the sleek black Jaguar that slipped in behind them and tailed them for 50 miles along the road from Dorset to London. The Jaguar pulled off to be replaced by a black Humber Pullman and, 20 miles from London, the Humber was replaced by a red MG whose passengers saw them park and go into the Cumberland Hotel at Marble Arch in the capital.

After checking in and freshening up, they re-emerged and travelled by Tube to Waterloo, oblivious to the dark-suited man carrying an umbrella and wearing a Homburg hat who had followed them to the Tube station and the man in the stained white mackintosh and trilby who took his place and travelled on the same train as them to their destination. As the couple walked through the subway that led to Waterloo Road, Harry was heard to say to Bunty: 'This is the way we came last time.' Arriving at the Old Vic theatre, they were joined by Gordon Lonsdale and the trio walked across to a small park opposite the theatre. They sat down on a bench and talked for around an hour. At one point during that time, the watchers saw Houghton pass to Lonsdale a package wrapped in brown paper and Lonsdale handed him a white envelope in return. The watchers heard them set their next meeting for four in the afternoon of 6 August. They parted, Lonsdale climbing into a Standard Vanguard parked in a nearby street.

On the appointed date, Houghton journeyed to London alone, by train this time, arriving at 3.40 pm, 20 minutes before the time of the rendezvous. He met Lonsdale and the two disappeared into a café for a drink but were closely followed by two MI5 officers armed with pocket tape recorders. Seated at an adjoining table, they listened in to the ensuing conversation:

Lonsdale (indicating a brown suitcase that Houghton had brought): 'You seem to have plenty in there!'

Houghton: 'Yes, I have more than my sleeping and shaving kit.'

Lonsdale: 'It certainly is fat. I reckon you've got a lot of work for me to do tonight.'

Houghton (laughing): 'You're right. You'll have to burn some midnight oil to get through it all in one go.'

They arranged to meet on the first Saturdays of both October and November before leaving the café, closely followed by their MI5 shadows. In an intricately executed ritual, in Baylis Road, Houghton went into a telephone kiosk where he opened the suitcase and took out a parcel and an envelope. He had a newspaper in which he wrapped them and the newspaper package was left in the kiosk when he exited it. Lonsdale then entered and grabbed the package. The MI5 men looked on from their hiding place in bemusement as this charade was played out. The point was, of course, for there to be no visible handover. As the two men walked back along the street, Houghton was heard to say: 'I don't want to be paid for that lot just yet. Leave the cash until our next meeting.'

Lonsdale

The question for MI5 at this point was: who was Gordon Lonsdale? He was known to have an office in Soho, but he was rarely there. He seemed to be something of a playboy, hanging out in the bars and clubs of London's West End, usually with a good-looking woman on his arm. Money was no object which allowed him to rent a flat at the expensive and exclusive White House on Albany Street. His car, too, was not cheap – a white Studebaker. MI5 called in Superintendent George Smith of Special Branch to find out all he could about Lonsdale and Houghton. The objective of this investigation was to discover the extent of their espionage, and whether or not they were part of a bigger spy ring. A case needed to be prepared.

Special Branch officers began following Lonsdale wherever he went and his office was under constant surveillance. On 26 August, he was followed from his office to the Great Portland Street branch of the Midland Bank where he placed a small attaché case and a large paper parcel in a safety deposit box. Smith obtained the necessary paperwork to enable him to access the items that had been deposited.

Extreme care was taken so that Lonsdale would not find out that his items had been disturbed. The parcel and case were driven to the secret MI5 laboratory near St Paul's Cathedral where, as well as Charles Elwell, the case officer for the Lonsdale investigation, an expert lock-picker was waiting. The parcel was unwrapped to reveal a brown leather briefcase and a small metal deed box. Soon they were both open, their contents photographed as they were removed so that they could be replaced in the exact order in which they had been found. There were some legitimate documents relating to Lonsdale's business, some letters and a couple of books – *Touch Typing in Ten Lessons* and *Contract Bridge Made Easy*. When a beam of light was focused on the pages of the books, it became apparent that indentations were visible on the paper, the marks left by someone writing on another piece of paper resting on that page. These were carefully recorded on film to be examined more closely later.

The attaché case revealed a Praktica camera with lenses, a cassette that held 100 feet of 35mm film and a couple of magnifiers. Amongst other items was a Ronson cigarette lighter with a wooden base that was found to contain a cavity. Inside were three miniature one-time cipher pads (OTPs) and a piece of paper that listed eight roads in the Kingston-on-Thames area as well as their grid references. The officers present immediately recognised the OTPs as being of the type used by the Soviets. They consisted of tiny plastic pages glued together. One section was red and the other blue, differentiating the codes used for incoming and outgoing messages. Unfortunately, the only way to photograph them was to break the glue to separate the pages and that would have alerted Lonsdale. Therefore, they were left intact. Everything was replaced and the items were returned to the bank.

While this had been going on, Lonsdale had left the country and he did not return to collect the parcel and case until 24 October. He was followed as usual but the MI5 agents lost him at Ruislip Manor tube station. It seemed an unlikely place for him to visit and they were puzzled, sufficiently puzzled, in fact, to increase the team of watchers by 20 people, mostly the wives of Special Branch officers. In Ruislip, they would not stand out as much as their gabardined and behatted husbands.

As had been learned at the café in Waterloo, Lonsdale and Houghton were next due to meet on Saturday 5 November. Houghton set off from Broadwey that morning and was followed to London, a cardboard box and a briefcase spotted on the back seat of his car. At Kingston, around 6.30pm, he stopped for Lonsdale to climb into the car. They sat talking before driving on to the Maypole pub where they talked and drank for a while before leaving. Just before that they exchanged briefcases. Fifteen minutes later, Lonsdale got out of Houghton's Dauphine, climbed into his Studebaker and drove off towards Ruislip. Around 9.45, he turned into Willow Gardens and proceeded on foot but the pursuing officers judged it too risky to follow him. His final destination remained unknown until he was seen leaving a bungalow, at 45 Cranley Drive, owned, it transpired, by a couple – Peter and Helen Kroger.

On 10 December, Lonsdale, Gee and Houghton met again in the Waterloo area, although it was not certain whether any items changed hands on this occasion. Afterwards, Lonsdale headed for Ruislip where, it was presumed, he was passing on something he had been given by the Portland couple.

Now the question was: who were the Krogers? Strangely, nothing about them could be found from before 1954. That year, they had appeared out of the blue in Catford. Neighbours were told they were from Canada, but learned nothing more about them. The following year, they moved to Ruislip and Peter Kroger rented a small shop in the Strand where he sold books. The shop had a high rent and there was little evidence that Kroger made much of a profit from his business, but he managed to keep it going as well as pay a big mortgage on the house in Cranley Drive. After three years, though, he closed the shop and began to run his business from home. The pair ingratiated themselves with their neighbours and became part of the local community. Superintendent Smith and his officers were puzzled by the fact that they seemed to have a very good lifestyle without any visible sign of real income, because the business was not making much. Their appearance in Britain from nowhere was also of concern.

Lock, Stock and Barrel

It was presumed that the next meeting for Lonsdale, Houghton and Gee would take place on the first Saturday in January 1961, a meeting that the authorities planned would be their last. At 7.30 that morning, the Dauphine drove away from Broadwey, heading for Bunty's house on Portland and by 8.45 they were crossing the causeway between Portland and Weymouth, *en route* to London. At Salisbury station, they parked the car but had missed the 11.50 to London Waterloo. They boarded the next one which arrived at 12.45pm. Smith gathered his team of ten men and two women Special Branch officers and briefed them. Police cars were parked in the approach to Waterloo station and the team were disguised, as railway porters, down-at heel men and match-sellers, amongst others. Superintendent Smith wore a natty beret and waited at platform 14 for the arrival of the Salisbury train.

Houghton and Gee disembarked from the train, Bunty carrying a shopping basket in which was a parcel. They walked out of the station and unexpectedly jumped on a number 68 bus in Waterloo Road. Fortunately, a couple of alert Special Brach officers also got on the bus. About 15 minutes later, they got off at a market at East Street in Walworth. After strolling through the market stalls, they took the bus back to Waterloo and by 4.30 were outside the Old Vic. Smith had already spotted the white Studebaker parked and, sure enough, Lonsdale arrived and greeted the other two. They began to walk down Lower Marsh Road, Lonsdale at one point taking the basket from Bunty. The transfer having happened, Smith gave the signal, a white handkerchief waved behind his back. While his officers converged on the scene, he ran towards the trio and stood in front of them, saying: 'You are all under arrest. I am a police officer.'

Houghton and Gee were, understandably, shocked. Houghton simply said 'What?' Ethel Gee gasped 'Oh'. Lonsdale, however, remained unmoved and said nothing. Police cars pulled up alongside them and they were taken away. The message that hit the police airwaves was 'Lock, stock and barrel', the code that signified a successful operation.

At Scotland Yard, when Lonsdale was searched, two envelopes were found, one containing £125, the other $300. Lonsdale told them when asked for his address: 'To any questions you might ask me, the answer is "no"'. He also asked them whether, as he looked likely to be staying the night, they could find a good chess player to play against. Smith obligingly ensured that there was a chess player in his escort. Harry Houghton's reaction was less sanguine. 'I have been a bloody fool,' he said. Bunty, meanwhile, was in denial. 'I have done nothing wrong,' she insisted.

But in the shopping basket she had brought to London was a parcel sealed with tape. Unwrapped, it revealed undeveloped film, 310 photographs of part of a secret Admiralty book that contained details of ships, fleet orders and drawings that were connected to the nuclear submarine *Dreadnought*. The culprits' homes were searched and more material was found. At Bunty's house, amongst other items was a document in her handwriting that presented details of anti-submarine equipment and its future development. The search of Houghton's cottage revealed documents, an Exakta camera given to him by Lonsdale and £650 hidden in a paint tin on the shelf of his garden shed. A Swan Vestas matchbox was discovered with a false bottom in which was a piece of paper bearing a freehand sketch of a part of London that highlighted a door between Westbourne

Park Road and Blenheim Crescent. This was used to arrange meetings. At Lonsdale's London flat, a number of incriminating items were found, including the Ronson lighter with the false bottom which contained some one-time pads, and £1,800 was discovered in the bottom of a Chinese scroll. A microdot reader and three negatives of transmitter signals were located in secret compartments in a tin of Yardley's after-shave talcum powder. A Canadian passport was found in Lonsdale's wardrobe, issued on 21 January 1955, in the name of Gordon Arnold Lonsdale, along with a birth certificate for him, issued in Ontario on 7 December 1954, certifying that he was born at Cobalt, Timiskaming District on 7 August 1924. A radio receiver was also found.

Meanwhile, a squad of Special Branch officers raided the Krogers' bungalow in Ruislip. As the couple made themselves ready for the journey to Scotland Yard, Helen Kroger tried to burn something she was concealing under her coat. It was a white envelope containing a coded message and the names of several streets with numbers typed beside each. This had been in the case belonging to Lonsdale that had been opened at the bank the previous August. There were also three microdots that were letters from Lonsdale's wife to him as well as one from him to her that was to be transmitted to Moscow. The Krogers, it seemed, provided the means by which Lonsdale communicated Houghton and Gee's information to Moscow Centre, something that was confirmed by the discovery of a radio transmitter hidden in the basement of their bungalow.

On 8 January, as their respective houses were being searched, the five spies were charged with 'conspiring together, and with other persons unknown, to commit offences against the Official Secrets Act 1911'. They were fingerprinted and the Krogers' prints, which were sent to the FBI in the United States, were found to actually be those of Morris and Lona Cohen who had disappeared from New York on 17 July

1950, the day that the spies Julius and Ethel Rosenberg were arrested. The Rosenbergs would later be executed. Since then, the Krogers, inveterate communists, had travelled the world and assumed new identities as Helen and Peter Kroger before arriving in Britain.

Trial, Sentence and Beyond

The five appeared in front of the Lord Chief Justice, Lord Parker, at the Old Bailey in March 1961, Houghton's defence insisting that his first handler, Nikki, had threatened him from the start and that he had once been beaten up by Russian agents. He claimed to have been very frightened. Bunty Gee agreed that she had taken Admiralty files, including the ones found on the day of her arrest, from the office and that she had posed as Harry Houghton's wife but she maintained that she had never been paid for her information. The Krogers denied that they had ever engaged in spying, Helen explaining away the microdots by saying that Lonsdale had asked her to look after the envelope containing them. For his part, Lonsdale attempted to take all the blame himself, telling the court that he had left all the incriminating items in their house without their knowledge.

It was all to no avail, as they were each found guilty. Describing Lonsdale as 'a professional spy', Lord Parker sentenced him to 25 years in prison. The Krogers were each sentenced to 20 years, and Harry Houghton and Ethel Gee were each sentenced to 15 years.

Eight months after the trial, it was revealed that Gordon Lonsdale was actually a Russian, born Konon Trofimovich Molody in Moscow in 1922. At the age of seven, he had been sent to California to live with an aunt but had returned to the Soviet Union at 16. While fighting with the Red Army during the Second World War, he attended a military spy school. He was sent to Canada in 1954, assuming the identity of Gordon Lonsdale before sailing to England in March 1955.

Lonsdale/Molody was a valuable commodity and, after only three years of his sentence, the British government cashed in his value by agreeing an exchange for Greville Wynne, a British businessman imprisoned in the Soviet Union for spying. Wynne, who had indeed been working for MI5, had been sentenced to eight years but was not bearing his sentence well. The two men were exchanged on 22 April 1964 at Checkpoint Heerstrasse, between East and West Berlin.

Little is really known about Molody after he returned home, but the acclaimed Russian spy movie, *Dead Season* is based on his activities. His autobiography, *Spy*, was published in Britain in 1965 and he died while picking mushrooms near Moscow five years later, aged just 48.

The Krogers, or Cohens, also served only a part of their sentences. They were exchanged for the jailed British lecturer, Gerald Brooke, in October 1969, after serving eight-and-a-half years. It turned out that they were American by birth, although the Russians insisted they were Polish so that they would not be extradited to the United States where they could have faced the death penalty for treason. They lived in Moscow for the remainder of their lives, Morris training spies. Lona died in 1992, aged seventy-nine, and Morris passed away three years later, aged eighty-four.

After serving a little more than nine years of their sentences, Harry Houghton and Ethel Gee were released on parole on 12 May 1970. Houghton travelled to Bournemouth and Bunty returned to her home in Hambro Street, Portland where her mother had died four years previously. A booing and jeering crowd awaited her.

Just before his release, Houghton released a statement that said: 'As long as I live, my main objective is to love and cherish Miss Gee and do all in my power to help her to get back to normality after nine long years of imprisonment. I was the one who was responsible for the tragic events in which she became involved and, in spite of this, she has never once reproached me… she is a woman in a million, such love is hard to find.' In a television interview he admitted to spying simply for money, saying that he was not an ideological communist. For her part, Bunty insisted that she never wanted to see Houghton again. Not long after, however, they were together again and married in April 1971 at Poole Registry Office. She moved into Houghton's house in Poole. Houghton's book, *Operation Portland: The Autobiography of a Spy*, was published in 1972 and he died in 1985, a year after Ethel.

George Blake:
'A Soldier in the Cold War'

From Rotterdam to Cairo

He was a walking contradiction – a Christian who was a communist; a lover of the House of Orange, despite his communism; a man of peace who was responsible for the deaths of upwards of 40 people; a lover of England who comprehensively betrayed the country he had adopted as his own. He was George Blake, possibly the most dangerous double agent in the storied annals of MI6.

Blake's exotic story began in Rotterdam in the Netherlands where he was born on 11 November 1922. His father, Albert Behar, was Jewish, a scion of a wealthy Constantinople family who had become a British citizen while fighting for Britain in the First World War. This also gave Blake British citizenship. By all accounts, George was a serious-minded boy, polite, conscientious and honest. He was very bright but did not make friends easily. The family was conservative and religious, leading him to harbour ambitions to be a pastor in the Dutch Reformed Church when he grew up. As a child he worshipped the Dutch Royal Family and this was still very much part of him decades later, despite his communist beliefs.

Albert had a small factory that made gloves for shipworkers, but it suffered badly in the Depression. Finally, in 1936, when George was 13, his father, who had been ailing for some time, died, and not long after, it was decided that George should go and stay with Albert's wealthy sister Zephira in Cairo where her husband, Daniel Curiel, was a banker. It was only as arrangements were being made that George learned for the first time that his father had actually been Jewish and not Catholic as he had pretended to be.

Suddenly, this Dutch boy was thrown into the melting pot that was Cairo. His home was a mansion set in a park in the midst of palm-trees in Zamalek, an affluent and exclusive suburb in the west of the city. There were servants and the Curiels were a cultured family whose hearts really lay in France where they summered every year. George was sent to an English school in Cairo and then a French one, and his conscientiousness and intelligence meant that he did well. Leaving the Netherlands had been a wrench, though, and he suffered from homesickness. His mind was occupied, however, by the lively discussion round the dinner table, often led by his cousin Henri, eight years older and something of a hero to him. Henri was in line to take over his father's business but, by the time George arrived, he was preoccupied with Marxism. He was particularly upset by the gap between rich and poor in Egypt, witnessing for himself the dire conditions in which the workers on his family's vast estate on the Nile Delta worked. This was Blake's first encounter with communism but he claimed that it had little influence on his political views at the time.

The Second World War

When the Second World War broke out in September 1939, the 17-year-old Blake was on a summer visit to Rotterdam which is where it was decided he should stay. The city was devastated by German bombs in May 1940 and the Netherlands surrendered to Hitler's forces not long after this. Blake's mother and sisters, who had been living in The Hague, managed to board a boat for England, leaving young George behind, forcing him and his grandmother to go and live with an uncle near Zutphen in the east of the country. Being British, he was interned with other foreigners by the Germans but, as he was under military age, he was released after a month.

Immediately, he joined the Dutch resistance and his life of subterfuge began. He was fortunate in that he looked much younger than his actual age and so was able to travel unhindered throughout Holland for a couple of years, working as a courier for Vrij Nederland (Free Netherlands), delivering illegal newspapers and carrying intelligence about the Germans that was sent on to England. His career as a spy had begun, but he decided he wanted to do more and resolved to get to England to join the British army. In 1942, therefore, he set out on a perilous journey, through Belgium, France and into Spain, finally crossing to England from Gibraltar on the RMS *Empress of Australia*. He was already looking to the future:

'I could have stayed in the Netherlands, but I wanted to be an agent for the English and Dutch service, and so I wanted to go to England and get sent back to the Netherlands. I thought – and it was true – that once I had got to England and had training there, then I could do much more than what I was doing in the Netherlands. I very much wanted to be a real agent.'

He was reunited with his family, who decided to change their name to the more English 'Blake'.

SIS Officer

Eager to fight, he enlisted in the Royal Navy but, on finishing his training, was summoned to London out of the blue for an interview at the Admiralty. Having taken notice of his resistance work in the Netherlands, the British Secret Intelligence Service (SIS) thought he might be useful to them and his father's service in the First World War further bolstered their belief that he would make a good officer. However, as Blake later pointed out to one writer, his allegiance in the war was to the cause of anti-Nazism, not to Great Britain. He joined P8, which was the Dutch section of SIS, given the task of escorting Dutch resistance fighters who were to board planes and be parachuted into the Netherlands. He also became involved in the interpretation of the often garbled messages that were sent back by these courageous people.

When the war ended 18 months later, Blake once again considered the ministry as a future career, but SIS retained his services, sending him to the Netherlands to wind down its Dutch operations. Although, like most of Europe, the country was in dire straits, he had a good time, enjoying requisitioned champagne and brandy as well as the company of attractive women. He fell in love with Iris Peake, a secretary in SIS. It has been suggested that the unsatisfactory dissolution of this relationship might have contributed to his decision to betray Britain. Iris was from a different social class altogether and would go on to become a lady-in-waiting to Princess Margaret. When Blake visited the family seat in Yorkshire, her father, Sir Osbert Peake – later Viscount Ingleby – a Conservative MP, informed him that he had no chance of marrying his daughter. Of course, the couple may never have had any intention of getting married – Blake himself denied that they did – but such a blatant example of snobbery can have done little to endear Blake to Britain's social hierarchy.

By 1947, the focus of Western security services had turned eastwards, the Soviet Union was now viewed as the enemy and Blake became involved in recruiting former German naval and Wehrmacht officers to work as agents in Germany's Russian Zone. Using former enemies against former allies went somewhat against his principles, however; he described it as 'the first breach in my ideological outlook'.

He was particularly well-liked by the SIS, although his colleagues found him a bit arrogant and often rude. But, he looked the part, tall and good-looking, without the obvious flaws of many of his fellows. Self-contained and confident, he appeared to be cut out to be a spy and was made a permanent member of the Secret Services. They sent him to Cambridge University for a few months to learn Russian.

Korea

After Cambridge, Blake was posted to Korea, an assignment that disappointed him. The Far East had never really interested him and he would rather have had a posting to the Middle East. In preparation, however, he read one text that made a lasting impression on him – a handbook on Marxism written for SIS officers by the SIS theoretician, Carew Hunt. Blake emerged from his reading believing that communist ideals actually differed little from those of Christianity. They made complete sense to him.

It was 1948 and the attention of the world would be focused on Korea in just a couple of years. After the Second World War, the country had been divided, the Americans in control of the south and the Russians the north. Even then, war seemed an inevitability and Britain's position would be one of neutrality,

Blake was told; he would be able to remain in Seoul. His superior in the Korean capital was Sir Vyvyan Holt, a career diplomat and Oriental scholar, and a man who became a bit of a hero to him. Blake's job was to recruit spies in the Russian east coast port of Vladivostok, some 450 miles north-east of Seoul. What his bosses had forgotten, however, was that to get there he would have to cross both the border into North Korea from the south and the border into the Soviet Union from North Korea. Blake had no chance of even getting into North Korea, let alone onto Soviet territory. He soon became disenchanted by the sight of poor South Koreans living a squalid existence on the streets while the Americans in the country lived privileged lives of luxury. The South Korean regime's opponents began to look more attractive to him.

The experience became even worse when it was announced that Britain was lending its support to America, taking the side of what Blake saw as a corrupt regime. The consequence of this decision for the British diplomatic contingent became clear one Sunday in July 1950, following the invasion of the South Korean capital by troops from the north. Three vehicles carrying North Korean soldiers arrived at the British Legation and took prisoner Sir Vyvyan and members of his staff, including George Blake and the Consul, Norman Owen. They joined around 70 civilians and 750 American prisoners of war and were marched north. It was winter and about half of the group died on the march, from starvation or cold or as a result of the North Korean guards' savage brutality. Blake never forgot the horrors he witnessed on that march and he was disgusted by the sight of huge US bombers destroying defenceless North Korean villages and equally defenceless North Korean lives. He questioned even more the West's mission in Korea.

Finally, he and his fellow British prisoners and some French nationals were taken to the comparative quiet of a farmhouse near Manpo in the north. They felt isolated and forgotten, but at least they had food and shelter and were safer than they had been in a while. The North Koreans brought them reading material – Lenin's book, *The State and the Revolution* and two volumes of Karl Marx's *Das Kapital* which Blake devoured, several times over, effectively becoming a communist through reading them. He decided that if and when he got back home, he had several options. He could find a new job; he could join the British Communist Party and work for it; or he could become a Soviet double agent. He opted for the most difficult option, resolving to become a double agent. To set the ball rolling, he handed the North Korean commander a note he asked be delivered to the Russian Embassy. Soon, he was talking to a KGB colonel, Nikolai Loenko who brought Blake bread, jam and chocolate. He gave him an assignment, asking him to write a paper on the structure of SIS. The Soviets compared what Blake described with what they had already received from Kim Philby and, when they saw that the two accounts were more or less the same, they knew that Blake was serious about becoming a double agent and could be trusted.

'Diomid'

After three years in captivity, Blake and his fellow-prisoners were released and returned to Britain as heroes. He was welcomed back into the SIS after a two-day debrief and was then given time off to recover from his ordeal. In September 1953, he resumed work in London, regarded as a heroic ex-prisoner of the North Koreans. He was also, of course, a Soviet agent, with the codename 'Diomid' – Russian for diamond – and at lunchtimes, when his colleagues went out to lunch, he would pull out his tiny Minox camera and photograph whatever top secret documents he could find lying around. He was given his own handler, Sergei Kondrashev, ostensibly the Soviet Embassy's first secretary for cultural relations.

They first met in October 1953, Blake delivering to him a motherlode of secrets, including details of the telephone taps and secret microphones the SIS used to listen into Soviet communications around Western Europe. Such valuable information further confirmed Blake's trustworthiness as an agent. They would meet every three weeks on buses or street corners in the suburbs and Blake would hand over whatever he had uncovered since their last meeting. The Americans estimated that Blake handed over 4,720 pages of material, some of which may have given the Soviets an indication of British negotiating positions at important international summits in the late 1950s. Dick White, head of SIS from 1956 to 1968, reckoned that Blake did more damage than Kim Philby. He was, quite simply, unique.

He had been dating a young SIS secretary whose father and sister also worked for the organisation and they married at Marylebone Registry Office in September 1954. The precariousness of his life had made him try to put her off, but she would not take no for an answer. Speaking on German television in the 1990s, he recounted how, during the Second World War, soldiers would often marry before they were sent to the front. He likened his situation to those men, saying 'I was a soldier in the Cold War'.

In April 1955, Blake was moved to Berlin as head of station. His work for the Russians was by this time bearing fruit. That month 521 'agents of western secret services' were arrested by the East German authorities, 105 of them believed to be British agents. It was a time of great tension and it was feared the world was hurtling towards nuclear catastrophe. Therefore, it was essential for each side, East and West, to be as up-to-date on the other side's intentions as possible. One way the British and Americans were achieving that was via a spy tunnel that they had dug under the Soviet sector of Berlin, designed to intercept communications. Operation Stopwatch/Gold was shrouded in the utmost secrecy, but, even before it was built, Blake had divulged its secrets to his masters in Moscow. Of course, if they had let on that they knew about the tunnel, serious questions would have been asked as to how they knew and those could have led to the exposure of Blake, this most valuable of assets. They had bent over backwards to protect him so far, and no more than three people in Moscow knew his true identity. Once a decent interval of time had passed – just over 11 months – the tap was 'discovered' and closed down.

Exposure and Trial

By 1959, it seemed that George Blake's luck was running out. He was transferred back to London possibly because SIS suspected him of spying for the Soviets. A year later, he was almost certainly under suspicion. His access to secret material was removed by sending him away, ostensibly to learn Arabic at a language school in Lebanon. At this point, he was exhausted by his double life and was looking for a way out. Nonetheless, Lebanon was a wonderful place to be in 1960, with a vibrant social scene, parties, a casino, skiing in the nearby mountains and swimming in the sea. He was happy with life with a good marriage and a third child on the way.

A reckoning was coming, however. In 1958, a letter from someone calling himself 'Heckenschütze' – 'sniper' in German – was received by the US ambassador to Switzerland. Claiming to be a senior intelligence officer in a communist country, this 'sniper' identified seven Russian spies working in America, Israel and Britain. Alongside this he sent a list he claimed came from the KGB, of a number of Polish officials that the British in Warsaw were trying to recruit as double agents. It was obvious that this list must have been passed to the KGB by a mole in the British Secret Service. This was denied by the British who said the names could have come from anywhere but it was then learned that the British had actually sent the exact same list to the CIA a year previously. This confirmed that there was a double agent in British intelligence. Only ten people in SIS had had access to the document and, after an enquiry, all ten were cleared of any blame. The British, however, were certain that they did have a mole. Too many operations were failing and too many agents were disappearing.

Heckenschütze, who defected in West Berlin in January 1961 and turned out to be Michal Goleniewski, a Polish counter-intelligence officer, identified Blake as the mole. Blake was summoned to London on the pretence that it was to talk about a new appointment. Some thought he might simply disappear and turn up in Moscow a few years later. Blake did suspect he was walking into a trap, but his handler reassured him that, according to Moscow, SIS did not suspect him.

Blake's worst fears were realised. On his return to London, he was immediately arrested. He said nothing for the first two-and-a half days of his interrogation but then cracked when it was insinuated that he had been tortured and blackmailed in North Korea which had led to him becoming a spy. 'No,' he blurted out. 'Nobody tortured me! No, nobody blackmailed me! I myself approached the Soviets and offered my services to them of my own accord.' He told them that his espionage had been carried out for purely ideological reasons, and that he had frequently turned down large sums of money offered by the Russians. He went on to confess to everything over the next few days. Meanwhile, back in Lebanon, his wife Gillian was told and immediately believed what they were telling her.

Blake's story was the latest in a long line of spy scandals that had blighted Harold Macmillan's Conservative government. Things were so bad that the Prime Minister disparaged the Secret Service, describing it as the '*so-called* Security Service'. On being told about Blake's arrest, he suggested that it might just be enough to bring down the government and even suggested that Blake be offered immunity to spare the government the intense embarrassment of a trial. But Dick White insisted that Blake should be the first SIS officer ever to be prosecuted for espionage.

Much of the trial, which began at the Old Bailey on 3 May 1961, was conducted *in camera*, so secret was much of the material to be discussed. Lord Chief Justice Parker presided and Sir Reginald Manningham-Buller, whose daughter Eliza would become director-general of MI5 in 2007, prosecuted. Blake was represented by Jeremy Hutchinson, reputed to be one of the people on whom John Mortimer based his character Rumpole of the Bailey. The main concern for the prosecution was that Blake would withdraw his confession, without which the prosecution would fail but, in the end, he did not. The judge laid the groundwork for what was to come, describing the case in his summing up as 'one of the worst that can be envisaged in times of peace'. For a moment, Blake was convinced that he was going to be sentenced to death but the maximum sentence for offences under section 1 of the Official Secrets Act 1911 is 14 years. He was convicted of three counts of spying for a potential enemy and sentenced to 14 years for each, to be served consecutively, a total of 42 years, the longest non-life sentence ever delivered in a British court.

The Prime Minister probably sat down that evening with a large Scotch and relaxed, thinking that was the end of the Blake case and the embarrassment it had caused him and his government.

How wrong he was!

Escape

Blake had been treated harshly by Lord Chief Justice Parker. After all, Anthony Blunt would be allowed to hold on to his knighthood until 1979 and to continue working as Surveyor of the Queen's Pictures. John Cairncross escaped prosecution after confessing and Philby was offered immunity from prosecution if he agreed to confess and cooperate fully, although he was too wily ever to confess. We are unlikely to know if the different treatment was due to the fact that Philby was viewed as 'one of us', a gentleman, while Blake was a half-Jewish foreigner. He was never liked by his colleagues and, for that reason, no one from within SIS was on his side. He had certainly been excluded from the establishment in Britain, but then again, it was probably a club of which he did not really want to be a member. He respected and admired the country, but his feelings never went deep enough to make him question betraying it. It was not his, after all.

In prison, he practised yoga and studied when he was not sewing mailbags. He taught Arabic, French and German to the other prisoners and helped them with legal questions. He befriended two peace activists, Pat Pottle and Michael Randle, jailed for protesting at a United States Air Force base at Wethersfield in Essex, who both felt that Blake's sentence was unduly harsh. Blake, for his part, had been planning his escape from the first minute he entered his cell. He asked Pottle to get a message to the Soviet Embassy when he was released. He told him:

'If you feel you can help me on your release, go to the Russian embassy, introduce yourself and say, "I bring you greetings from Louise". Between 10 and 11 o'clock we exercise in the yard outside D Hall. If a rope ladder is thrown over the wall at the spot I have marked X [there was a sketch enclosed] as near to 10.30 as possible, I will be ready.'

If the Russians were in agreement, they should put an advert in the personal column of the *Sunday Times* saying: 'LOUISE LONGING TO SEE YOU'. That would let Blake know that the breakout would take place on the following Sunday. Meanwhile, there was bad news. Gillian had met another man and wanted to marry him.

Blake found another accomplice in a rebellious Irishman named Sean Bourke. On his release, he made contact with Randle and Pottle and purchased a rope ladder and two walkie-talkies, one of which was smuggled to Blake in prison. On the evening of 26 October 1966, after the message had appeared in the paper, Bourke parked his car outside Wormwood Scrubs and, at 6.55, Blake scrambled up the rope ladder that Bourke had thrown over the wall and leapt to the ground from the top, breaking his wrist and gashing his forehead.

After hiding out in London for a few weeks, he was smuggled to West Berlin through Belgium and West Germany in a camper van in which Michael Randle and his family were pretending to have a holiday. In West Berlin, he made for the border crossing between East and West and introduced himself to an astonished East German border guard. He had made it.

Moscow

When Randle and Pottle were finally prosecuted in 1991 for helping Blake to escape – Sean Bourke having died in 1982 – they claimed there was a moral justification for their actions – Blake's sentence was excessive and inhuman. Astonishingly, they were acquitted.

Blake, meanwhile, had settled into life in Moscow. Initially, he had shared a flat with the Irishman Bourke who, ever on the lookout for adventure, had travelled to Moscow. In 1968, however, Blake married Ida Mikhailovna Kareyeva and they had a child. He was given the rank of colonel in the KGB, but found a job as a Dutch translator for a Russian publisher. It was not terribly exciting and he found it to be a solitary occupation but, eventually, he was employed as a Middle East expert by the research institute, the Institute of World Economy and International Relations.

The British government was still vengeful towards him. When a British publisher published his autobiography, *No Other Choice*, in 1990, he was paid £60,000, but the government intervened, preventing him from receiving a further £90,000. Taking the case to the European Court of Human Rights, because it took the government nine years to come to a decision, he was awarded £5,000 compensation.

He socialised occasionally with Kim Philby and his wife, but they fell out. His best friend in Moscow was his fellow spy, Donald Maclean, who, he said, gave him good advice and helped him to settle in the Russian capital. The two were made for each other; both were of an intellectual bent and both kept others at arm's length. Their flights from the UK had been similar, too – there was an element of drama and both left behind families, although Maclean's joined him eventually.

George Blake lived to the grand old age of 98, dying on Boxing Day, 2020. He is buried in Troyekurovskoye Cemetery on Moscow's western edge. He remained a Marxist-Leninist to the end and, when accused of being a traitor, he explained that he had never felt British, adding: 'To betray, you first have to belong'.

John Vassall: The Dandy Clerk Who Became a Traitor

Looking for a Future

In the 1950s, being gay was not easy. Homosexuality was illegal, for a start, its status changing only with the passing of the Sexual Offences Act in 1967. Before that time, it was very much something to be concealed, especially in view of the demonisation of homosexuals that took place in the 1950s. This reached a crescendo with the arrest of the actor Sir John Gielgud at a public toilet in Chelsea and his subsequent conviction for importuning men. The world of espionage also brought moral outrage on account of the sexual tendencies of its practitioners. Guy Burgess and Donald Maclean were both victimised in the press as homosexuals. The link between homosexuality, communism and treason was well-established in the years after the war.

John Vassall was gay, but he was never a communist. He was born in 1924 to a father who was chaplain at St Bartholomew's Hospital in London and a mother who was a nurse at the hospital. So far, so good – a good family with ancestors who had been respected figures in education and who had enjoyed sporting success. Vassall attended several prep schools before going to Monmouth Grammar School, a public school for boys. By the age of 12, according to his autobiography, he had already had his first homosexual experience, at a boarding school at Seaford in Sussex.

After leaving school in 1942, he tried to enlist as a pilot in the Royal Air Force but his application was rejected. While awaiting call-up, he worked as a clerk in a City of London branch of the Midland Bank, but remained there only briefly before a friend of his family found him a position as a temporary clerk in the Victualling Department of the Admiralty. He was eventually called up to the RAF in 1943 and, as was so often the case throughout his life, he found the tasks he was called upon to perform demeaning, beneath his dignity. Things improved when he was transferred to the photographic branch and was sent to north-west Europe. He was now responsible for taking, developing and printing photographs for the RAF.

Honourably discharged in 1947, he worried about the path his life was taking. To try to resolve the issues with his sexuality, he wondered if religion might provide an answer. He had a dilemma, as his father was a Church of England vicar, but his mother, to whom he was very close, had chosen to adopt the Roman Catholic religion, understandably a source of some discord in his parents' marriage. He decided, therefore, to become a Catholic, taking instruction before being received into the Catholic faith. At this time, he was living at home, spending several evenings a week drinking at West End clubs and bars wearing the expensive clothes he was able to buy. His sex life blossomed and he often spent weekends with men of means who lavished him with gifts and compliments in return for sexual favours.

But he was unhappy. His career and, consequently, his finances were not prospering. He failed several times to obtain the promotion he sought which he took as an affront to his increasingly inflated sense of himself. Suddenly, he seized upon an opportunity to advance his prospects and satisfy his taste for foreign travel, gained during the war – an advert for the position of clerk to the naval attaché at the British Embassy in Moscow. To his delight, he was offered the job and, at the age of 30, flew to Moscow. He was immediately captivated by the snowy Red Square and the sight of the Kremlin.

Partying in Moscow

His accommodation was a flat shared with two other junior embassy officials. He was soon thrown into a full social life but the restrictions of life in Moscow were anathema to him. There were certain parts of the city forbidden to westerners who were spied on everywhere they went. Although he dined with the ambassador, and socialised with all the other senior officials, he was lonely and critical of the fact that the embassy employees were left more or less to fend for themselves. However, he had met a gay Polish interpreter, Sigmund Mikhailski, who worked at the embassy and who was happy to provide him with tickets to concerts and plays. What he did not realise was that he had been marked by the Soviets as a potential traitor.

Mikhailski and he often partied together and, on these occasions, he was introduced to a number of cultured and charming men. He was particularly attracted to one who arranged a number of dinner parties that Vassall attended. One night, he ended up at the Hotel Berlin, a luxurious establishment in the centre of Moscow. In a private dining room, after drinking a large amount of alcohol, he was advised to lie down on a large divan and he was persuaded to remove his clothing. Soon, there were three men in bed with him and he later recalled photographs were taken as the men had sex. In March 1955, after another party, he was in bed with another man when there was a knock at the door and he was asked to come into the adjoining room. There he found two men in dark overcoats and a couple of guards at the door blocking his escape. He was interrogated over a period of several hours, and informed that he had committed a serious criminal offence. They asked him questions about his personal life, finally enquiring whether he was homosexual. Vassall was shocked, but confirmed that he was, indeed, homosexual. Next they produced a box of photographs taken at the parties he had attended. He was pictured naked, grinning for the camera, or indulging in anal and oral sex with a variety of men. Of course, the whole point of it was blackmail. If he failed to do as they asked, the photographs would be shown to his employers and his family. His career would be over. Furthermore, he could go to prison in Russia, not a prospect to be relished. Eventually, he was released and his career as a spy for the KGB began.

Initially, they quizzed him about simple things such as the Embassy personnel he liked or disliked, but gradually over a period of eight months they began to require more, asking him to provide documents and files. He was unable to withstand the pressure and he was soon passing to them hard copies of important documents. In order for the documents to be copied, they had to be taken out of the embassy. He would put the material in question into an envelope and simply smuggle it out under his coat or in his briefcase. In the evening, the envelope would be passed to the Russians to be copied and was then given back to him to be returned the following morning. Of course, he was only able to provide them with material with which he came into contact but they seemed happy with that. And he was soon financially rewarded for his work, his new-found income enabling him to take trips to Rome and Frankfurt.

Return to London

When, after two years, his tour of duty in Moscow ended, Vassall wondered if, perhaps, that would mark the end of his espionage. His Russian handlers had other plans for him, of course. To his great disappointment, at his last rendezvous in Moscow, he was introduced to a man named Nikolaj Korovin whom he was instructed to meet on his return to London. Korovin explained to him the complex signals that were to be used. They were to be pencilled in a telephone box. The figure '1' in a circle was a sign that Vassall should be at a certain spot at a given time the following night; a number '2' in a circle meant that there would be a meeting on the Monday of the following week; a '3' in a circle meant that there would be a meeting on the first day of the second week; an 'X' in a circle gave warning that there should be no contact for a month. Pencilled brackets were the worst of all – they indicated that Vassall was being watched by Special Branch. Returning to London, he was given three months' special leave from his job, a time he spent travelling to Sweden, Canada and the United States, a trip mostly paid for by the KGB.

Back at work, he took up a position as a clerical officer in Naval Intelligence at the Admiralty. Soon, he had his first meeting with Korovin, at the distinctly unglamorous Frognal station in Finchley Road. Bizarrely, Vassall's instructions were that he had to wear a green Tyrolean hat, sporting a feather at the side, and carry that evening's newspapers under his arm. He was told he would be approached by Korovin who would utter the words: 'Can you please tell me the best way to get to Belsize Park tube station?' Vassall's response was to be: 'It is a long journey from here; the best way is to take a taxi.'

Korovin was a professional and had adapted to being in London, dressing like a city gent with an exquisitely cut Savile Row suit, a trilby and a rolled umbrella. They discussed Vassall's new job and the material to which he had access. Korovin gave him a bundle of large envelopes that he was to use to get documents out of the Admiralty. Meetings would be on Mondays at 7.30, always in different places. If Vassall suspected he was being followed to a meeting venue, he should signal this by kneeling down to tie a shoelace.

Meanwhile, Vassall tried to make progress in his career, but was always turned down by the promotions board which felt that he quite simply did not have the intelligence to do much more than he was already doing. He finally managed to get a move after a year, transferred to the private office of the Civil Lord, a position responsible for managing the Royal Navy's supporting civilian staff, as well as the works, buildings, departments and lands owned by the navy. The incumbent was the Conservative MP for Hillhead in Glasgow, Tam Galbraith. The move was a disappointment to Korovin because not a great deal of sensitive material passed through this office but Vassall loved being at the centre of government. He also got on very well with Galbraith, to the extent that, after his arrest, questions were asked about their relationship although there was nothing untoward in it.

Vassall was moving up in the world. He moved into a flat in

the exclusive Dolphin Square in Pimlico even though the rent amounted to half his total annual income from the Admiralty. To allay any suspicions from his colleagues as to how he could possibly afford to live in such an expensive location, he dropped hints about receiving legacies in the wills of friends and relatives. That year, Galbraith was moved in a Cabinet reshuffle. Vassall also moved, this time to the military branch of the Admiralty, a posting more to the liking of his Soviet handlers. Now he had access to all kinds of material of interest to them, documents dealing with torpedoes, radar and anti-submarine equipment. Vassall would meet with Korovin in expensive restaurants and pass him classified material.

His world was rocked in January 1961 when the arrests of Ethel Gee, Harry Houghton and Gordon Lonsdale – the so-called Portland spy ring – hit the headlines. He was terrified he would be next, but even so, kept his next appointment. The man he met was not Korovin who appeared to have been summoned back to Moscow. In reality, Korovin had fled when he heard of the arrests of the Portland spies, fearful that he was going to be implicated. Vassall's new contact was Nikolai 'Nikki' Karpekov. He informed Vassall that, in spite of the arrests, all was well, although operations were being temporarily suspended.

Arrest and Trial

Months passed, the Portland spies were convicted and jailed, but there was no increase in security at the Admiralty. Vassall began to relax. He was off the hook and felt secure enough to return to his espionage activities. He used some of the money given to him by the Russians to have a holiday in Capri and was due to fly to Rome for another holiday on 15 September 1962. Three days before that flight, he looked out of the window of his office and spotted a car parked in Whitehall with three men sitting in it. He panicked at once and, grabbing his hat and briefcase, ran to the north-west exit of the Admiralty, away from the main exit, only to run straight into the waiting arms of a couple of Special Branch officers. He had actually been under suspicion since the previous June and Superintendent George Smith, known as 'Spycatcher' Smith because of his involvement in a number of cases of espionage, had spent the months since building a case against him.

Vassall's exposure as a spy came courtesy of Anatoliy Golitsyn, a senior officer in the KGB, who defected to the United States in 1961. Another defector, Yuri Nosenko, who handed himself over in 1964, confirmed Vassall's espionage. It is also thought that material provided by yet another defector, Michal Goleniewski, contributed to the case against John Vassall. Needless to say, Vassall was horrified by the turn of events, later writing: 'Their faces were expressionless and somehow I knew it was all over. The whole of my blackmail experiences and my life as a spy had suddenly come to an abrupt end. I felt a lost soul who could not look to anyone for a word of comfort.'

In the car, on the short journey from Whitehall to Scotland Yard, Smith asked Vassall if he had any cameras and Vassall readily replied that he was in possession of an Exakta and a Minox, the tools of the spy. 'There is a film in the Exakta,' he added. 'I think you will find on it what you are looking for.' His flat was searched and the cameras and 14 rolls of film were found, the film hidden in a concealed compartment in a bookcase, some of it containing secret documents. After an interrogation lasting a number of hours, Vassall signed a confession, his head, by this time, 'spinning with nausea, physical and mental.'

On 16 October 1962, John Vassall pleaded guilty to four charges under the Official Secrets Act, 1911 and was sentenced by Lord Parker, the Lord Chief Justice, to 18 years' imprisonment. The judge said at one point: 'I take the view that one of the compelling reasons for what you did was pure selfish greed.'

The Macmillan government was thrown into turmoil by the

exposure of yet another spy, hot on the heels of the Portland case. Macmillan, who was about to be rocked by yet another scandal, this one involving his Secretary of State for War, John Profumo, was reported to be very unhappy that the case was going to be made public. 'When my gamekeeper shoots a fox,' he is reported to have said, 'he doesn't go and hang it up outside the master of foxhounds drawing room; he buries it out of sight. But you just can't shoot a spy as you did in the war. There will be a great public trial. Then the security services will not be praised for how efficient they are, but blamed for how hopeless they are. Then there will be an enquiry. There will be a terrible row in the press. There will then be a debate in the House of Commons, and the government will probably fall. Why the devil did you catch him?'

He was right. There was a furore in the media. In the *Daily Mirror*, of 23 October, for instance, this appeared: 'What manner of man was John Vassall? Vanity and greed were his twin gods, and they turned that dandy clerk into a traitor. He gave away thousands of secrets to his Russian masters so that he could parade in elegant suits and silk shirts and live the life of a man about town.' Other papers made insinuations about homosexuals in top government posts. The First Lord of the Admiralty, Lord Carrington, was criticised by the press for the Admiralty's failure to spot Vassall's excessive spending.

Finally, Harold Macmillan announced an inquiry into the Vassall affair. The Vassall Tribunal, conducted by Viscount Radcliffe, Mr Justice Barry and Milner Holland QC, found that Vassall had worked independently and had not been helped by others, and the press was heavily criticised for its treatment of the case. During the proceedings, two journalists, Brendan Mulholland of the *Daily Mail* and Reg Foster of the *Daily Sketch*, famously refused to name the sources for their stories and were jailed for contempt of court, for six months and three months respectively.

John Vassall served 10 of the 18 years to which he had been sentenced, in Wormwood Scrubs, Maidstone and Durham prisons. A model prisoner, he was released on parole in October 1972. His autobiography, *Vassall: The Autobiography of a Spy*, was published in 1975, after he had spent time in a monastery writing it. He changed his name to Phillips and lived in St John's Wood, working as an administrator at the British Records Association as well as for a firm of solicitors in Gray's Inn. He died following a heart attack on a bus on 18 November 1996, aged 72.

Geoffrey Prime:
The Inadequate Traitor

'Yes, Mr Cole,' he said, looking at the clock and then back at his interrogators. 'At four o'clock today, 26 June 1982, I now wish to tell you the whole truth of this tragic affair. I cannot go on talking about my wife whilst I am continuing to tell lies. It will take a long time. Could we have a short break, then I'll start from 1968 when this affair started.'

Having uttered these words to Chief Superintendent David Cole, Geoffrey Prime sat back in his chair and smiled, as if he had suddenly had a heavy burden lifted off his shoulders, the weight of 14 years of duplicity, lying to his bosses, fooling his colleagues and betraying both of the women he had married. It had taken 19 exhausting hours to arrive at this point, but finally he was there. He would make the confession needed to gain a conviction.

A Loner

Geoffrey Prime was born in Alton in Staffordshire to parents who were already in their forties, his mother, Annie, almost dying in childbirth. She was obese and would spend what was left of her life confined to her bed for long periods. For the rest of his life, Geoffrey could not escape the guilt he felt for what he had put her through and, as a child, he was often reminded of it by his parents. His father was a semi-skilled wire-drawer at a copper and brass works who worked hard to keep his family together, what spare time he had given to managing the family's smallholding. He was a hard, uncompromising man with little time to spare for his children. Geoffrey's two brothers and sister were considerably older than him, and he became isolated and introverted, which continued at school where he struggled to make friends and maintain relationships. Nonetheless, he was bright and, aged 11, won a scholarship to St Joseph's Roman Catholic College in Stoke-on-Trent. In order to attend the school, he had to get up at 5.45 every morning and was not home until early evening. He was cut off from life in the village and had little chance of making friends, even if he had wanted to. His only interest was Stoke City football club. In adolescence, he had his first sexual experience when an older relative seduced him. This gave him a fear of rejection by the opposite sex which undoubtedly contributed to his later sexual deviance.

His family had little interest in his academic progress. No family member had ever previously gone to grammar school as he did and, when he was 16, his father insisted on him taking a job, as a junior wages clerk in the factory where he worked. He was paid £50 a year but it was grindingly boring. He devoured books, however, and worked hard to lose his Potteries accent. At 18, like every other young British man at the time, he was called up to do National Service and it was life-changing. That year he joined the Royal Air Force and his mother finally gave up her struggle and died.

He found life in the RAF hard, loathing the absence of privacy and the strict discipline of military life. His discomfort was heightened by his introverted nature which manifested itself as a form of superiority that did not make him any friends. He also came across as prudish in the eyes of the other young men who were far more experienced sexually. Found to suffer from colour blindness, a career as aircrew had to be abandoned. Instead, he ended up working in the stores, stacking shelves and issuing items. It was not long, however, before his facility for languages was spotted, a talent that had first emerged at school. At the time, the military was desperate for Russian-speakers but he would have to sign on for a longer period if he was going to take the course. Prime signed on for nine years, the prospect of foreign travel, more money and improved promotion prospects convincing him. He went to Scotland to begin his course and, a month later, he was promoted to acting sergeant and sent to London University to further his Russian studies. Sadly, he lasted for only three months at university, blaming his social and intellectual status and claiming his fellow students received preferential treatment. This was not the first time he had blamed others for his failure and was not to be the last. Losing his rank and privileges, he returned to serve a further six years in the mundane world of the stores.

It was during his only overseas posting – to Kenya – that a social and political conscience began to awaken in Geoffrey Prime. The living conditions of the Kenyan people affected him greatly and he started to blame capitalism and the evils of colonialisation for their suffering. Only communism, he thought, as practised in the Soviet Union, could free people from poverty and hardship. He was not afraid to make his views clear to anyone who listened, but at no point did anyone in authority hear any alarm bells. While in Kenya, he indulged his language skills, learning to speak Swahili, but more importantly, he enjoyed his first relationship with a woman, a Kikuyu prostitute seven years older than him. She was hardly likely to subject him to the pain of rejection.

In 1962, with just three years to serve, he returned to Britain, working in Surrey for the Air Ministry. However, fearing life in the outside world, he resolved to have one more go at language training and signed on for a further three years. This time he applied himself, gaining an O-Level in Russian which led to the reward of a posting to Gatow in Berlin. Within a short time, he had picked up German. For four years, he worked as a voice radio operator in signals intelligence, attaining the rank of sergeant. He might reasonably have been expected to have extended his service because, after all, he was single, had no personal responsibilities and enjoyed being in Germany. But, instead, in 1968, aged 30 and having served 12 years, he suddenly quit. Returning home, he quickly found employment, as a linguist with the Government Communications Headquarters, more commonly known as GCHQ.

GCHQ

He worked in London, in a GCHQ office – the London Processing Group – that provided written versions of Russian broadcasts. Meanwhile, his private life still a wasteland, he signed up to a marriage agency, through which he was introduced to 28 year-old Helena Organ, head of the English department in a large London comprehensive. Within three weeks of meeting, they were engaged, and the marriage took place six months later. However, Prime was unable to consummate the marriage which sent him into a downward spiral of depression and despair. It seemed that sex for him only worked through being with a prostitute, making obscene telephone calls or indulging in voyeurism. Parting after four years, he and Helen were divorced in 1975. He shrugged off London and his failed marriage with a transfer to GCHQ in Cheltenham.

Now working with highly sensitive material, he seemed to regain some sense of self-worth. He was happier, and this change in attitude which his superiors ascribed to the end of his difficult marriage, led to promotion to a position where he was responsible for allocating work and supervising a team of seven translators. His happiness also stemmed from an improvement in his private life when Rhona Ratcliffe became his landlady and then his wife. A bubbly woman and a Christian, she had emerged from an unhappy marriage with three sons and a house in Cirencester Road in Cheltenham. She fell for the introverted and careworn Geoffrey Prime after he became a lodger at her house, accepting his inability to have sex and appreciating how well he looked after her boys, especially the youngest, Craig, with whom Prime developed a close relationship. They married, but three months later, he suddenly resigned from his job at GCHQ, blaming overwork, an outdated management style and a lack of sympathy with his nervousness when he was expected to deliver lectures to junior colleagues. As ever, none of it was his fault.

He worked as a taxi-driver for three years, but the money was only half what he had earned at GCHQ, and as at other times, he did not fit in. His fellow drivers found him odd, especially as he would spend his time in his cab, reading Russian newspapers and listening to foreign radio stations. Eventually, he left, but whispers had already started. He was approached by another driver who had received a complaint from a neighbour whose 13- and 16-year-old daughters had been offered 50 pence by Prime to get into his taxi. The mother of the children was swayed by Prime's pleas not to go to the police and he escaped investigation.

After taxi-driving he embarked on a disastrous career as a wine salesman, disastrous because customers took an instant dislike to him and he knew absolutely nothing about wine. Rhona feared financial ruin and began to wonder how he had managed to sustain their lifestyle in the four years since he had quit his well-paid job.

Unacceptable Urges

It was a cardboard box filled with small index cards, some 2,287 of them. They had been marked up meticulously, each referring to a single female child and recording Prime's contact with them, as well as details of the comings and goings of the girl's parents, when they were home, when they were not. It was his habit to peruse local newspapers for any mention of a young girl, perhaps for winning a competition, or for a notable hobby or interest. If there was a photograph, it was pinned to the relevant card so that he was able to visualise the particular girl when he was speaking to her on the telephone. A few weeks after the girl's appearance in the newspaper, he would make contact, finding out what he could about her family. Everything would be recorded on the card relating to that girl. He would call a number of times and, when he thought it was the right moment, introduce suggestive comments into the conversation. Finally, after effectively stalking the girl for months, he would make filthy suggestions. Amazingly, there was never a complaint about him to the police, even after thousands of calls.

It is well-known that men with such a predilection graduate to more serious offences and Prime's excesses began to involve physical abuse of his victims. He would phone a girl when her parents were not home and insist that he was a plumber or painter whom her father had asked to provide a quote for a piece of work. Telling her he was in the area, he would suggest that he could come round and look at the job. Once there, he slipped on a mask and ordered the terrified child to strip or he would look up her skirt while he satisfied himself. Naturally, these incidents were reported and the police were so concerned that a major investigation was launched. After one attack, in late 1982, a diligent officer discovered a fingerprint on the lavatory cistern in the house. Then, a farmworker came forward saying he had seen the perpetrator leaving the scene in his car which he identified as a two-tone, brown Cortina Mark IV. All owners of such a car were visited and interviewed, and their fingerprints were taken.

Eventually, Prime was interviewed as he was the owner of a Mark IV Cortina in the right colour but he insisted he had been picking up his wife from work around the time of the assault the previous week. They took his fingerprints and spoke to Rhona who confirmed that he had indeed picked her up. However, officers were convinced he was their man and, with careful calculations, worked out that he could have picked up his wife and would still have had time to carry out the assault. That night a tortured Prime confessed to Rhona that he was indeed the man they were looking for. After speaking to a solicitor, he contacted the police. Prior to their arrival at the house, he drove Rhona into Cheltenham where he paid off all their outstanding debts. She had no idea where the money had come from, but at least she would not have that to worry about in addition to everything else.

The following day, Prime confessed and was charged with indecent assault. Detectives took the opportunity to carry out a search of his house. As well as the box of index cards, some other curious items were found, such as a black leather briefcase, personal papers and a diary.

Microdots and One-Time Pads Under the Bed

Rhona had challenged Geoffrey on several occasions, her suspicion aroused by the odd telephone calls he had received, his strange behaviour and things she had come across in the house.

Then, on the night he confessed his sexual crimes to her, he also told her about his espionage. Hardly believing it, she kept this momentous secret to herself for an entire month, until, on 24 May 1982, she finally went to the police. Under the bed, she had found a carrier bag containing notes about microdots and two pads of clear cellophane sheets on which were printed columns of numbers. There were also envelopes addressed to places in East Germany. She worried that she and her sons might be in danger if someone came to collect this material.

At first, there was incredulity amongst police officers but Prime's previous employment at GCHQ began to pique their interest and the contents of the bag seemed to confirm her claims that her husband had been involved in espionage. The pads and columns of numbers were what was known as one-time pads. A further search revealed a schedule of radio contact, with frequencies, Prime's call-sign, books, magazines, audio-tapes and writing material. Prime, it seems, had never been terribly good at keeping things secure.

Meanwhile, Prime believed he was being held only on the sexual assault charges, certain that Rhona would not divulge his other crimes. This changed on 8 June 1982 when Chief Superintendent Cole and Detective Chief Inspector Picken of West Mercia CID arrived at Prime's prison to interview him. For a short while, Cole talked about the crimes with which Prime had been charged before dropping his bombshell: 'It may also not surprise you that because of your behaviour and the nature of your previous employment at GCHQ, Cheltenham, you have been put under the microscope in the past few weeks. I have carried out a number of enquiries and I now believe that you have been engaged in passing information to a subversive agency.' Prime's disbelief grew, as Cole began to produce some of his espionage tools – his radio, the reel-to-reel tape recorder, the one-time pads, addressed envelopes and the radio schedule. He became flustered, tried to justify the equipment, the trips abroad – to Potsdam and Vienna. The Russians had tried to recruit him, he claimed, but he had resisted, even when they gave him £4,000.

At the next interview, with Picken and Detective Chief Inspector Keith Smith, Prime mentioned a briefcase, about which, at that time, Smith knew nothing, although he did not let on that he was unaware of it. Prime was anxious about it and claimed that it had been left at his sister's house for him by Soviet agents. Inside it, he told them, was a false bottom concealing espionage equipment and a sum of money. But they continued to throw questions at him. How did he know there was a false bottom? How did he know how to open it? How had they told him?

The first part of the third and decisive interview, nine days later, lasted from after lunch until nine in the evening. At the end of it, Cole produced a tape machine on which he played a coded message in German that had been found in Prime's house. It dated from 1970 when Prime had been stationed in Berlin. Prime said it was merely a random recording he had made but it must have been rattling around in his brain as he tried to get to sleep in his cell that night.

The following afternoon, Cole changed tactics and made the interview more personal, by bringing Rhona into his questions. Prime's disquiet was immediately visible. He was even worse when they talked about his stepson, Craig. It was at that point that Prime agreed to make a full confession.

The Making of a Spy

The reasons for Geoffrey Prime's betrayal of his country will never be fully known. It is a matter of fact that he was obsessively enamoured of the Soviet system and saw it as the only hope for the poor and underprivileged of the world. He was also very anti-American, disgusted by US involvement in Southeast

Asia at the time and enraged by the treatment of blacks in the USA. He was vehemently against apartheid in South Africa and appalled at the British government's refusal to allow self-determination to Rhodesia's black population. Undoubtedly, he was 'talent-spotted' by the Russians, although he insisted that he engineered his own recruitment, claiming he had thrown a note, wrapped round a stone, through the glass hatch of a sentry box on the road corridor to Berlin. Farcically, the guard, terrified that it was a bomb, had thrown it back, but after some discussion, Prime managed to convince him that he wanted to help the Soviet Union.

He suggested a meeting two weeks later at a restaurant on Leibnizstrasse but he waited in vain, as the Russians were understandably wary of such an approach. They may already have had him in their sights. His job and his liking for sleazy nightlife made him an ideal target for entrapment. In fact, they did not contact him until two months later when he found a cylinder containing a handwritten note attached to the door of his car. It gave him a date and time to be at Friedrichstrasse underground station in Berlin. This was risky as the station, the gateway to the Eastern sector of the city, was off-limits to Allied personnel. A woman approached Prime as he disembarked from the train. Her name was Valya and the partner to whom she ushered him was called Igor. They established during that first meeting that he was everything they had hoped for. The work in which he was engaged made him very valuable, but he was also eager to help, compliant even. As usually happened when a new spy was being recruited, he was given a relatively simple first task – to bring them a copy of his unit's telephone directory – but in the coming weeks, they would get to know everything about him. Every Wednesday afternoon was spent at a flat in the military Kommandatura at Karlshorst in Berlin's Russian Zone where he was well fed and drank the finest brandy. He was instructed in tradecraft including the use of invisible ink, one-time pads and microdots, and was also taught how to use a 'dead-letter box'. He was given the codename 'Rowlands'.

The Soviets asked him about everything at his base at Gatow, even mundane details that would outwardly appear to be of little interest. He also used a Minox mini-camera to photograph classified documents, and gave them details of secure radio frequencies. From the length of time that the Soviets utilised his services – from 1968 until his arrest in 1982 – it can only be imagined just how much material he was able to pass to them.

Unusually, Prime met his handlers abroad: in Vienna in 1969; Ireland and Rome in 1970; and Cyprus in 1972. Once he was working at GCHQ, he would receive Russian radio messages by night and used the Minox to photograph secret documents that he would then post as microdots to an address in East Berlin. He used dead-letter drops in various places, employing Coca-Cola cans as well as trees that were signalled with chalk-marks. He was smuggling out so much classified information, however, that these methods were not adequate and, more often than not, he had to meet his handlers in person. While working at the London Processing Group, he was in a position to inform the Soviets which of their lines was being listened to and what information the listeners had managed to get. He was being well paid for this work; in 1975, when he had a rendezvous with his handlers in Vienna, he came home with £800 in his pocket, about £6,000 in today's money.

After resigning from GCHQ, Prime had been tempted to follow in the footsteps of Burgess, Maclean and Philby and defect. He had been told by his handlers at the start that if he was ever in danger of exposure, he should fly to Helsinki and go straight to the Soviet Embassy there. Twice he booked an airline ticket to the Finnish capital, but, on each occasion, he backed out, the second time, in 1977, as he was driving to the airport. At that point, he was no longer working for the Soviets and had been ignoring the radio messages. Crucially, however, he failed to dispose of the incriminating evidence.

The KGB made an effort to bring him back into the fold in April 1980 when he was invited to Vienna to go on a cruise on the Danube with some agents. He refused to work for them full-time again, although he handed over some 15 reels of film of documents he had copied before leaving GCHQ. For that, he received £600 and in November 1981, he received £4,000 for further material. The large sum reflects the significance of what he handed over, 'the most damaging of all', according to the security head at GCHQ.

The documents Prime passed to the Soviet Union were, indeed, significant. His clearance at GCHQ permitted him to see material that came in from two American Signals Intelligence (SIGINT) spy satellites – Canyon and Rhyolite – that were employed to detect and collect information about Russian missile launches, and intercepted material from Soviet, Vietnamese, Chinese and Middle Eastern radio and telephone communications. The material received was substantial and Americans had asked the British to help them interpret it. Learning about Canyon in 1975, the Soviets put procedures in place to prevent the interception of their radio communications. Geoffrey Prime was likely to have been the source of such information about Canyon. But the most damaging material Prime gave the Soviets is likely to have been information about the initiative known as 'Project Sambo', a programme designed to intercept the secret radio transmissions of Soviet submarines.

Guilty

Geoffrey Prime pleaded guilty at the Central Criminal Court in London to seven charges of espionage and three of sexual offences against children aged 11 to 14. His trial was held *in camera* and the media were prevented from reporting on him until after his trial. He was sentenced to thirty-eight years, thirty-five for offences under section 1 of the Official Secrets Act 1911 and three for the assaults on the girls. Prime stated in court that his spying was '… as a result of a misplaced idealistic view of Soviet socialism which was compounded by basic psychological problems within myself'.

He served half of his sentence, released on licence from Rochester Prison in March 2001 and placed on the Sex Offenders Register. The press discovered his address and he had to be quickly relocated. Rhona subsequently wrote a book about her marriage in 1984, *Time of Trial*, and remarried.

Michael Bettaney: The Traitor the Russians Ignored

Two Envelopes

Oleg Gordievsky has been described as the most significant British agent of the Cold War. Working as a double agent for 11 years, he was the only person that British intelligence officers ever managed to exfiltrate from the Soviet Union. Having joined the KGB in 1963, he was posted to London in June 1982 where, in April 1985, he became *rezident*-designate and bureau chief, MI6 making sure his superiors were thrown out of Britain to aid his advance in the KGB ranks at the Soviet Embassy. Gordievsky had been spying for Britain since 1974, his disgust for the Soviet system triggered by the Soviet Union's brutal crushing of the Prague Spring movement in Czechoslovakia in 1968, while he was working at the Soviet Embassy in Copenhagen. Learning to speak English, he persuaded his superiors to send him to London where he rose through the ranks. In the course of his work at the embassy, he learned that there was yet another Soviet spy working within the Secret Service.

The spy had come to Gordievsky's attention in extraordinary circumstances. On 3 April 1983, Arkadi Vasilyevich Guk, a murderous, ambitious and astonishingly ignorant man, ostensibly First Secretary at the Soviet Embassy, but, in reality, the KGB *rezident* in London, returned to his flat at 42 Holland Park to find an envelope had been pushed through his letterbox. On opening it, he was astounded to find a classified document that laid out the case for the expulsion of Igor Titov who had been declared *persona non grata* by Great Britain and had been expelled, along with two GRU officers, the previous month. The document further explained that the three men had been identified as working for Soviet intelligence. The signature at the bottom of the note that accompanied the document read 'Koba' – a nickname adopted by the Soviet leader Stalin as a schoolboy. What's more, Koba promised to reveal more secrets with a complicated set of instructions on how he could be contacted. If Guk was interested in pursuing this matter, he was to place a single drawing pin at the top of the right-hand banister of the stairs that brought passengers up from platforms three and four at Piccadilly Underground station. Koba's acknowledgement would take the form of a piece of blue adhesive tape wrapped around the telephone cable of the middle telephone box in a row of five such boxes in Adam and Eve Court, a narrow lane off Oxford Street, east of Oxford Circus. Once all this had been done, Koba would tape a roll of film containing classified information under the lid of the cistern of a gents' toilet in the Academy Cinema in Oxford Street. The offer would be open to Guk until 25 April.

Guk was nothing if not suspicious. In fact, he could have been described as verging on paranoid. His first reaction was that this letter was a trap set by the British Secret Service, the aim being to catch him out and then have him expelled. Understandably, he decided to ignore it. After all, he reasoned, his place must be under surveillance. Which MI6 officer would risk being seen by his colleagues delivering an envelope to the home of a Soviet Embassy employee? What he had not added in to his calculation, however, was that, if the envelope had been delivered by an MI6 officer, that person would surely have checked the surveillance rota to ensure that, when he pushed the envelope through the letterbox, he would not be seen.

For two months, Guk forgot about the clumsy attempt to attract his attention, but on 12 June he woke up to find another envelope pushed through his letterbox. Opening it, he was astonished to find a list containing the name of every Soviet intelligence officer in London. Next to each name were the legends 'fully identified', 'more or less identified' or 'under suspicion of belonging to the KGB station'. There was an offer once more of further secrets and another elaborate communications system. This time, if Guk was interested in taking it further, the note – again signed 'Koba' – told him to park his Mercedes at the parking meters on the north side of Hanover Square in London at lunchtime on 2 or 4 July. If this was done, on 23 July Koba would leave a Carlsberg can filled with film containing classified material at the base of a broken lamppost that leaned to one side and lacked a shade on the footpath that ran parallel to Horsenden Lane in Greenford, a suburb of West London. As if that was not enough, Guk was then to leave a piece of orange peel at the foot of the right-hand gatepost of the first gate of St James's Gardens in Melton Street, a thoroughfare located close to Euston Station. Guk still insisted it was an elaborate plot by the British but consulted with Moscow Centre in any case. Equally suspicious, they ordered him to do nothing.

It was at this point that Gordievsky was told that a British spook was offering his services to the Russians. Shown the list of names by Guk, he was relieved to see that he was in the 'more or less identified' category meaning that the creator of the list was unsure whether he was a KGB man or not, and as such, could not know that he was a double agent.

Gordievsky was confused, however. If Guk was right and this was a sting operation, why had his British handlers not warned him? He also doubted whether MI5 really would be foolish enough to let the KGB know that it had identified all its agents in Britain. An hour after seeing the list, he met MI5 officers in a safe house and told them that someone in their organisation was offering to spy for the Russians and that he had already provided them with classified information. MI5 was now faced with the prospect of a mole hunt but, of course, if the mole got wind of it, it would become evident to him that the knowledge of his existence could have come from only one source – someone inside the *rezidentura* itself. That would immediately open Gordievsky to exposure and, so far, it seemed that the mole was unaware of the Russian's activities. So, it was evident that Koba was not a member of the team – known as NOCTON – that dealt with Gordievsky. If he had been, he would have been fully aware that his approach to Guk would be reported back to MI5. And, of course, Gordievsky's status as a double agent would have been the first thing that Koba would have passed on to Guk. A hunt – codenamed ELMEN – was initiated to discover Koba's identity. The team, consisting of members of NOCTON, was headed by John Deverell, Director of K, MI5's counter-intelligence department. The ELMEN team, working in secret from Deverell's office, nicknamed themselves 'the Nadgers'.

The Nadgers' first job was to narrow down the list of suspects. The document that was part of the first mail drop by Koba, detailing why the three Soviet spooks were sent home, had been distributed in the Foreign Office, the Home Office and 10

Downing Street. The contents of the second envelope – the list of KGB officers – had been sent to various departments of the Secret Service. The task was to work out all those who would have seen both of those documents.

The net was tightening.

Michael John Bettaney

Michael Bettaney was born in 1950, in Stoke-on-Trent, his father a toy factory employee and his mother a cleaner. A bright pupil, even though he failed his 11-plus the first time he sat it, he managed to get into Pembroke College, Oxford but his time there seems to have been quite shocking. He displayed a liking for the Nazis, goose-stepping around the quad and playing the speeches of Adolf Hitler at high volume on a gramophone. He affected the tweeds, brogues and pipe of a country squire and is said to have once set himself on fire after a party. The Stoke accent he grew up with changed to an upper-class one. Despite this, and the obvious inferiority complex he displayed at Oxford, he was recruited by MI5 in 1975.

In June 1976, Bettaney was posted to Northern Ireland which was in the midst of the 'Troubles' and, not long after arriving, he was injured when a car bomb exploded. He ran agents inside the IRA, and engaged in a great many dangerous and grim actions. While posted there, he lost his parents. His father died in 1977 and his mother a year later but, despite this double tragedy in his life, and the traumatising nature of his work, his tour of duty was extended. He eventually returned to London in 1978, obviously damaged by his experiences, but no help was offered by his employers. He just had to get on with his life and career.

Bettaney worked for a while in the newly-created anti-terrorist branch before being transferred in December 1982 to K4, the MI5 department that dealt with Soviet espionage in the United

Kingdom. Meanwhile, he was living alone in a house that was home to a large statue of the Madonna, Russian icons, Nazi war medals and a large trove of pornography. He was lonely and insecure and drinking heavily. When drunk at parties, he could be heard shouting: 'I'm working for the wrong side!' and on one occasion bellowed: 'Come and see me in my dacha when I retire'. His drinking became increasingly dangerous and by 1983 he was consuming a bottle of spirits a day. Arrested in London's West End on one occasion for being drunk, he yelled at police officers: 'You can't arrest me, I'm a spy!' After being fined £10, he tendered his resignation to MI5 but it was rejected and he carried on working, having committed to giving up alcohol.

After six months on the wagon, however, he hit the bottle again and, around April 1983, he began to memorise secret documents and type them up at home. He also started photographing them, especially when he was on night duty with no one else around. He later said that he had become a Marxist in 1982 and that his espionage was done for purely ideological reasons. He had been angered by Prime Minister Margaret Thatcher's government and what he called its 'slavish adherence to the aggressive and maverick policy of the Reagan administration'. He accused the government of deliberately increasing unemployment in order to further enrich the wealthy. MI5, he reckoned, used 'sinister and immoral methods... not merely to remove the Soviet Government and Party, but also to destroy the entire fabric of society in the USSR'. World peace, he insisted, was his goal. It was all nonsense, of course; he never displayed an iota of political sensibility.

No Response

Bettaney was shaken by the Soviets' lack of response to his efforts to spy for them. None of his elaborate instructions were followed; the drawing pin never appeared on the banister; the Mercedes was never parked on Hanover Square. His attempts to become the centre of attention, if only in his own head, seemed to have failed.

However, he was beginning to become the centre of attention elsewhere. The Nadgers, beavering away in their office on Curzon Street, had narrowed the list of suspects down to just three with Bettaney their favourite. He was put under surveillance which was complicated as Bettaney knew the Watchers, as MI5's surveillance team was known. The only way was to use the members of MI6's NOCTON team, all of whom were unknown to him and therefore unrecognisable. They codenamed him 'Puck' and started following him.

By now, he was becoming desperate. He had visited Hanover Square on several occasions and the Mercedes was still nowhere to be seen. So, he decided to have another go and on 10 July, after midnight, he dropped a third envelope through Guk's letterbox. The envelope contained a note inquiring whether Guk had received the first two and if anything was going to happen as a result. He also wrote that he would place a telephone call to the Soviet Embassy the following day at 8.05 am and ask for Guk. Guk was to answer with a phrase given him in the note to show he was interested in what Koba had to offer. When Bettaney called the next morning, Guk refused to take his call.

Meanwhile, Bettaney was behaving bizarrely in the office at Curzon Street, discussing Guk in an obsessive way and asking for files that were not connected with his work. When he asked a colleague a few days after his telephone call, 'How do you think Guk would respond if a British intelligence officer put a letter through the door of his house?', the game seemed to be up. Or was it? There was still not enough evidence to prosecute him. Bizarrely, Guk's house had not been under observation when Bettaney posted the third envelope, and a tap on his telephone and search of his house had produced nothing. It became increasingly evident to MI5 that short of catching him in the act, only a confession would lead to a conviction.

They finally decided to bring Bettaney in for questioning after he began to tell people that he was going on holiday to Vienna. This appeared to be a trip designed to allow him to approach a Soviet agent there, a suspicion confirmed by the discovery of documents referring to a KGB officer, expelled from Britain, and now working in the Austrian capital. On 15 September, Bettaney was summoned to the MI5 office in Gower Street, ostensibly to discuss some counter-intelligence business. When he got there, however, he was surprised to be taken immediately to an apartment at the top of the building where his interrogators, John Deverell and Eliza Manningham-Buller, later Director General of MI5, presented their evidence to him. One item shown to him was a picture of Guk's front door, giving the impression that he had been seen making his deliveries, which, of course, he had not.

Bettaney was, of course, stunned by what he was being shown, but, although nervous, he remained in control. He said some strange things, intimating his guilt by noting that he would be a fool to confess. Of course, it was all hypothetical because, as yet, he had not been put under caution or arrested. The MI5 officers listening in a room below were increasingly concerned that their chance was slipping away. Bettaney was asked to stay in the flat that night and he agreed although he had every right to go home. All he required, it seemed, was a bottle of whisky which was duly delivered. The questioning continued until three in the morning when he collapsed, no doubt, into bed.

The next morning, he declined breakfast, even though he had not eaten for the entirety of the previous day. He had woken up hungover and angry, declaring that he would not confess. But at 11.42 that morning, his mood suddenly changed, something that was not unusual for him. 'I think I ought to make a clean breast of it,' he said to Deverell. 'Tell Director K I wish to make a confession.'

Meanwhile, his house had been searched and the tools of the spy's trade had been uncovered – details of KGB officers he wanted to meet in Vienna were concealed in an electric shaver box. In the coal cellar, buried under rubble was found photographic equipment. Also found were notes on top-secret matters sewn into a cushion, hidden in a cardboard box and in a laundry cupboard.

Trial, Conviction and Prison

In April 1984, Michael Bettaney arrived at the Old Bailey to be tried on ten charges of breaching the Official Secrets Act. The trial was held in great secrecy, much of it in camera, because the Secret Service and the government were trying to protect their double agent, Oleg Gordievsky. Bettaney pleaded not guilty but, as was fairly inevitable, was found guilty of all ten charges. Summing up, Lord Chief Justice Lane described Bettaney as 'self-opinionated and dangerous'. He added: 'You would not have hesitated to disclose names to the Russians which would almost certainly have led to the death of more than one person.' He was sentenced to 23 years in prison.

Bettaney's pursuit of attention through passing on secrets is rumoured to have continued while he was on remand before his trial. He is said to have passed to IRA prisoners details of MI5 agents who had infiltrated their movement and he passed similar information to the National Union of Mineworkers who were also in dispute with Margaret Thatcher's government. Through time, his initial hopes of an exchange for a British prisoner being held in Russia dwindled and he settled into his long sentence, most of it spent in solitary confinement, studying and exercising. He learned Russian while inside and considered taking holy orders. He wrote for the communist newspaper,

Workers' Weekly under the name Michael Malkin and finally, after serving fifteen years and six months of his sentence, was released on licence in 1998.

The Aftermath

British intelligence wrought its revenge. Arkadi Guk was expelled in May 1984. Of course, as the man who had turned down the chance to work with a potentially valuable asset, he was not received warmly in Moscow. His departure brought a welcome bonus because, with Guk gone, Gordievsky moved up the KGB ranks in London *rezidentura*. Before long he was appointed head of the KGB in London.

In 1985, Gordievsky came under suspicion and was recalled to Moscow. There, in an operation codenamed Operation Pimlico, he was exfiltrated from the Soviet Union, the only Soviet agent to whom this happened. He was sentenced to death *in absentia* by a Russian court but now lives in an undisclosed location in the English Home Counties.

Naturally, after the Bettaney case, just the latest in a long line of such cases, MI5 was at its lowest ebb. As was public confidence in the Secret Service. A Security Commission, convened to look at the matter, was critical of the senior figures in MI5, leading to the replacement of the Director General, John Jones, as well as the officer in charge of its vetting process. The Intelligence and Security Committee was created in 1994 and the Investigatory Powers Tribunal in 2000. But there was also concern about the way that staff in British intelligence were treated, following the lack of care for Bettaney after Northern Ireland and the deaths of his parents. Steps were taken to show greater care for the wellbeing of employees.

Of course, there was also the issue of how a man like Bettaney – insecure, unstable and attention-seeking – could have been employed by British intelligence in the first place and have remained employed, despite his bizarre personality traits and drunkenness. 'Enhanced positive vetting' was introduced by the Security Commission, featuring more personal references and financial checks. These are now carried out on a regular basis for all employees.

On leaving prison, Michael Bettaney lived in Ware in Hertfordshire with Marion Johnstone, a committed socialist, who corresponded with him in prison and visited him hundreds of times. He found a job in a shop and eventually died of alcohol intoxication at home on 16 August 2018.

Bibliography

The files of the National Archives proved invaluable in writing this book, as did the following books:

Andrew, Christopher, *The Defence of the Realm*, London: Penguin, 2012

Andrew, Christopher, *KGB: The Inside Story of its Foreign Operations*, London: HarperCollins, 1990

Andrews, Geoff, *Agent Moliere*, London: IB Tauris, 2020

Barnes, Trevor, *Dead Doubles: The Extraordinary Hunt for One of the World's Most Notorious Spy Rings*, London: Weidenfeld & Nicolson, 2021

Bulloch, John and Miller, Henry, *Spy Ring*, London: Secker & Warburg, 1961

Burt, Leonard, *Commander Burt of Scotland Yard*, London: Heinemann, 1959

Carter, Miranda, *Anthony Blunt: His Lives*, London: Bello, 2017

Close, Frank, *Trinity: The Treachery and Pursuit of the Most Dangerous Spy in History*, London: Penguin, 2020

Cole, DJ, *Geoffrey Prime: The Imperfect Spy*, London: Robert Hale, 1998

Curry, JM, *The Security Service 1908-1945*, London: PRO Publications, 1999

Griffiths, Richard, *Fellow Travellers of the Right*, London: Faber & Faber, 2015

Griffiths, Richard, *Patriotism Perverted*, London: Constable, 1998

Griffiths, Richard, *What Did You Do During the War?*, London: Routledge, 2016

Hemming, Henry, *M: Maxwell Knight, MI5's Greatest Spymaster*,

London: Arrow, 2018

Hermiston, Roger, *The Greatest Traitor: The Secret Lives of Agent George Blake*, London: Aurum Press, 2014

Holmes, Colin, *Searching for Lord Haw-Haw*, London: Routledge, 2016

Hutton, Robert, *Agent Jack: The True Story of MI5's Secret Nazi Hunter*, London: Weidenfeld & Nicolson, 2018

Ireland, Josh, *The Traitors: A True Story of Blood, Betrayal and Deceit*, London: John Murray, 2017

Knightley, Phillip, *Philby: KGB Masterspy*, London: Andre Deutsch, 2003

Kuper, Simon, *The Happy Traitor: Spies, Lies and Exile in Russia: The Extraordinary Story of George Blake*, London: Profile Books, 2021

Lownie, Andrew, *Stalin's Englishman: The Lives of Guy Burgess*, London: Hodder, 2016

Lucas, Norman, *Spycatcher*, London: WH Allen, Virgin Books, 1973

Macintyre, Ben, *A Spy Among Friends: Kim Philby and the Great Betrayal*, London: Bloomsbury, 2015

Madeira, Victor, *Britannia and the Bear: The Anglo-Russian Intelligence Wars, 1917-1920*, Woodbridge, Suffolk: Boydell & Brewer, 2016

Moorehead, Alan, *The Traitors, The Double Life of Fuchs, Pontecorvo and Nunn May*, London: Hamish Hamilton, 1952

Page, Bruce; Knightley, Phillip; Leitch, David, *The Philby Conspiracy*, New York: Doubleday, 1968

Penrose, Barrie and Freeman, Simon, *Conspiracy of Silence: The Secret Life of Anthony Blunt*, London: Grafton, 1986

Phillips, Roland, *A Spy Named Orphan: The Enigma of Donald Maclean*, London: Vintage, 2019

Quinlan, Kevin, *The Secret War Between the Wars*, Woodbridge, Suffolk: Boydell & Brewer, 2014

Smith, Christopher, *The Last Cambridge Spy: John Cairncross,*

Bletchley Codebreaker and Soviet Double Agent, Stroud: The History Press, 2019

Tate, Tim, *Hitler's British Traitors: The Secret History of Spies, Saboteurs and Fifth Columnists*, London: Icon, 2018

Thomas, Rosamund, *Espionage and Secrecy: The Official Secrets Act 1911-1989 of the United Kingdom*, London: Routledge, 2016

Urban, Mark, *Big Boys Rules: The SAS and the Secret Struggle Against the IRA*, London: Faber & Faber, 1996

Vassall, John, *Vassall: The Autobiography of a Spy*, London: Sidgwick & Jackson, 1975

Volodarsky, Boris, *Stalin's Agent: The Life and Death of Alexander Orlov*, Oxford: Oxford University Press, 2014

Weale, Adrian, *Renegades: Hitler's Englishmen*, London: Lume Books, 2021

West, Nigel, *Mask: MI5's Penetration of the Communist Party of Great Britain*, London: Routledge, 2005

West, Rebecca, *The Meaning of Treason*, London: Macmillan, 1949

Wilson, Ray, *Special Branch: A History: 1883-2006*, London: Biteback, 2015

Index

INDEX

INDEX